Management for Professionals

More information about this series at http://www.springer.com/series/10101

Tony McNulty • Robin Marks

Management by Permission

Managing People in the 21st Century

 Springer

Tony McNulty
Northwood
Middlesex
United Kingdom

Robin Marks
Faversham
Kent
United Kingdom

ISSN 2192-8096   ISSN 2192-810X   (electronic)
Management for Professionals
ISBN 978-3-319-79758-8   ISBN 978-3-319-25247-6   (eBook)
DOI 10.1007/978-3-319-25247-6

Springer Cham Heidelberg New York Dordrecht London

Printed on acid-free paper

Springer International Publishing AG Switzerland is part of Springer Science+Business Media
(www.springer.com)

Foreword

This book is a 'page-turner', a strong candidate for 'Management Book of the Year', and an essential guide for those who manage others. Written in an engaging, and at times, humorous style, it combines academic rigour with practical advice and guidance for anyone in a management role, whatever their level. It makes for a compelling combination. Having personally recommended the book to a number of senior managers and executives, I am also using it in my own role as Faculty Dean, managing a high-profile medium-sized enterprise with a multimillion pound turnover. I find that whenever I am wrestling with a management problem, *Management by Permission* continually comes to the rescue.

The thesis of the book rests on an important **value judgement**, summed up perfectly in the first chapter's opening 'quotation from the greats': Abraham Lincoln's sentiment that no one is good enough to govern another person without that other's consent. Such a world view may be timeless—but it is especially pertinent in the contemporary world of organizations.

The book's authors help us both intellectually and practically in the struggle to attain the consent of others to work with us, under our direction and guidance, so as to achieve things of value through organizational endeavour. The authors know that the resources required for organizational endeavour are limited and need to be applied purposefully and with the greatest care to avoid the risk of being squandered. As far as possible, we must apply people's **spirit, creativity, and time** willingly to change the world for the better, as judged by multiple stakeholders.

This book will have wide appeal, therefore. The value derives from the fact that the authors bring their own mix of rare characteristics to their craft: (1) they are 'accredited' in scholarship—underpinning argument with theoretical reflexivity and rigorous research know-how; (2) they are 'bloodied' from engagement in real-world practice; and (3) they can write clearly and engagingly. That's why it's a page-turner, helped at times by the adept application of humour. One further special attribute: they're passionate about their discipline, to share practical lessons learned, and to help contemporary managers to manage by **permission** (defined early in the text), as opposed to edict, diktat, or soulless bureaucracy.

In setting out how people in the modern world are managed by permission, the book directs attention towards securing systematic control, managing expectations, navigating blockages that interfere with people's capacity to secure goals, and continuously developing individuals and groups. As I read the book I was struck by the extent to which these elements are also helpful in advancing both thinking and practice within my own research passion: corporate governance.

Governance is currently a hot topic in the business literature and in policy settings, with interest heightened post the financial crisis in the 'advanced' economies. For governance to be effective, permission is necessary from various stakeholders if senior executives are to run organizations effectively. Not only will managers' capability to do their jobs be enhanced through embracing and applying the principles described by Tony and Rob, I believe that organizational investors, policymakers, and regulators will learn plenty from working through the book's contents.

Management by Permission will, in my view, enable twenty-first century enterprise, productivity, consensual corporate endeavour, and all-round happiness. Please try it.

Stephen J. Perkins
Corporate Governance,
London Guildhall Faculty of Business & Law
London, UK

Praise for *Management by Permission*

"*Management is getting harder but is no less valuable. In this readable and practical book the authors spell out the key challenges facing managers and how they can address them. The central question is how you win permission to manage—in straightforward language this book shows you how.*" **Professor Rob Goffee, London Business School**

"*This is a great book. Given the challenges of today's business world, there is perhaps nothing more important than an empowered and committed workforce. As younger generations join our organizations, be they Millennials or Generations "X" or "Y", we desperately need a more collaborative management model in order to engage them.* Management by Permission *offers an extraordinary road map, providing us with an approach that is as timely as it is effective. The book is loaded with management best practices and tips, a few of which I have used and many more which I wish I had used. If you have time for only one management book in your life,* Management by Permission *would be an outstanding choice.*" **Greg Thompson, President, Markel Specialty**

"*As a female leader, for me this book is a treasure into the insights and practicalities of management. Great use of illustrations and I particularly like the 'Remember' summaries throughout. You will not just read this book once. It will continue to remain part of your business life.*" **Anna Maria O'Shea, Head of Finance, AIB Group**

"*McNulty and Marks are acute and analytical observers of people and how they work together. Their key insight and the premise of this book is that in a modern, less hierarchical organization a manager needs to have the permission of those being managed in order to be effective.* Management by Permission *cuts through all the apparent muddle and noise of the modern workplace to identify the keys to effective management practice. A tightly written volume which manages to be easy to read, thought-provoking, and entertaining, it draws on a great depth of organizational experience, offering concentrated common sense in an incisive, practical, and essential guide for the time-strapped 21st-century manager. In short, it's excellent.*" **Ed Moffatt, Managing Director, Elevation Learning**

"*No 'guru speak' but actionable advice.* Management by Permission *is a 'must read' for anyone on the line management ladder. Amongst all those aspirational ideas of leadership and new organizational models, there are some fundamentals of management forming the prerequisites to success. McNulty and Marks refocus us on the core principles and equip managers with a fresh guide to face the evolving challenges of today's work environment. Embracing the consequences of modern organizations, flatter structures, and the power shift to the employee, the authors capture the wisdom of prior management generations in an up-to-date, practical framework along four ground rules. Workplaces often do not role model clearly enough what good management looks like, leading to people having to learn the 'hard way.' This book gives any reader a head start in navigating organizational pitfalls for themselves and their teams."* **Dr Janine-Nicole Desai, Regional HR Director, Hilton Worldwide**

"A testament to how good this book is: I just read it cover to cover in three hours. I really like the structure. Control, Work Management Systems, and Development are really well explained. I like the management boulders, and the calling out of key points and summaries is very useful." **James Allan, Managing Director, Barclays Corporate Banking**

Acknowledgements

This book is the result of a number of years of research, consultancy, and hands-on management experience in organizations both large and small. Our ideas have been refined and shaped in a variety of ways.

Our time spent as managers, project and team leaders, as well as, in our earliest days, individual contributors, has given us a perspective on organizational life at various levels. As organizational consultants, between us we have worked for a range of predominantly private sector clients in more than 20 countries. We have conducted interviews and research in a large number of organizations, often as part of consultancy assignments. In testing and refining our ideas, we have then worked with clients to help implement the findings. We have facilitated top-level meetings, run seminars, spoken at conferences, conducted benchmarking assignments, as well as carried out a large number of what we call 'taking the temperature' organization reviews, often involving in-depth interviews at all levels in a variety of organizational settings. We have also acted as one-on-one executive coaches and personal advisers to company chairpersons and chief executives, as well as to managers working at operational levels. Together, all these experiences have given us ample opportunity to observe, reflect upon, test, and establish what works and what does not.

Unless otherwise stated, all of the case study material in the book is drawn from our work and research. The various situations and settings have been disguised in order to protect individual identities. In addition to thanking these anonymous colleagues and clients, including past and present participants at our two-monthly 'Executive Leadership Group' meetings,[1] we would also like to thank a number of 'critical friends' who have read or commented on various drafts of the book or contributed in some other way. These include in particular: Professor Paul Evans of INSEAD, Professor Rob Goffee (Tony's former doctoral supervisor at London Business School), and Professor Stephen Perkins of the London Guildhall Faculty of Business & Law. We would also like to extend our thanks and appreciation to

---

[1] Each Group comprises around seven senior level professionals from different organizations who act as a 'Board' of trusted advisers for each other. We facilitate an all-day meeting of the Group every 2 months, enabling members to share problems and dilemmas, test ideas, and get advice and guidance from each other (tony@mcnultymanagementconsultants.com).

Christian Rauscher, Senior Editor at Springer, who was not only enthusiastic about our book from the very beginning but also needs no instruction in how to manage people (even authors) with their permission.

Finally we would like to thank our wives, Wendy and Sue. As a co-consultant in two of our businesses, Wendy McNulty has been involved in a large number of the assignments from which we have subsequently drawn insights and information. And both she and Sue have provided the emotional and practical support necessary to getting the book finished, as well as having had to listen to us talking about it for long enough. Like Victor Borge before us, having thanked our spouses for making this possible, we would also like to acknowledge the part played by our children in making our continuing work necessary—in Tony's case, Joe, David, and Olivia, and in Rob's, Laurence and Sally.

Contents

List of Figures

Introduction

1

No man is good enough to govern another man, without that other's consent

Abraham Lincoln

Leaders must devote as much of their time looking backward to make sure that the people continue to follow, as looking forward to find where they should go

Theodore White

My MBA taught me a great deal, but I still had lots to learn when it came to managing my current team

Executive Leadership Group participant

My job's like the trenches in the First World War. I'm happy if I can get to the end of the day without being shot at

Director

Somewhere along the line, managing others became much more difficult. There are many reasons. We keep running into four in particular:

- Firstly, leaner and flatter organizations have invariably increased managers' spans of control, putting more pressure and heavier workloads onto managers and staff alike
- Secondly, there is an increasing distrust towards institutions of all kinds, allied to a general decline in respect towards those in positions of authority
- Thirdly, managers have to deal with a more assertive, demanding and often diverse workforce
- Fourthly, many managers are simply less well equipped to do their jobs. With fewer intermediate levels in organizations, the opportunities for gaining management experience are more limited, and there are fewer organizational role models from whom to learn.

Yet we desperately need competent and effective managers. Without them: fuel does not reach the pumps; trains never run on time; museums do not open; planes have difficulties in landing safely; cash machines run out of cash; life changing

© Springer International Publishing Switzerland 2016
T. McNulty, R. Marks, *Management by Permission*, Management for Professionals,
DOI 10.1007/978-3-319-25247-6_1

operations get delayed; parcels and examination papers fail to arrive in time; the lights go out; and at the extreme, economies collapse ... the problems are legion. Management is key to so many of the tasks and services which we take for granted and upon which we all depend.

As management and organizational consultants, we have worked with large numbers of executives and managers as they have struggled with the challenges of managing people in this much more difficult world. We have helped to devise, develop and implement solutions, and we have also gone back and helped refine the solutions when it has proved necessary.

These experiences, together with our own and others' research, have led us to conclude that we are going to have to be much smarter in the way we manage people in the modern world. It calls for a new approach. We call it, "*Management by Permission*" (*MBP*). It recognizes that, irrespective of periodic recessions, and booms and busts, the balance of power in modern organizations has now shifted. Almost all staff are now able to subvert management's intentions with impunity, with the result that *the majority of people can only be managed with their active cooperation and consent*. How managers can secure that cooperation and consent, whilst still getting the work done, is the subject of this book.

1.1   How Does This Book Relate to Other Books on Management and Leadership?

There is a plethora of management and leadership books available, written from a number of different perspectives. The writers include business leaders, politicians, sports stars, military figures, historians and researchers as well as business school professors. Inevitably such a vast output varies in quality, and the extent to which practising managers find it helpful. Bennis and Nanus (2003) dismiss some of it with the words: "Never have so many labored so long to say so little."

This book aims at providing a readily accessible and practical guide for those responsible for managing others in the modern world. We set out an approach to management that acknowledges the changing attitudes, aspirations and behaviour of the people being managed, and one which secures their cooperation. The core ingredients we propose are as relevant to those at the very top, as they are to those starting out on their first management roles. In his highly regarded book, Tony Watson (1994) states that he considers management as "at the same time both simple in principle but difficult in practice." This book is our attempt to set out the core *principles* for managing others in a modern world, whilst providing advice and guidance as to the *practice*.

Unlike some nineteenth and twentieth century doctors, whose work appeared to be finished once they had identified a problem, and attributed their names to it for all eternity, we prescribe some solutions to the problems of twenty-first century management. *Management by Permission* consists of four main ingredients, which taken together, will get the organization's work done, whilst meeting many of the individual objectives of the staff. This book is *not* designed to help organizations decide what businesses to be in, nor help them define their markets and business strategies. These issues need to be worked through by those who are knowledgeable in a particular field or industry. However, once the strategy is decided, this book will help managers to implement it in the most efficient and effective way.

There are a number of management and leadership books from which useful ideas and insights can be obtained. The core management text of Peter Drucker (2009) is a recognized classic in the genre, and although it may have become dated in some respects, it remains a useful primer for any manager whatever their level. Goffee and Jones (2006), having challenged leaders to consider how to make best use of their own unique skills and characteristics, provide a useful blueprint for helping individuals to succeed in the task. These selfsame authors have also helpfully turned their attention to the specific challenge of leading "clever people", those talented individuals with the potential to create disproportionate amounts of value from the resources available to them (Goffee and Jones 2009). The latter book contains a number of detailed case histories, which act as a useful catalyst for considering how best to lead an organization's smartest and most creative people.

As well as providing an excellent summary and critique of research carried out into management and leadership down the years, in *Managing*, Henry Mintzberg examines the challenges and dilemmas facing senior managers in a variety of contexts (2009). His book presents a thought-provoking model setting out the key tasks to be achieved, and highlighting the varying roles managers must play. Birkinshaw (2013) helps managers obtain insight into their own management models, and consider whether these models are fit for purpose. He shows how making changes can lead to better informed and smarter choices with a greater likelihood of success.

Various attempts have been made to differentiate between "management" and "leadership", although there is not always agreement as to the precise boundaries between the two activities. Covey (1989) sees management as the organization of activities, while leadership for him is more concerned with deciding on the direction. So when a team is using machetes to cut its way through a jungle, it is the manager who organizes the work schedules and makes sure the machetes are kept sharp. The leader is the one who climbs up the tallest tree, surveys the scene, and calls out, "Wrong jungle!"

Kotter (2013) considers the two as "radically different": management being, "a set of well-known processes, like planning, budgeting, structuring jobs, staffing jobs, measuring performance and problem-solving, which help an organization to predictably do (*sic*) what it knows how to do well." Leadership, on the other hand, "is about vision, about people buying in, about empowerment, and most of all, about producing useful change."

Mintzberg (2009) finds difficulties in understanding what the distinction between leadership and management might mean in the everyday life of organizations. While Birkinshaw (2013) finds the dichotomy as described in the work of Bennis and Kotter as "inaccurate and, frankly, insulting."

Certainly, and perhaps only until quite recently, books on leadership seem to have taken precedence over books on management. Birkinshaw suggests that one reason for management's demise was owing to its practitioners having been seen as passive, inert and narrow-minded, whilst leaders were visionary agents of change. As a consequence, there was a need, "to make room for leadership." To this we would add our own observation that the concept of "leadership" (as opposed to "management") has traditionally been much more revered within certain cultures.

Management is now seen as "making a comeback" after a number of years during which business writers felt compelled to diminish its role, despite the few "lonely voices" (notably Mintzberg and Drucker) who continued to remind people of its importance (Birkinshaw 2013). Certainly Hamel (2007) has argued that finding an appropriate form of management is a vital ingredient to securing innovation. And as Collins pointed out in the Foreword to Peter Drucker's updated book on Management, "the very best leaders are first and foremost effective managers" (Drucker 2009).

Ever since people have been writing about management, various theorists have set out any number of skills and competencies that managers need to acquire, as well as lists of tasks and activities which managers need to carry out. And our four ingredients do indeed draw on some of the work of these prior management theorists. However, unlike some authors, we avoid the confusing, interminable, and often overwhelming lists of skills, competencies, and techniques which managers are expected to master. Instead, we have distilled from our work the four essential ingredients to managing in the modern world. *Our experience is that if managers can get these four ingredients right, then these ingredients will entail most of the rest.*

Whenever and wherever we, or others have applied the principles set out in this book—in management, consulting or coaching—it has led to improved performance, control, employee engagement, morale and retention.

1.2   A Map of the Book

Figure 1.1 provides an overview of the book.

Chapter 2 sets the scene by explaining in more detail how a number of factors in the modern world are conspiring to make it much harder for managers to manage. It highlights the good and the bad news regarding this state of affairs. We also discuss why although being poorly managed may initially confer great freedom to staff, its ultimate consequences are far from idyllic. In fact, being poorly managed is usually a real problem for any employee.

Chapter 3 deals with the first of the four ingredients: *keep things under control.* We argue that effective control works for the benefit of both managers and the people they are managing. Without proper controls, managers cannot be sure that work is being progressed, the targets are being met, and even what work is being done. For those being managed, inadequate controls are ultimately demotivating. Your contribution goes unrecognised, and any subsequent attempt at appraising your performance is likely to be a farce. Whilst the precise methods for achieving

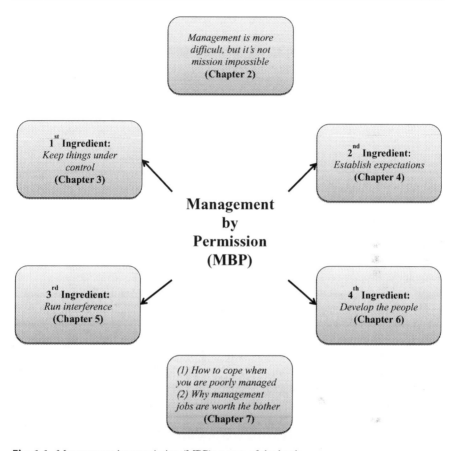

Fig. 1.1 Management by permission (MBP): a map of the book

effective control will differ from organization to organization, we suggest three tried and tested ways, which are most effective when used in concert.

Chapter 4 describes the second ingredient: ***establish expectations***. Both managers and their direct reports need to know what each expects of the other, for their own benefit as well as for the benefit of their organizations. Surprising though it might appear, expectations are often communicated badly, and sometimes hardly at all. The chapter suggests some ways in which managers and their staff can work together in order to reach agreement and ensure expectations are communicated.

Chapter 5 highlights the need for managers to ***run interference*** for their staff. Running interference has its origins in American football, and describes the practice whereby certain players are detailed to get in the way of opposing players, thus preventing them from tackling the player with the ball. In this context it means helping to protect staff from the organizational or other problems that might prevent these individuals from getting their work done. Many managers ignore this responsibility, yet if there is too much organizational and other noise competing for people's attention, then employees can get diverted and underachieve. This chapter suggests ways in which managers can act as an 'umbrella' in order to protect staff from those matters (such as the consequences of poor organizational design, or an excessive number of "initiatives") which can get in the way of effective performance. The chapter also advises how a manager can help anticipate, identify and tackle some of the 'boulders' which can appear on an employee's racetrack, including boulders which the employees themselves sometimes put in the way.

Chapter 6 addresses the fourth and final ingredient: ***develop the people***. Employees increasingly view their continuing development as part of their informal contract with their employers. It is a contract which is rarely made explicit, yet more and more staff consider it as part of the *quid pro quo* or "deal." In our experience, high levels of individual performance tend to go hand in hand with the continuing development of knowledge and skills. Furthermore, employees who feel that they are developing tend to remain much longer with their organizations, even when the financial rewards might be greater elsewhere. The chapter provides some insights into how managers can help develop their staff, both in their current roles, and in preparation for any future roles to which these staff might aspire.

Finally, Chap. 7 draws together the various strands of the book by addressing two main issues. Firstly, we discuss how, if you are being badly managed by your own boss, you can use the four ingredients to improve matters and get your organization to manage you more effectively. Secondly, in the light of the levels of opprobrium directed at managers from so many quarters, we examine whether the rewards for being a manager in the modern world can ever be worth the extra hours, the responsibility and the effort. We think that they can, and we explain why.

Managers at all levels want to know what it is they should be doing. Not all management or leadership books have been that helpful in this regard. The words of historical heroes and the thoughts of some contemporary business figures, which often adorn such texts, can undoubtedly be stirring. So are many of the anecdotes about these and other renowned figures. On closer examination, however, some of these exemplars may well have succeeded *despite* some of their actions or idiosyncrasies, and not because of them. And the real trouble is, that clever quotations and one-off war stories seem to be of little practical help, for instance, to an anxious manager facing an uncooperative, recalcitrant team on a Monday morning.

If managers pay appropriate attention to the four key ingredients, our experience is that the members of their teams will actively cooperate, and the work of the organization will get done. Not only are people more than delighted to be managed in this more professional way, somewhat surprisingly, even the most difficult amongst them will very often become a pleasure to manage, as well as becoming more effective performers.

The changing circumstances in our organizations mean that employees will continue to assert their independence, be more demanding, push back and more frequently challenge, as deference towards those in authority becomes more of a distant memory. Books such as this one not only reflect and disseminate this change, they also tend to confer a certain legitimacy as regards the change. We believe that the sorts of management practices we describe will become more and more necessary for the effective management of people at all levels. The *Management by Permission* genie has escaped from the bottle, we think it unlikely he will go back.

1.3 Who Is Our Audience?

The overall aim of the book is to set out an approach, which we call *Management by Permission,* to help ensure that people are managed effectively, in their own interests, as well as the interests of their organizations, leading to improved performance. As a consequence, we have several audiences in mind.

Our principal audience is *practising managers.* The book should interest anyone responsible for managing others, from the Chairperson, Chief Executive and the members of the Board, down to those embarking on their first management jobs. Although the scope of these roles may be different, the core principles of *Management by Permission* apply. Our aim is to provide a practical guide to help managers in solving the day-to-day problems they face in the modern world, rather than war stories about fashionably successful, charismatic or renowned public figures and leaders, who are often working in very specific contexts and circumstances.

Perhaps unusually for a 'management text', this book also contains a number of messages for *those being managed.* Of course, while many of us are in roles in which we have management responsibility, almost all of us are in roles in which we are, or should be, managed. At times during our careers, both of the authors of this book have been on the receiving end of poor management. And in our research and consultancy, we have seen some people managed quite appallingly. As noted above, being badly managed is unpleasant and stressful, as well as being an enormous problem, and there is precious little advice available about how to cope with this situation.

Contrary to what some might think, few people actually mind being managed. *What people object to is incompetent management.* When it happens it can lead to stress, resentment and underperformance. Those who are badly managed can get isolated from the mainstream of the organization. They can become uncooperative, depressed, petulant, or simply opt out, sometimes focusing only on what interests them. Even if their own sense of self-correction kicks in, they still face real difficulties. All of us probably feel we should be managed properly, but this is not going to happen by magic. At various points in the book, and specifically in Chap. 7, we provide some practical advice on how to proceed if you are badly managed, and how you can improve matters.

A third and final audience is our *colleagues in the consultancy and business school worlds, as well as those who write about leadership and management.* Consultants, including those engaged in executive coaching, will find insights and models to help identify and tackle the key management tasks faced by their clients. Academics may find the book useful as part of MBA, management or executive development programmes. Besides their professional interest in management, the majority of this third group may well spend some or all of their time working in organizations, wherein their activities will be 'managed.' In addition to the practical applications of this book in their own day-to-day activities, they may be interested in our observations and prescriptions as regards management in the modern world.

We know from our work in organizations that there are increasing numbers of people who have decided that, for a variety of reasons, management is not for them. Sometimes this is because they have seen managers living with constant stress, or spinning like out of control tops. As we argue, management does not have to be like that, and our hope is that downstream, the book may also encourage some of these individual contributors to remain in or take up managerial positions. Our organizations, be they public sector, private sector, business schools, trade unions or charities, all need talented and capable managers.

Like many authors before us, in one sense we have written the book that we wished we could have had when we embarked on our own careers. If it only helps some managers and their staff understand better how they can contribute more effectively in their organizations, with greater levels of personal and career satisfaction, *Management by Permission* will have achieved a useful purpose.

1.4   Guide for Readers

The opening sections of Chaps. 3–6 are emboldened and provide an overview of each chapter's content. Within the chapters themselves, each major section is signposted, and there are periodic summaries of the important messages. Textboxes are used throughout the book and these contain case studies, illustrations, checklists or other material relating to the main text. "Management books" sometimes make dull reading. At various times, in an attempt to reflect in a humorous way the points being made, we introduce cartoons. Many of these feature the fictitious Arnie Blenkinsop, the hapless modern manager who never quite gets it right.

The list of references at the end of each chapter is a guide to further reading and will enable academic colleagues and others to explore further some of the ideas, as well as locate other sources of guidance. Practising managers and those more interested in examining the potential application of the ideas to their current situations may wish to focus principally on the main text.

One optional use for the book is as a catalyst for discussion between managers and the members of their teams. The ideas and approaches suggested here should help to bring the important issues to the surface, get a way forward agreed, and establish more effective ways of working. Less ambitiously, selective use of some of the cartoons contained in the various chapters could also be used to help raise some of the issues in a light-hearted way.

References

Bennis, W., & Nanus, B. (2003). *Leaders: Strategies for taking charge*. New York: HarperCollins.

Birkinshaw, J. (2013). *Reinventing management: Smarter choices for getting work done*. San Francisco, CA: Jossey-Bass.

Covey, S. (1989). *The seven habits of highly effective people: Restoring the character ethic*. London: Simon & Schuster.

Drucker, P. F. (2009). *Management: Tasks, responsibilities, practices*. New York: HarperCollins.

Goffee, R., & Jones, G. (2006). *Why should anyone be led by you?* Boston, MA: Harvard Business School Press.

Goffee, R., & Jones, G. (2009). *Clever: Leading your smartest, most creative people*. Boston, MA: Harvard Business School Press.

Hamel, G. (2007). *The future of management*. Boston, MA: Harvard Business School Press.

Kotter, J. P. (2013, January). Management is still not leadership. *Harvard Business Review*.

Mintzberg, H. (2009). *Managing*. Harlow: Pearson.

Watson, T. J. (1994). *In search of management: Culture, chaos and control in managerial work*. London: Routledge.

Management Is More Difficult, but It's Not Mission Impossible

2

> *The truth always turns out to be simpler than you thought*
> Richard Feynman
> *We are now overled and undermanaged*
> Henry Mintzberg
> *Our organization is now so lean and mean, we're like the Cheshire cat. The grin is there, but precious little else*
> Marketing Executive
> *You never notice management unless it is poor*
> Software engineer

2.1 Managers Under Pressure

Management has always been a challenge. But managing in the modern world has become ever more difficult and time-consuming. Not only are people harder to manage, we seem to have created organizations in which many of our managers are now even less well equipped for the task.

Consider the following examples, all drawn from real life. Each describes someone in a management role, at a different level in their organization's hierarchy, struggling with the demands of their job.

> *The Chief Executive had been in post for nearly a year now, and the clock was beginning to tick more loudly, for him as well as the Directors. His appointment had initially been accompanied by a great fanfare. The Chairman had announced that things had gone slack under the previous administration, but that the new CEO would, "sort it all out." However, the share price had hardly moved, and little progress had been made by way of reorganization. None of the Directors ever disagreed with the decisions made at Executive meetings, but little seemed to change. Everyone was getting frustrated and some were beginning to fear for their jobs. "I feel like I have a number of buttons here", the CEO told us. "And they all have labels: 'Stop'; 'Start'; 'Change'; 'Reorganize'. The trouble is, when I press a button, it doesn't seem to be connected to anything."*

> *As the first meeting with his new team approached, Paolo was about as relaxed as a long tailed cat in a roomful of rocking chairs. A thirty-year old software specialist, he was one of*

© Springer International Publishing Switzerland 2016
T. McNulty, R. Marks, *Management by Permission*, Management for Professionals,
DOI 10.1007/978-3-319-25247-6_2

fifteen engineers in an IT department. Until recently he had never really considered a management career, but found he had quite enjoyed supervising small teams of graduates engaged in project work. When the IT Manager post fell vacant, following some major cost overruns, Paolo was flattered to be offered the job. None of his colleagues wanted it; their interests lay in solving hardware and software problems. After a weekend of soul-searching, Paolo accepted. He knew it was going to be tough: it would not be easy tackling the cost overruns, endemic in IT; staff turnover was high, and most of the younger engineers were very marketable; and finally, he did not have the best of relations with all the staff, especially two of the older engineers, who were of a similar age to the previous manager.

An economist in international headquarters, for the last six years Katherine had success-fully managed three teams of economists. Following a reorganization, she was put in charge of a new department of forty. In addition to her old group she was now responsible for a team of lawyers. Although Katherine was well respected amongst the economists, there was considerable resentment of her amongst the lawyers. They had only ever known reporting to a manager with a legal background. They were concerned about their career prospects, felt that the legal department was being "punished" for its previous manager's performance, and feared that Katherine would not appreciate the special problems of legal work. Katherine wondered whether she was up to it.

Whilst each of the above is not without its difficulties, the sorts of problems faced by these managers are not really that new. All Chief Executives know that it is rare for top-level decisions to be implemented entirely smoothly, and at the sort of pace they would like. In common with the IT Manager, most of us were more than a little fearful when we first stepped onto the managerial ladder. And supervising staff with a different professional background to our own—the task facing the international economist—has always been a stretch, and certainly in the initial stages.

So why does this Chief Executive feel quite so frustrated at his lack of progress? Why is Paolo so concerned about his ability to manage a team of talented professionals, none of whom wanted his job? And why should an experienced and successful manager like Katherine begin to doubt her management skills in an organization with which she is so familiar?

2.2   Difficult Times, More Challenging People

There are a number of reasons why management in the twenty-first century seems to have become harder. We would highlight four in particular:

2.2.1   Reason One: Leaner and Meaner Organizations

Driven by the need to reduce costs, the trend towards more streamlined organizations—taking out levels of management and reducing overall numbers of staff—has placed many more demands on everyone, and especially managers.

Greater responsibility falling on fewer shoulders has inevitably led to heavier workloads, with the potential for longer hours and more stress for both managers and employees. Very few managers depart for the day with an empty inbox, and it is only the most disciplined who leave their phones permanently switched off when returning home.

Wider spans of control in many organizations have meant a greater distance between managers and their direct reports. This often leads to management by rules, procedures and metrics, and staff sometimes feeling that their performance ratings and salary decisions are arrived at unfairly, by managers who have had limited direct contact with them. When an individual complained about this in one organization, he was told: "Yes, but I know lots of people like you."

Increasing numbers of part-time workers and independent contractors, as well as greater use made of outsourcing, have placed greater demands on a manager's ability to specify outputs and deliver results. In addition, with knowledge advancing and becoming more complex in many technical fields, some managers are called upon to supervise and appraise professional staff when they neither understand, nor necessarily appreciate, these individuals' professional skills. And whatever the merits of matrix organizations, they have done little to make lives easier for the managers involved: even more people to be consulted; a degree of ambiguity about reporting lines; and more difficulties in working out 'who is responsible for what?'

Fewer staff means that managers are now much more dependent on a smaller complement of individuals. Many organizations used to strive for "backup" coverage for management and technical posts at various levels (McNulty 2000). Reductions in the number of layers and downsizing have often turned this into a luxury, with backup support and successors now much thinner on the ground. One effect of this "delayering" is that posts which were once deemed important to an organization, even if not mission critical, have now become of greater consequence.

By way of an example, in an HR Department in which formerly two people looked after payroll and headcount reporting, they would provide backup coverage for each other. In the 'lean and mean' structure, one person alone is given the responsibility. An unplanned absence can now cause a major crisis. The work has to be done, but no-one is sufficiently knowledgeable to do it to the required standard. Worse still, if the incumbent becomes uncooperative, falls ill, or resigns at short notice, there is no-one to train a successor. Thus larger organizations are now facing what has always been a problem for SMEs: they are even more reliant on smaller numbers of staff, some of whom may be doing fairly routine work. Such staff members have become more indispensable, and the smaller the department or the business, the greater the proportion of individuals critical to its future. In organizations in which the number of part-time employees has increased, these problems are exacerbated. While outsourcing can be a solution, it can also be costly, and it is often a struggle to specify the precise nature and level of services required, when demands can change so rapidly.

Overall, there is now much more pressure on managers to deal with ambiguity and uncertainty, to plan for peaks and troughs, and to deal with rapid changes when the one-time goalposts suddenly turn into hanging baskets.

2.2.2 Reason Two: Less Respect for Organizations, People in Authority and Those in Management Positions

Amongst the general public there has been a progressive waning of trust in almost all organizations—public or private sector institutions, churches, banks or hospitals. It is an endless list. The public's confidence has been gradually eroded by a variety of factors including spin, lies, exploitation, profiteering, corporate scandals, misleading information, cover-ups, mismanagement and administrative incompetence, as well as by the abuse of power for reasons of self-interest, greed, personal advancement or self-gratification.

Those in positions of authority no longer automatically command respect, whether they are public figures, politicians, managers at work or even sports referees, the latter frequently facing abuse and even violence (Elleray 2004, pp. 7–11). Little by little, the public has learned to be sceptical non-believers of anyone who dons the cloak of authority. Although some sources of information are more reliable than others, checking 'the facts' has become easier through Twitter, Facebook, the Internet and other sources.

Large pension pay offs for senior executives, especially when these are seen as a reward for failure, have contributed to a deeply ingrained cynicism towards organizations and some of those in charge. Any public apologies for misdemeanours carry little weight. People are suspected of apologizing only because they have been found out. When questionable practices cease, it is assumed to be because people can no longer get away with them.

Very few reputations—including those of lauded historical figures—seem to survive the penetrating and intrusive scrutiny to which they are now subjected. The French philosopher Montaigne informed us that few men were wonders to their families, and in a similar vein, a seventeenth century French society hostess and woman of letters told us, "No man is a hero to his valet."[1] Modern investigative journalism and research, as well as organizational whistle-blowers, have provided similarly intimate portraits on many of those in the public eye, with people sometimes proving flawed and all too human in their frailties. Few areas of investigation are now taboo, and few reputations entirely survive the intensive scrutiny to which they can be subjected.

Whenever there is a problem in an organization, management almost always gets the blame. In the minds of many people, management has come to be associated with unnecessary controls, bureaucracy, rules, downsizing, micromanagement, incompetence, and a whole set of roadblocks which get in the way of performance.

---

[1] "Il n'y a pas de grand homme pour son valet-de-chambre" (Mme A. M. Bigot de Cornuel).

"I'm not sure Blenkinsop's quite got the hang of managing the Millennials"

The profession of management is generally less respected and in some quarters even despised. Any regard for an individual manager is conditional and depends on how people continue to assess that manager's competence, capability and credibility, and whether they are perceived to add value. While managers might hold down a formal position of leadership, authority and status by virtue of where they sit in an organization structure or hierarchy, managers now have to earn the right to be in charge. This point is rather neatly captured in the provocative title of the book: *Why should anyone be led by you?* (Goffee and Jones 2006). To earn this right, managers have to act professionally, with all that that entails. They will not succeed by trying to effect the latest trends, nor trying to win staff over by pretending to be 'one of them', like the hapless Blenkinsop.

These various trends have affected the balance of power in the organizations in which we work, with any managerial authority now much more open to challenge.

2.2.3 Reason Three: A More Demanding, Self-assured and Diverse Workforce

It does not seem to matter whether they are baby boomers, migrants settling into a new country, Millennials, or whether they are described as belonging to Generations X, Y or even Z. As deference towards authority has declined (Layard 2005, pp. 91–92), people are generally much more confident, assertive and self-assured in their day-to-day dealings with others.

In public, whether it is on the public highways, public transport or in stores, people are much more demanding and likely to insist upon what they consider to be their inalienable rights. Similarly, those working in organizations also tend to assert a greater sense of freedom and independence in relating to other people. Some people's rights have been reinforced and legitimated through equal opportunities, affirmative action and anti-discrimination laws and programmes.

Employee attitudes towards employers have undergone some subtle changes in many places. With fewer individuals knowing the meaning of 'job security', many people feel less loyal to their employers as they work harder for the same or less money, contribute more towards their pensions, and face a later retirement. During an in company seminar, one of us jokingly remarked that a modern mission statement for staff in many organizations might read: "Be happy, for less money, and work harder and longer." One of the participants called out: "Who said anything about being happy?"

And not only have attitudes towards employers altered. The composition of the workforce in many countries is much more varied, and this often adds an extra layer of difficulty as more and more managers take charge of teams with a diversity of gender, culture and background. This can make management more time-consuming, as well as make it more difficult to understand some individuals, and anticipate and interpret their reactions and motives.

Many modern employees are not shy in letting others know about their knowledge and skills, and very often their self-assessments of their value and capabilities are indeed well-founded. Similarly, more and more people consider that their own opinions on almost any subject are as valid as the next person's, regardless of whether all of these opinions are equally informed. In the workplace many employees feel they are both qualified and entitled to make critical judgements in a range of fields far beyond the confines of their own.

Notwithstanding the effects of periodic recessions, which bring with them momentary concerns about job prospects, employees in firms large and small can display a belligerent self-confidence in their ability to secure employment in other organizations, or even to resign in order to run their own businesses should they so wish. In many organizations, some of the more experienced employees have attained a level of financial independence which means that they feel they do not have to work, and certainly not necessarily for you.

As a consequence of all these trends, most modern employees expect to be consulted about matters that affect them. This does not automatically mean that they will disagree with what management is proposing, nor does it necessarily mean they will be obstructive. It is just that they do not expect to be treated as cannon fodder, on the receiving end of whatever gets doled out. Most people want more two-way communication: to be asked for their views on topics beforehand, rather than just be notified about decisions after the fact. Such a process can certainly improve the quality of decision-making and help with subsequent implementation, but it is also harder, and invariably more time-consuming for the manager.

Not only do many staff have the knowledge and ability needed to solve the problems their employers may face, they also know where most of the organizational bodies are buried. This has made many of them much more conscious of their power, freedom and autonomy. It is as if horses suddenly realized that they were stronger than their riders. People have sensed that managerial authority is less potent than previously, and there is less to fear if they disobey or subvert management intentions. Even if they wanted to use them, there are precious few sanctions available to modern managers. Staff can often fail to cooperate with impunity. And many managers tell us that if they do try and impose discipline, their organizations are not always willing to support them.

In truth, people have always had the potential to subvert authority or avoid doing what they did not want to do. With leaner organizations and often greatly expanded spans of control, the demands on management are greatly enhanced, and the time to supervise the activities of increasing numbers of direct reports plummets. Most of us will recall our schooldays and what tended to happen when the teacher left the classroom. Gouldner (1954) showed that when employees in a gypsum plant were no longer subject to systematic observation, they could ignore management rules. Similarly Shepard and Blake (1962) studied industrial employees and found a significant decline in output when supervisors were absent at their daily meetings.

Modern managers are deluded if they think that their instructions will always be followed to the letter when they are not present. And this is despite some of the more sophisticated monitoring and surveillance techniques now available—tachographs, the recording of telephone calls, monitoring of email and Internet usage, controlled electronic access to buildings and various office locations, as well as the practice of clocking in and out, which continues in many places.

If the aim of these techniques was to make sure employees always followed instructions and rules, then they have failed. Instances of "time theft"—defined as perpetrating a fraud by claiming and receiving financial rewards for work not done—continue to be reported (see, for instance Humphreys (2013), who cites the dismissal of 29 Canadian road workers following time theft allegations; also Fitzgibbon (2014)). People have been caught out 'clocking in' absent colleagues, and taking extended breaks. And how many of us know colleagues who have made excessive use of company time and facilities in order to conduct personal business via email and telephone?

Ehrenreich (2001), who took a series of low level jobs in order to explore the difficulties of surviving in America on a basic wage, was lectured about time theft in one organization. Based on her experiences, she concluded that without constant supervision and monitoring, it would be very difficult to envisage how "management" could force staff to work all of the time.

According to David Bolchover (2005), many office employees are "switched off and zoned out" and he cites evidence from a number of sources:

- In one survey, nearly 15 % of US workers admitted surfing nonwork related Internet sites *constantly* (his emphasis)
- At the Department for Work and Pensions in the UK, an investigation into Internet usage found that, over a period of 8 months in 2004, 2.3 million pages of pornographic material had been accessed
- In another survey, employers reported that each week workers spent on average 8.3 hrs. (more than an entire working day) accessing nonwork related websites
- One in three all-day visitors to a theme park admitted taking the day off from work on a dishonest pretext

- In 2004, a Finnish tax auditor died at his desk, and it took the hundred people working on the same floor two days to notice.

Paulsen (2014) cites international statistics suggesting that what he calls "empty labor"—defined as private activities carried out at work by employees—accounts for an average of 2 hrs. per employee per day. He also interviewed some extreme cases who spent half of their time on nonwork activities, as well as one person who wrote a postgraduate thesis whilst at work. Some of Paulsen's interview sample actively resisted attempts to get them to carry out their employers' work, while others simply did not have enough to do. In her controversial book, EDF employee Corinne Maier (2006) even recommended employees to do little work if they wanted to advance in the hierarchy.

In our own research and consultancy we have uncovered numerous examples of employees subverting management intentions, or ignoring instructions which they did not 'own':

- A group of staff employed on the late shift in a processing plant had organized a rota which enabled them to schedule small group visits to a local bar
- A Chief Executive in the public eye, renowned for outspoken utterances on a number of business topics, and especially those relating to staff efficiencies, would be surprised to observe the relaxed ambience which pervades at head office during his frequent absences overseas. In contrast with the frenetic atmosphere he creates whilst there, when he is abroad, office staff enjoy long lunches and take extended breaks. Sometimes they even organize office games
- In a study into management and executive succession in a global corporation, it was found that some subsidiaries would sometimes submit the names of patently unsuitable candidates as successors on replacement planning charts ("people we would not appoint to those roles in a million years", in the words of one subsidiary director). Subsidiary staff behaved in this way in order to meet corporate form-filling requirements and avoid subsequent sanctions
- Following the appointment of a new Head of an international firm, one senior staff member openly ignored an instruction to stop working on his existing programme. He told us: "I don't agree with the new strategy and I am continuing to use my staff as well as other resources on the project. And I will carry on doing so. One day they will want to pursue this area again and I will be prepared"
- When a newly-appointed HR manager visited a plant during the night shift, he discovered that some of the employees had formed a rock band, and were spending several hours each night rehearsing
- The top management of an engineering company decided to focus on a smaller range of products, and as a consequence decided to cease production of a particular component. One of the engineering managers disagreed with the decision and kept on sending samples to customers, who in turn continued to order them. The directors then took away the manager's staff, whereupon he started borrowing staff from elsewhere in the organization. In the end the directors gave in and the product was reinstated.

Sometimes people are openly insubordinate, at other times covertly so. Others pretend to follow instructions and then do not. What is clear in the modern world is that if individuals do not wish to do something, and feel they can get away without doing so, then sometimes they will. Most of us can only be managed with our consent.

2.2.4 Reason Four: Managers Often Less Well Equipped to Do the Job

In a previous era, large numbers of managers would be able to perform most of the jobs reporting to them, often at least as well as the incumbents themselves. In some organizations, the ability to handle each of the jobs in a given department was a prerequisite to a supervisory appointment. These days have long gone. The managerial equivalent of Renaissance Man (or even Woman), expert in all of the work performed by his or her staff, no longer exists.

Opportunities to develop management skills have become fewer, given the reduction in the number of intermediate management positions in many organizations. Posts such as Section Leader, Unit Leader, Deputies and Assistants are much rarer. If any manager dares to propose an organization structure containing these sorts of roles, he or she will often be challenged by top management or by external advisers, and the structure will be revised.

Formerly, fledgling managers had the chance to cut their teeth by, in a first instance, taking responsibility for smaller groups or teams. The consequences of any errors were not so great: there were more managers above them in the structure to go to for advice and guidance. Flatter structures tend not to allow such a luxury, and many managers find themselves appointed to their first management post, and one with a wide span of control, with relatively little supervisory experience, and practically no safety net. Furthermore, technical specialists and experts who have no supporting staff tend not to bequeath their expertise to anyone in the organization. When they depart, much of their knowledge usually departs with them.

One consequence is that many managers now live in permanent fear of the words: "OK boss, you tell me what to do and I'll do it." Managers hearing this know they are in serious trouble. At best, the work would get done no better than they could do themselves. Modern managers rarely have the technical knowledge to do their subordinates' jobs. And even if they do have this knowledge, no manager can be sufficiently close to the detail of every job to be sure where the current elephant traps might lie. In most instances, managers can only tell their staff what is necessary to meet the overall strategy, where the employee's work fits into that strategy, and the context in which their work is being carried out. At worst, managers can be on the receiving end of "malicious obedience", whereby the person given an instruction obeys that instruction even though they know it is misguided and can lead to problems.

Another consequence is that there are fewer organizational role models that less experienced managers can observe, and from whom they can learn. Frequently senior managers have less time available for coaching and mentoring their more junior counterparts.

"I think Arnie needs to speak to his executive coach"

It is little wonder that many of those with management potential seem less interested in management roles. Try engaging your "high potentials" in a discussion about possible managerial posts. Whilst some are interested, many others head off faster than rats up a drainpipe. Not everyone wants the trouble of trying to manage demanding people like themselves, and people believe that they can get career satisfaction in other ways.

We have seen a number of attempts to force such high potentials into managerial roles, resulting in their poor performance as managers, and even in some cases their resignations soon after, as they return to roles as individual contributors elsewhere. Sometimes it is the poorer professional performers, or those motivated by financial or other pressures, who apply for the management positions. Many such individuals can lack credibility in a management role.

Given this background, it is hardly surprising to learn that organizations world-wide are more and more obsessive about the quality of their overall management "bench strength" and the length of time it would take to replace certain key employees should they resign.

2.3 The Bad News for Employees: You Pay a High Price for Being Poorly Managed

At first sight, the various difficulties facing management might seem welcome news for those being managed. As their confidence has increased and they have become more assertive, at the same time many of those managing them have become less self-assured and less secure in their positions. The result in some cases has been ever more freedom and autonomy, enabling staff to concentrate more of their time and energies on whatever they want—interesting technical challenges, the Internet, pet projects, personal development, extensive "networking", keeping up with the latest developments in those fields that interest them, or simply playing in their particular sandpits.

If there are some tasks these staff do not wish to perform—perhaps because they do not agree the tasks are important, or they are opposed to elements of their organization's strategy, or they prefer to be otherwise engaged—first of all they may delay matters by arguing at length. If this does not work, they will do the tasks grudgingly, poorly, or perhaps not at all. Micromanaging them is not a solution. As well as being time-consuming and undesirable, at its worst, person-to-person marking by the supervisor can be like watching an old-style screensaver: you can see some activity, but you are not sure what, if anything, is being accomplished.

But, as in the old tale of the Monkey's Paw (Jacobs 1902), staff should be careful what they wish for. As Oscar Wilde put it, "The Gods have two ways of dealing harshly with us—the first is to deny us our dreams, and the second is to grant them." Poorly managed employees face some real difficulties and are destined to pay a high price if the situation continues. Even assuming their jobs survive, if they are ambitious, they face an immediate problem. As was pointed out by Peter Drucker some years ago, in the real world few subordinates are promoted over the prostrate bodies of incompetent bosses.

But promotion prospects are actually the least of their difficulties. If all of us are to deploy our talents effectively, in our own interests as well as our employers', we need a proper context in which to operate. Poor management will deny us this. Starved of proper direction and control, where we focus our efforts may not be what the organization requires. And when it comes to assessing us, or considering us for bonuses or salary reviews, or even as potential promotion candidates, it does not matter how many problems we have solved. We will not get the credit because few people will know what we have achieved.

Progressively cut off from what matters in our organizations, deprived of quality information and feedback from above, we risk becoming marginalized, our ability to carry out satisfying and significant work very much reduced. Increasingly ignored as an irrelevant or annoying presence, we have fewer opportunities for development, lack role models, and can be in danger of sinking quickly into a narrow technical cleft, as we join others in an organizational isolation ward.

When this happens, our frustrations mount, and we are destined to discover that being badly managed is an unpleasant as well as a corrosive experience. Many of us have long hankered after more freedom, but Godot has always been a disappointment whenever he has turned up. We might appear to be getting what we want. However, as our liberty turns into licence, some of us become like the barking dog that always ran after the car. When the car stopped one day, the confused animal just did not know what to do.

Curiously, excessive freedom has a tendency to hamper professional development. Our career opportunities can be derailed because decisions about us get made on spurious criteria, by individuals with whom we have had minimal contact. Progressively, our importance and status in the organization declines, and our market value drops. If we are poorly managed, there is little documented evidence as to our effectiveness, no-one has much idea about our level of contribution, and there is no credible supervisor at hand to send out the lifeboat for us. As our professional reputation and performance decline, we become less employable elsewhere. At worst, unable to resign, we just remain in resignation, until we leave or get fired.

Yet managed well, most employees can and do perform, and the future success of any organization can be built around them. Managed poorly, they are a nightmare for their employers. If they become dissatisfied, they can withdraw their cooperation and become difficult. When this happens, if you are lucky, they leave your organization. But sometimes they stay, disturbing others, taking up valuable time and resources, or wreaking havoc. If and when they do finally depart, they can leave behind them a legacy of landmines—poor records, inadequate files, missing information, soured relationships with customers and others—a myriad of problems.

2.4   The Death of Autocratic Management?

Despite the above, 'management by fear' is still to be found in some places, along with some of the more old-style coercive and directive approaches to managing people—the macho management "square them or squash them" philosophy, in the words attributed to one-time British Prime Minster Lloyd George. However, the effectiveness of such styles does seem to be in decline, even if the species itself is unlikely ever to be entirely extinct. There will always be some individuals in whom the desire to dominate, overpower and even bully, is hardwired. And they may well be lucky in finding organizations in which for a time they can get away with it, or compliant subordinates prepared to put up with it. Similarly, when organizations are in crisis, some of the niceties can momentarily take a back seat, and employees will often accept the necessity for strong direction and a degree of autocracy for short periods.

Autocratic management *can* work for a limited time, but it tends not to work in perpetuity. The 900 pound gorilla with the loaded machine gun does get some things done. But, as soon as he turns his back or gets out of range, blind obedience to his authority has a tendency to stop. Furthermore, if people are treated aggressively and without consideration when they are in a weak position, such as during a business or economic downturn, they will remember it later when they are in a stronger one. They will also watch to see how you treat their colleagues. When the economy improves and businesses look up, those who feel that employees have been treated poorly will become more difficult, or take steps to move elsewhere.

2.5   The Good News: "Management by Permission"

We have described a world in which: management is more challenging; there is more 'push back' from below; insubordination may be harder to spot; and organizations increasingly rely on fewer and fewer key individuals. Against such a background, can managers hope to manage?

The *good* news is that they can. We have seen it done. People *can* be managed effectively, in their own interests as well as in the interests of their employers. But it requires a different management approach, which we call *Management by Permission (MBP)*. It is neither a directive "command and control" style, nor is it permissive management, which is so focused on the needs of people, that the staff are free to do as they please. *Management by Permission* is hard-nosed consensual management. It is hard-nosed because certain elements, such as control, are non-negotiable, and it is consensual because it involves the willing cooperation and commitment of the staff.

Management by Permission still requires managers to manage. Employees are still subject to direction from above, but control is increasingly exercised *with the active cooperation and consent* of those who are being managed. Managers need to expend time and energy in order to secure this active cooperation. But the time and energy has to be spent in the right ways. Managerial control is still exercised, but the rationale for decisions is explained, whenever possible, and people's concerns and ideas are listened to. At its heart, *Management by Permission* is based on a mutuality of interests: the work of the organization gets done, and employees are rewarded for deploying their talents in a meaningful context in which their contributions are fully recognized, and their personal and professional development needs are addressed.

Not all of them will readily admit it, but most people are in fact desperate to be managed properly. They: (1) want to get the credit and be recognized and rewarded for their achievements, in a context in which they are focused on the right priorities for the organization; (2) want to know what is expected of them; (3) need their managers to help and protect them so they can get on with their jobs; and (4) want to grow and develop their capabilities. These are the four principal ingredients to *Management by Permission*. When all of these elements are present, everything falls into place, and work can actually be enjoyable.

We already spend large portions of our lives at work, which for many people now plays a significant role in providing our lives with meaning (Handy 2001; de Botton 2009). If financial and other considerations mean that the majority of us are going to have to retire much later, then we need to get as much satisfaction as we can whilst we are at work.

A client once told us that people should come with an operating manual so that their managers would know how to deal with them. In a sense, this book is our attempt at such a manual. However, we believe that the people being managed would also benefit from consulting the manual. Both managers and managed need concrete and practical advice on what to focus on and what to do in their day-to-day work environments to ensure effective working. The alternative many of us adopt, when faced with difficulties, is to imitate the horse in Orwell's *Animal Farm* (2000). We simply work harder. However, unless you are doing the right things, working harder will not solve your problems, it will just make you even more tired and frustrated. Based on our experience, this book sets out those "right things" which managers need to be doing, so that they will be better equipped to do their jobs.

References

Bolchover, D. (2005). *The living dead: Switched off, zoned out the shocking truth about office life*. Chichester: Capstone.

de Botton, A. (2009). *The pleasures and sorrows of work*. London: Hamish Hamilton.

Ehrenreich, B. (2001). *Nickel and Dimed: On not getting by in America*. New York: Henry Holt and Company.

Elleray, D. (2004). *The man in the middle: The autobiography*. London: Time Warner.

Fitzgibbon, M. (2014). *What is wilful misconduct under the Ontario employment standards act?* Thoughts from a management lawyer—Commentary on Canadian labour and employment law issues (Labour Law Internet Blog).

Goffee, R., & Jones, G. (2006). *Why should anyone be led by you?* Boston, MA: Harvard Business School Press.

Gouldner, A. W. (1954). *Patterns of industrial bureaucracy*. New York: The Free Press.

Handy, C. (2001). *The elephant and the flea: Looking backwards to the future*. London: Random House.

Humphreys, A. (2013, January). Hamilton fires 29 city roadworkers who allegedly ran personal errands when they should have been patching potholes. *National Post Canada*.

Jacobs, W. W. (1902). The monkey's paw. In *The lady of the barge*. London/New York: Harper & Brothers.

Layard, R. (2005). *Happiness: Lessons from a new science*. London: Penguin.

Maier, C. (2006). *Bonjour laziness: Why hard work doesn't pay*. London: Orion.

McNulty, A. (2000). *Rationality and the process of succession in a global corporation*. Unpublished Ph.D. thesis, London Graduate School of Business Studies.

Orwell, G. (2000). *Animal farm: A fairy story*. Harmondsworth: Penguin Modern Classics.

Paulsen, R. (2014). *Empty labor: Idleness and workplace resistance*. Cambridge: Cambridge University Press.

Shepard, H. R., & Blake, R. R. (1962). Changing behavior through cognitive change. *Human Organization, 21*, 88–92.

The First Ingredient: Keep Things Under Control

3

> *Trust, but verify*
>
> Russian proverb
>
> *The uninspected inevitably deteriorates*
>
> Dwight Eisenhower
>
> *As a rule, he or she who has the most information will have the greatest success in life*
>
> Benjamin Disraeli
>
> *Check at least two reliable sources*
>
> Classic rule in journalism

A "MUST" FOR MANAGERS, EFFECTIVE MONITORING AND CONTROLLING ALSO BRINGS CONSIDERABLE BENEFITS TO THOSE BEING MANAGED

For many people, "control" is a bad word, with connotations of authority for its own sake, Big Brother, the imposition of inappropriate targets and measures, micromanagement and bureaucracy. *But an organization not under proper control is one out of control.* And out of control organizations tend to fail, putting everyone's futures at risk.

In this chapter we show how a combination of three key control techniques enables MANAGERS to:

- Know what work is underway and pending in their areas
- Help ensure this work is carried out to time, cost and quality
- Delegate with confidence, without losing touch
- Balance departmental workloads
- Cope with and incorporate flexible work practices
- Ensure effective, relevant communications
- Use the resources of all team members in decision-making and problem-solving

© Springer International Publishing Switzerland 2016

T. McNulty, R. Marks, *Management by Permission*, Management for Professionals, DOI 10.1007/978-3-319-25247-6_3

- Capture the "departmental memory"
- Concentrate development and coaching activities so these are both timely and effective

We will show how these control processes are also in the interests of THOSE BEING MANAGED in that they help staff to:

- Have more freedom to work in their own manner and style and reduce micromanagement
- Gain recognition for their work and be assessed on their whole contribution
- Have an opportunity to have their views taken into account when decisions are made
- Have fair, fact based appraisals
- Be kept informed about the changing organizational context of their work
- Use the experience, networks and authority of their managers
- Get effective and timely coaching and development

Whenever we conduct individual fact gathering discussions as part of consulting assignments or what we call, "taking the temperature" reviews, towards the end of every interview we usually ask: "If you could only give this organization one piece of advice, what would that be?" The answers help in focusing on what people really consider important. And if you were to ask us, on the basis of all of our experience, what is the one piece of general advice we would give to managers, we would answer: *"Make sure that you have got things under control."*

In a world in which more and more people can only be managed with their permission, keeping control nonetheless remains a must for all managers. If they do so nowhere else, control is the one area in which managers must exercise their authority. Every manager, like the Chief Executive in the case study at the beginning of Chap. 2, gets into trouble when this basic requirement is ignored. And when managers fail to control, it causes real difficulties for those being managed.

As a manager, without an effective overall control system, you have no real handle on the work going on in your area. The result is poor follow-up to the decisions made, no proper monitoring of progress, unclear ownership of the issues, and rising levels of stress for all concerned. Under these circumstances, it is usually only a matter of time before something goes wrong. In our experience, losing control of the work is one of the main reasons managers lose their jobs. It can lead to bad publicity, negative headlines in newspapers, and organizations subject to ridicule and censure. In the worst cases it can lead to disasters, lawsuits and even the demise of the organization itself (Leeson 1996; Fox 2003).

From the staff's point of view, a lack of control means they do not necessarily get the support and information they need to perform effectively. In addition, they rarely get the credit for what they have done, and the way their performance is subsequently assessed can sometimes be little more than a farce. Performance review meetings turn into "blamestorming." If control is poor, staff may enjoy more freedom, but it is often no more than the freedom to fail.

This chapter highlights and describes three of the main methods for keeping control: (1) those based on *monitoring and reviewing quantitative data* or metrics (in short, 'tracking the numbers'); (2) what we call a *Work Management System* (keeping an up to date list of jobs and reviewing them at set intervals); and (3) a range of *informal methods* (which include simply walking the patch). Our experience suggests that most managers will probably need to draw on all three of these approaches in concert, with each one often informing the others.

If you are relatively new to management, the chapter can help you to decide on what should be controlled in your area and how to go about it. More experienced managers who already have their control systems in place may find the chapter helpful in reviewing their current practices, and considering whether certain of their control processes should be updated or tightened.

> THE THREE TECHNIQUES OF CONTROL ARE:
> **(1) Track the numbers**
> **(2) Use a Work Management System**
> **(3) Use informal methods including Management by Walking Around (MBWA or "walking the patch")**

3.1 Technique Number One: Track the Numbers

In this section we will:

- *Discuss briefly how measures are used in some organizations*
- *Describe the three main pitfalls managers need to avoid when using measures*
- *Discuss some of the factors involved in setting measures in your own area*

A standard set of key numbers, statistics or measures has traditionally formed part of most attempts at monitoring and controlling the performance of both organizations and those working in them. If anything, this emphasis on "metrics" has become ever more formalized, moving beyond areas such as manufacturing, where output, quality, and other measures have always been tracked. Many organizations now have well established "balanced scorecards" or "dashboards" which monitor and review key targets and measures in line with the organization's strategy (Kaplan and Norton 1996).

Some firms use a "traffic light" system in presenting the important data, so that deviations from plan are highlighted and remedial action can be taken. And these high level numbers are usually then disaggregated in order that they can be passed down in the form of departmental and ultimately individual targets. In some organizations, weekly or monthly performance data are posted publicly so that different departments or units can compare themselves against others. In some cultures this exerts a powerful motivational effect on the performance of in-house teams.

The types of data, performance indicators, and measures used vary widely according to organization and industry. For instance, many global firms employ a number of standard measures for their country marketing or sales organizations. Typical examples of these measures would be: orders; revenues; headcount; customer satisfaction; profitability; and cash in the bank. Some of the measures are sometimes combined with other information, to calculate further indicators of business health, and compare productivity levels at different locations or across business lines.

Professional services firms tend to track a number of elements including: potential sales in the pipeline; sales achieved; hours/days billed; work in progress; and individual utilization. Again, these figures can subsequently be used to develop further measures, such as profit per partner or employee, which can be compared against industry or sector norms.

Metrics can also be useful warning signs of possible problems with an organization's processes or help inform further action. For instance, universities might monitor: numbers of applicants for courses; attendance figures at lectures; numbers of new graduates obtaining jobs and their starting salaries. In the retail world footfall is an important measure. Amazon has been known to monitor closely CPO ("contacts per customer order"), since a higher number of contacts can be an indicator of, for instance, the effectiveness of customer communications or possible defects in the quality of Amazon's processes. Analyzing the reasons why customers need to get in touch can be an indication of the need to improve aspects of operations (Hubbard 2007; Price and Jaffe 2008). Some organizations now measure customer satisfaction by means of a "Net Promoter Score" (NPS) based on customer responses to 'the ultimate question': whether they would recommend an organization, product or service to others (Reichheld 2011).

There is, however, an extensive literature on the pitfalls of an over reliance on measures and targets (Weber 1968; Merton 1968; Watson 1994). In our experience, managers need to avoid three dangers in particular.

3.1.1 First Danger: Misleading, Incomplete or Inappropriate Data

Managers must make sure that the data and measures they are using are reliable and fit for purpose. This is not necessarily an easy task. As management writer Peter Drucker put it: "Tell anyone over the age of twenty-one to find a set of statistics to support a predetermined conclusion, and they will be able to do it."

Drucker was highlighting the fact that, whether intentionally or unintentionally, data can mislead. So, for example, to assess heart surgeons solely on the survival rates of their patients could penalise those surgeons engaged in treating the more complicated cases. As a result, the competence of some outstandingly capable surgeons could be called into question, and it could also encourage changes in how patients with certain complications are treated.

In a similar vein, it is sometimes forgotten that some of the numbers managers use are based on "best guesses." Staff estimates of the hours they have spent working on projects, jobs, or for particular clients tend to be in this category. The fact that they are estimates does not mean that we should not use them, but we should be aware that we are not always dealing with precise measurement. Often our measures are nothing more than indicators of what we may be interested in. For example, staff absentee rates can be a guide to morale, but they may also highlight a flu epidemic or a sports fixture.

"Do please hurry Arnie, the Chief Executive is waiting for this month's sales figures"

In the context of misleading measures, consider also the case of one firm which had an industrywide reputation for "best in class" performance on a "revenue per employee" ratio. On closer examination it became apparent that the firm had maintained its premier position by laying off full-time employees on Fridays, only to rehire these selfsame employees as "agency staff" on the following Monday (Pfeffer 1992).

Traps such as these are more common than is generally realized, and they often remain undiscovered. For this reason, in addition to keeping any measures they use under continual review, we always advise managers to: (1) get to know who is compiling any data they are using; and (2) understand how these individuals collect and process this information. Record-keepers may perform a more conscientious (or even different) job if they know interest is being shown in how they go about their work, and that the results of what they do are being reviewed or used for a particular purpose.

Talking to the individuals responsible for data-gathering and compilation can be an eye-opener. We were working in one firm whose new Chief Executive was attempting to compare payroll costs month by month. After a large increase appeared one month, it transpired that differing categories of payment methods were rendering monthly comparisons difficult: some staff were paid weekly, some fortnightly, and some monthly. This meant that some "months" contained five weeks of data for the weekly paid, and three sets of payments for those paid fortnightly.

If you are making comparisons over time, check that the measurement method is consistent. Published statistics on suicides in Prussia showed an increase between 1882 and 1883. However, the change was found to have coincided with a transfer of responsibility for recordkeeping from the police to the civil service, who were presumably more diligent about data recording (Webb et al. 2000).

3.1.2   Second Danger: Unintended Consequences

The law of unintended consequences (Weber 1968; Merton 1968; Watson 1994) points out that the actions people take to achieve their goals often lead to unantici-pated consequences: Prohibition in America created Al Capone. Similarly, whilst mandatory seat belts can reduce the number of deaths amongst vehicle occupants, the sense of security they bring to drivers can lead to increased fatalities amongst cyclists and pedestrians.

Sometimes the "means" we choose can undermine the objective to the extent that they achieve the precise opposite to what was intended. And when our metrics become more than indicators, they have a habit of turning into ends in themselves rather than means to ends.

For example, when a measure was set in the UK National Health Service whereby outpatients had to be seen within a given time period, there were reports that some patients were seen by a nurse for an initial "consultation"—which consisted of some form-filling, after which they were weighed—and then returned to the waiting room where they sat for a further 3 hrs. The measure designed to improve the service offered to patients had been successfully met, but the service and frustration experienced by patients had worsened.

Some further examples of unintended consequences in organizational settings are described in Fig. 3.1. The message for managers is: by all means use measures to monitor performance and track progress. You are missing an important trick if you fail to do so. But measures can have a tendency to become contaminated over time. So keep the measures you use under continual review so as to ensure they are meeting your requirements and are still measuring what you think they are measuring.

3.1.3   Third Danger: Using Measures as a Stick Rather than as a Guide

Setting measures and targets can be helpful in indicating the expected standards of performance required. Some people find these motivating: they like to test and measure themselves against a set of standards or goals.

However, other people have had poor experiences with such organizational measurement systems, to the extent that they will rebel against any attempts at introducing them. Often this is because some managers impose sanctions or otherwise berate those who fail to meet particular measures or targets. If you use measures as a stick to beat the staff, you are almost certainly doomed to failure. People will become resentful and uncooperative and it will also ruin your attempts to manage in most other areas. Those on the receiving end of sanctions may well try to interfere with whatever measures you are using, or develop quite clever ways of undermining them.

Measures should be treated as a guide to "how we are doing." They should alert those concerned to the need to investigate, not become an objective of management. And they can usually only be applied successfully in collaboration with those being managed.

3.1.4   Which Numbers Should I Track in My Area?

So if you are a manager, how do you decide which numbers to track?

You must develop your own scorecard, "dashboard", or set of key numbers to give you the information you need. If you know your own field well, most of the elements will be obvious to you. If you are supervising in an unfamiliar area, you need to find someone who can identify the appropriate numbers, and explain any possible traps. In many cases the answer can be as simple as tracking four or five key numbers on a monthly basis.

Three cases of unintended consequences of measures (or "We would never do this in our organization, would we?")

How a perverse incentive rewarded the under achievers in a Drawing Office

A Drawing Office manager in a high tech engineering company was under pressure to improve the productivity of his department. So he let it be known that he would judge each individual's performance on the number of drawings they released each week. Most draughtsmen set to work with a will, not to work harder or more effectively, but to increase their output of drawings. When calling for new washers or screws, instead of updating a general data sheet they produced new drawings. This took longer but met the measure. Furthermore, as all similar components were no longer on the same sheets, many were duplicated. The office worked more slowly and stock management in the factory became a nightmare. Under this regime the less skilful people producing the "hack" drawings thrived, while those given the "knotty" technical problems were penalised.

Achieving the opposite of what was intended in a professional services firm

The partners in a management consultancy, concerned about cash flow, imposed sanctions on any consultant who recorded work on their monthly utilization sheets, without immediately invoicing that work to the client. Some consultants responded by not declaring work they had done during a given month, because they had not yet raised the relevant invoice. As a consequence, the partners had achieved the precise opposite of what they had intended: (1) the consultants had a further month's grace for raising invoices, and as these were generally raised later than would otherwise have been the case, the cash flow issue was exacerbated; (2) monthly consultant utilization figures – which management had previously used to attempt to balance consultant workloads – were rendered meaningless; (3) when invoices finally were raised, consultants then billed this work at the same time and ended up being praised either for having little 'work in progress' or for their ability to 'pre-invoice', when they probably should have been 'punished' for delaying their invoices.

Never mind the quality …

An international firm on the acquisition trail wanted to increase its flow of potential deals. Top management announced that they would assess the Acquisitions Department on the basis of the number of potential deals in the pipeline. Not surprisingly, the result was an immediate increase in the *quantity* of deals. The problem was, the deals were not always of the required *quality*. The firm solved the problem by developing and publishing criteria against which the quality of potential deals would henceforth be assessed. Contrary to what some of the "quality gurus" might hope, when introducing measures you will not always 'get them right first time.'

Fig. 3.1 Three cases of unintended consequences of measures

Each manager's situation is so different that it makes no sense recommending a standard set of statistics. However, the following pointers should help you in getting to the right answer for you.

3.1.4.1 Consider What Is Already Available

Start by looking for measures where the data are already available in your organization. Use measures which suit your own purpose, people and function, rather than necessarily apply downwards those measures which are being applied to you.

3.1.4.2 Identify the Mandatory Numbers

Some of the measures you need to monitor may well be mandatory. For example, certain statistics may have to be reported on for legislative reasons, and the Finance Department or HR may require certain information to be collected at specific intervals. Similarly, some data may be required for inclusion in your organization's balanced scorecard, where this exists. Senior management may also have certain "hot topics" they wish to track at a certain moment, for instance outsourcing costs or headcount figures. Certain individuals in senior positions sometimes have particular data "hot buttons", and it is worth finding out what these might be.

3.1.4.3 Pinpoint What You Should Track at Your Particular Level

What individual managers need to track often depends on their organizational level. For instance, in a private sector firm, the Chief Executive and the Board may require statistics relating to overall sales. Meanwhile, the Sales Director may also track sales by region and large accounts, whilst the Regional Sales Manager is likely to focus more on sales per sales representative.

Having managers review data at different organizational levels can be important. For example, an IT manager may only be concerned about statistics relating to employee defections to a competitor within his territory. However, when a more senior manager reviews the statistics nationwide, it may reveal an underlying trend whereby a competitor is systematically poaching a firm's staff. Spotting the pattern enables consideration of a timely response.

3.1.4.4 Consider How Often You Should Monitor the Numbers

The frequency with which metrics are tracked depends on the nature of the activities in which an organization is engaged. In a factory context, output data are invariably tracked at short intervals. Similarly, retailers need to monitor sales of individual lines closely to enable reordering and trend spotting. Again, depending on the area of activity and industry, regular reviews of key indicators can take place daily, weekly or perhaps monthly. The timeframes for tracking information will sometimes need to alter, for instance during periods of organizational crisis, when the critical numbers receive almost constant attention. One obvious example would be safety statistics in the wake of a disaster or a public outcry.

3.1.4.5 Build in Early Warning Signs So You Have Time to Take Action

A minimum standard is to ensure that you have at hand those metrics which will provide you with an early warning of any unpleasant surprises. You need sufficient time to be able to take appropriate remedial action. Other useful questions to ask (and not only for reasons of trying to pinpoint the important numbers) are: What would give me sleepless nights if it were not regularly tracked? What is the worst thing that could happen in my department?

3.1.4.6 Track an Appropriate Number of Measures

Trying to track too many measures at once can become confusing. If it seems that this might cause you a problem, then it can be helpful to distinguish "first order" as opposed to the supporting or "second order" measures. On the other hand, the consequences of focusing on too few measures taken in isolation can also be problematic. In one organization, a monthly focus on monitoring an overall employee headcount figure led to a gradual reduction in lower paid, but essential workers. Meanwhile a full complement of more expensive managers had been retained to supervise the reduced output of fewer individuals.

3.1.4.7 Consider the Lessons of History and Benchmarking

A useful approach in helping to decide on priorities is to conduct a historical review of basic data relating to a department, organization or business. Figure 3.2 shows the data selected as part of a review of one firm's overseas acquisition. The sorts of measures set out here can be adapted for a review of any business.

Those new to a job can often make an immediate contribution by casting a fresh eye over some of the available statistical information. In one firm, the newly appointed Head of its International Division requested a historical analysis of each international subsidiary's performance, going back 5 years. He noticed a pattern: subsidiaries would perform well and consistently for a couple of years, but there would be a subsequent decline, with poor results perhaps in the third or fourth year. He concluded that a successful few years in a subsidiary seemed to lead to some slackening of the pace. Perhaps the members of the subsidiary management were resting on their laurels, or perhaps senior management had started paying less attention to these subsidiaries. Whatever the explanation, henceforth he took steps to ensure that the pattern was not repeated, and kept up the pressure on successful subsidiaries by aggressively raising the bar and keeping performance under continual review.

It has been known for a new Chief Executive—brought in because an organization has been seen as sleepy and underperforming—to try and create an atmosphere in which staff are made to feel on edge and insecure. In such circumstances having to hand an up to date set of numerical performance indicators provides evidence that a department is performing and can help protect its members.

Benchmarking can provide further sources of insight. Consider those in similar roles to yourself in your own organization as well as in other firms. Check which numbers they use to monitor and measure performance. Sometimes insights can also be obtained by carrying out benchmarking in organizations in completely

Measures used for assessing an overseas acquisition in trouble

As part of a consulting assignment to review a firm's overseas acquisition, we first asked for details of the overall cost of the investment and then compared this with its estimated current value. We then tabulated monthly and cumulative data relating to performance on a number of measures over the three years since acquisition. The measures selected were:

- Budgeted revenue
- Forecasted revenue (i.e. local management's monthly revised estimates in the light of events)
- Actual revenue
- Profit (i.e. revenue minus fixed and variable costs)
- Headcount – permanent employees
- Headcount – sub-contractors
- Costs – permanent employees
- Costs – sub-contractors
- Cash collected
- Cash in bank
- Outstanding debts (unpaid invoices, long-term debts)
- Bad debts (written off and unable to be collected)
- Wastage (cost of goods purchased minus goods in stock and goods delivered, all figures collected at cost price)

Reviewing the results provided an indication of the overall health of the business, pinpointed areas for attention as well as suggesting further hypotheses for testing. For instance, the owners had been called upon to inject further working capital at several points. So it was important to check the historical trends in the overall cash position. The analysis highlighted several issues – such as high wastage figures and bad debts – which were then followed up.

Fig. 3.2   Measures used for assessing an overseas acquisition in trouble

different fields to your own (McNulty 1993a, b). Many innovations and scientific advances are taken from one setting and successfully adapted in another (Schon 2001). Henry Ford invented the production line in the wake of visiting a local abattoir (Hargadon 2003).

In conclusion, despite the potential difficulties, managers must find out what numbers they should be monitoring, set up systems for doing so, and then track these numbers. The numbers should provide useful feedback on the important areas of performance. *Without* this feedback you are likely to have three immediate problems:

- The department may fail to reach its targets, and by the time the shortfalls become clear, it could be too late to take any remedial action. If key departments fail to reach their numbers, then it is likely that the organization as a whole will underperform. When that happens, all employees can get tainted by association, which may affect their individual rewards or future career prospects
- It can be difficult for staff to have a sense of progress and achievement, and their motivation can decline. It is normal that people want to be associated with those departments or organizations known to be successful and to have a positive image
- You cannot provide senior management with evidence of effective operation. Lacking confidence, they are then likely to "ferret" for information, and they may obtain inaccurate or misleading figures. Alternatively, members of senior management may interfere in the activities of the department, taking up more of everyone's time, and curtailing employees' freedom to get on with the work in hand.

Remember
- You track measures so that you and your staff can spot when things may be going off track and need looking at
- Choose measures that suit your needs, not because someone else uses them
- Ideally choose measures where the data are easily obtainable from current systems
- Keep measures under review to ensure they are meeting their inventors' intentions
- Do not use measures to punish your staff, or as the sole basis on which to reward them. Clever people can often meet your measures at the expense of doing the job
- Measures can only be applied successfully in collaboration with those being managed

MEASUREMENT IS NOT A SUBSTITUTE FOR MANAGEMENT

3.2   Technique Number Two: Use a Work Management System

In this section we will show you:

- *A simple Work Management System, how to design it, run it and get more from it*
- *Why every manager needs a Work Management System*
- *Why those being managed also need a Work Management System*

3.2.1 Developing and Implementing Your Work Management System

Of all of the three control processes we describe, some form of Work Management System, with its Job List and accompanying regular meetings, is the most important one. *It is an absolute "must" for any manager.* Its benefits are legion and it is the cornerstone for the day-to-day management of a department or group. Work Management is not a command and control system but a forum for a collaborative working relationship, bringing benefits to both managers and their direct reports.

At its simplest, it comprises a list of the jobs which staff are working on, a regular meeting with these staff (individually, or as a group or a combination of these two), and a willingness to discuss progress on each job openly, examine the implications, and agree the next steps.

Jobs are added to the list as required, and as soon as they are complete, they are crossed off the list.

There is no need to provide an example here of a sample list of departmental jobs. However a more detailed form of the basic job list, and one which we ourselves have used and also recommended to others, is illustrated in Fig. 3.3. Variants of this type of list are to be found in many organizations. This format seems to suit the circumstances of most managers, and it can be especially helpful when a manager first introduces a Work Management System.

Whilst the purpose of most of the columns is self-evident, some points can usefully be made.

Column One: "Job Number"
Allocating a number to each job sequentially helps to keep track of jobs and is also useful in subsequently locating information about those which have been completed. Relevant reference material or information relating to finished jobs can be stored electronically and/or archived using the job number.

Column Two: "Responsible"
This column records the name of the person from your department who is responsible for the work. Although in some instances more than one team member may be involved, it is usually preferable to define jobs such that one person 'owns' a given activity.

Column Three: "Client"
In addition to the name of the client, sponsor or customer, if desired, an internal "cost code" can also be recorded in this column.

Column Four: "Date of Request"
As you track progress on a job, it can be useful to have a continuing reminder of when the work was first commissioned.

				Work Management System		
			Current Job List following 20 March Monthly Team Review Meeting			
Job Number	Responsible	Client	Date of Request	Description of job	Progress	Date for Completion
212	Alan Clancey	Carlo Crespo	27 Jan	Develop client plan for Acme to include target revenues for fiscal year	Reviewed client plan model developed by senior management group. Plan was circulated and finally approved on 6 March	Completed Filed in SharePoint under "Client plans, 2013"
213	Per Miller	Peter Wurz	28 Jan	Develop Annual Report proposals for Finance Director review	Paper now ready and will be discussed at forthcoming Finance meeting	3 April
222	Sheila Jackson	Ajay Patel	14 March	Respond to request for overseas support	Benchmarking review now complete. Katherine will present proposals to KW and SP next week	15 May
223	Rebecca Ross	Paul Orwell	18 March	Complaint from Finance re. delays in submitting sales data	Identified problem territories and have discussed with territory sales managers. Will review again with Finance after April data are submitted	12 May
224	Etc.	Etc.	Etc.	Etc.	Etc.	Etc.

Fig. 3.3 Sample Work Management System

Column Five: "Description of Job"

In describing a job, many managers find it helpful to use certain key words or the standard terminology in regular use in their organizations. Doing so will later enable activities relating to particular topics to be easily referenced or searched.

Column Six: "Progress"

Once a job has been reviewed, the manager uses this column to update progress and outline the next steps, prior to reissuing a revised Jobs List in the days following a review meeting. In between meetings, further changes can be made to the list—new jobs often get added, for instance.

We always recommend that managers also send out the notes on the meeting as soon as possible afterwards, and an updated Job List (including any new jobs) around 3 days in advance of the next Work Management Meeting. This gives people sufficient time to take action and move some items forward immediately prior to the review. It is remarkable how many jobs get completed during this 3-day period, especially those little nuisance jobs or routine chores which staff might otherwise not quite get around to doing. The impending meeting, and the requirement to share any progress with colleagues seems to act as a spur to getting things done.

Column Seven: "Date for Completion"

Whilst the work is in progress, this column acts as a constant reminder of the project completion deadline, and enables everyone to check that jobs are still running to schedule. *It is the real date.* We have worked with managers who wished to build in a "hedge" perhaps by advancing the date. We have always argued against this. In a world of *Management by Permission*, people do not appreciate their managers playing games with deadlines. If managers want to build in 'hedges' for wider organizational consumption, then they should produce a different document for this express purpose. Managers should never compromise their own Work Management System.

3.2.1.1 Once a Job Is Complete

As soon as a job or task is finished, it is marked as "Completed" and the location of the relevant files, information and reference materials is noted (for an example of a finished job, see job Number 212 in Fig. 3.3). The completed job can now be removed from the current list and transferred to a "Completed Jobs" list, which then becomes the historical record for the Department. It makes sense to use the same format as in Fig. 3.3 for these completed jobs.

The list of completed jobs can be usefully consulted, for instance at performance review time, or when searches are being made of the archive to find out "who worked on what?" or "who knows about what?" It becomes an important document which contributes to the 'institutional' or 'corporate memory' (i.e. the permanent archive of work done). Without ready access to such records, there is a risk of wasted effort and subsequent duplication or wheel reinvention.

3.2.1.2 A More Ambitious Work Management Scheme

Whilst we have found the format in Fig. 3.3 to be adequate for most purposes, some managers wish to include further detail. For instance, we have worked with several people who have included a column for recording time estimates for new work, and later compared these estimates against the actual time taken. Doing this sharpens everyone's estimating capabilities, as well as helping managers to make more accurate assessments of how much further work their departments could carry out, without compromising the quality of any work already underway.

The Appendix provides an example of such a format. We have found that those working in technical or project based departments sometimes prefer this more detailed approach. It could be considered once the more basic approach has been successfully applied. As against this, you should avoid the temptation to overcomplicate matters. Staff tend to find an excessively sophisticated system somewhat tiresome and they lose interest. The aim is to get the work done, not win a design award for a Work Management System.

3.2.2   Four Common Questions on Work Management Systems

- *Should jobs be reviewed one-on-one, or as part of a meeting with the entire team?*
- *How do managers make sure team Work Management Meetings are efficient and effective?*
- *Should all jobs carried out by my team be included on the Work Management List?*
- *How does the Work Management System link to Organizational Project Management Systems?*

3.2.2.1 Should Work Be Reviewed One-on-One, or as Part of a Meeting with the Entire Team?

As a manager, you have three fundamental choices in reviewing jobs. You can:

(a)   Review them with each of your direct reports singly, and as often as required
(b)   Review them with your direct reports as a group, as part of a regular team meeting
(c)   Use a combination of these two

In our experience, most managers using a Work Management System adopt the third approach. They hold a regular team meeting—its frequency can vary, but monthly is a popular choice—to review those jobs of interest and relevance to the whole team. In addition, they hold one-on-one meetings as circumstances dictate, such as: when an individual requires in-depth coaching; when it would be inappropriate to share the subject matter with the entire team; or when the topics are small jobs or ones of limited general interest.

The benefits of the team review approach are considerable and we would highlight six in particular:

First Benefit: Group Pressure Helps Everyone Meet Their Deadlines
In most people's experience, setting a deadline for any task is one of the best ways to get it done. When tasks and deadlines appear on a published departmental list, and the items are subsequently reviewed in front of colleagues, this acts as a further incentive. People seem not to want the embarrassment of an unfinished item behind schedule. The looming Work Management Meeting helps get the job done.

The psychological effects of the approaching meeting affect the manager as well as the staff, and if you are managing a mature team, you can take advantage of the power of group pressure by putting your own jobs on the list. If you find that you are struggling to meet the deadlines for your own jobs, then it might mean you are failing to delegate. Putting your own jobs on the list also helps to build trust with your team. They get to know what you are doing, and it educates them as to the priorities at your level.

Second Benefit: Work Quality and Problem Solving Are Improved Overall

Provided the review meetings are run efficiently, the process seems to keep everyone that much sharper. The overall quality of the work done is invariably improved, and the process provides learning and development opportunities for all members of the team. As each job is discussed, team members have the opportunity to contribute their experience and knowledge, and they often suggest new approaches or further avenues of enquiry. Being able to draw on the resources of the entire team is especially useful to the manager who is not an expert on all aspects of the topic under discussion.

Like ageing sons who suddenly find themselves grunting like their fathers when getting up from the armchair, patterns tend to repeat themselves, in work as well as in life. When team members see the potential for the same errors to be repeated, they can share their experiences. And when jobs run into difficulties, sometimes an experienced team member will have faced a similar situation and will be able to provide advice, and sometimes even the solution. In this way the less experienced members of the team learn from the more experienced—how they tackle certain issues, the way they structure their thinking, their general approaches to solving problems (see Figs. 3.4 and 3.5).

The meeting attendees also gain knowledge from the questions that the manager and others ask. They learn to anticipate questions, and to be ready with the answers. This not only improves their preparation for this and other meetings, it also tends to enhance their general performance, and sharpen the quality of their thinking. Thus they are better prepared more generally to tackle the problems they face. Incidentally, staff learn from the jobs which are going well, as well as those jobs where there are problems.

For most of us, having others critique and review our work should be a part of daily professional life. To perform at our best, we all need to be challenged—sometimes gently, sometimes more robustly—even if we may not always immediately appreciate it. If a "peer review" of a job becomes a "rock throwing session" or degenerates into "blamestorming", as can happen, managers can intervene as they see fit to ensure that the matters are kept under some control and egos are provided with a degree of protection. Nevertheless, managers need to be aware that, especially after a robust exchange, certain people may still need 'picking up' after the meeting. Egos can be more fragile than they sometimes appear.

Third Benefit: Communications Are Better

When managers communicate information as part of a team review, it ensures that one consistent message is transmitted to everyone. It also saves time in that managers do not have to go over the same issues repeatedly with different people.

Reviewing the jobs underway greatly reduces the chances of a manager failing to communicate the latest organizational intelligence and thinking from above. In the course of a working day, busy managers sometimes find it hard to remember to communicate all of the information a team needs. With a Work Management System, as each job is discussed and reviewed in turn, it tends to trigger the important contextual and background information which everyone on the team

Problem-solving: Two red flags for managers

People working together in teams to solve problems can be prone to error. For example, "Groupthink" is a well-known phenomenon whereby individuals on a team sometimes have a tendency to avoid exploring any possible conflicts about the best solution, and instead focus on maintaining harmonious relations amongst themselves. Often, the result is poor decision-making.

In the context of team review meetings, we have observed two problems in particular which managers should guard against.

Mistake number one: accepting uncritically either a client's definition of a problem, or their solution to it

Accepting a *client's* definition of a problem or indeed their proposed solutions is a common trap. Clients will often mistakenly define a problem in terms of *their* solutions. Begin by working on defining the problem accurately, *not* on other parties' solutions.

Mistake number two: Solving the immediate problem at hand without taking steps to prevent a recurrence

Very often the more difficult problems that get raised in review meetings require two sorts of solution. The first priority is to solve the immediate problem at hand, or 'stop the bleeding.' Once this is done, consideration should then be given to any actions, such as a change in policy, which will prevent a similar problem occurring in future. Most people seem to manage the first step quite well, whilst often ignoring the second.

Fig. 3.4 Problem-solving: Two red flags for managers

The power of asking simple questions

The ancient Greek philosophers considered the effective question to be a "midwife" that would give birth to ideas. Questions should never be underestimated as powerful problem-solving tools. Some useful questioning techniques include:

- Kipling's six "honest serving-men" (What? Why? When? How? Where? Who?) which can be employed to help cover all of the angles

- The "Five Whys" technique, which involves repeatedly asking, "Why?" as a way of challenging assumptions (this is a form of "root cause analysis")

- Asking: "Everything is like something. What is this like?" The philosopher Isaiah Berlin suggested using this E. M. Forster question as a way of thinking about a problem. Making comparisons in this way often helps to open up a new avenue of enquiry.

Fig. 3.5 The power of asking simple questions

needs. Managers provide this information, and in addition often other team members will also have important "nuggets" or intelligence to share.

In passing on your latest intelligence, you keep your staff calibrated and help ensure that their proposals and any decisions they may take are appropriately informed and relevant. A change in thinking at a higher level can often potentially affect your staff in ways that you cannot necessarily envisage. It is a source of intense irritation to staff when they believe they are not given the information they require to do their jobs, and they often complain when their manager fails to pass on this "soft" information. This feeling is particularly acute if they feel that they would be made to look foolish in front of others through being uninformed.

When matters are going well you have the opportunity to recognize publicly an individual's contribution. The importance of public recognition for a good idea or a job well done is often underestimated. When we hold discussions with people in organizations, as part of organization reviews, a recurring theme at all levels is the annoyance many feel when they do not get the credit for their ideas and contributions. Such recognition is not only motivating, but is an important method by which standards and expectations are set and reinforced for the whole team.

Fourth Benefit: Knowledge Is Shared More Widely and Also Captured for the Future

The knowledge sharing which naturally and inevitably takes place during review meetings gives team colleagues an understanding of what is happening in other people's areas. When information gets shared in this way it contributes towards reducing an organization's dependence on one individual: what is a by-product of the Work Management System manages to address wholly or partially a problem which might otherwise require a specific initiative to keep one or more designated colleagues up to speed.

When lists of jobs are kept in the manner we suggest above, over time this results in the development of a departmental "memory." This written record of the content and nature of the jobs done, and the location of the relevant files, enables subsequent searches of types of project or activity, and maintains a record of who has worked on what. In addition to reducing the chances of 'wheel reinvention'—always frustrating for all of those involved—the records which build up provide factual input to salary reviews, as well as performance and succession management.

Fifth Benefit: The Manager Obtains Important Data as Regards Individual and Team Development

The Work Management System provides a manager with endless possibilities for gathering detailed information and insights about individuals and the team.

If you are the manager, then review meetings help to highlight *individual* development needs and provide opportunities for on-the-spot coaching and development. You also have an opportunity to assess people's capabilities and their performance:

- How do they set about jobs?
- Can they carry jobs forward on their own initiative, or do they continually need support and guidance?
- Do they fight fires, or light them?
- How well do they work with their colleagues within the department and elsewhere?
- Who is well networked?
- Who needs more attention and help from you?
- Who needs more of your time as a sounding board?

With regard to your *team*, the Work Management Meeting provides some insight into the chemistry and degree of cooperation between staff:

- Who networks with whom?
- Are there any cliques or sub-cliques within the team?
- Are there any interpersonal difficulties in the team requiring your intervention?
- Who does, and does not talk (and listen) to whom?

You become aware of any emerging problems in the team and it gives you an opportunity to address them.

3.2.2.2 When Not to Use the Team Review
Despite the considerable advantages of the team review, as was pointed out earlier, there are some circumstances in which one-on-one meetings might be preferable.
Some examples are when:

- Someone is working on a job which is inappropriate for discussion amongst the entire team (for instance, it could be a highly sensitive project, or an assignment which might lead to unhelpful rumours circulating)
- The topics are small jobs, or ones of limited general interest, and it would be very tedious for the others to work through these jobs in detail with the one subordinate report who needs that level of attention
- Some of the topics are contentious, and if you have any "loose cannons" on your team, you are afraid they might use the meeting as a platform for misbehaving
- You have only just started managing the group and you are not yet sure that the members are sufficiently mature to behave appropriately
- You are not happy with someone's work, or they need in-depth coaching and development in the context of their present workload.

3.2.2.3 How Do Managers Make Sure Work Management Meetings Are Efficient and Effective?
We do not propose wasting readers' time by setting out the basics involved in running a meeting, nor how to work one's way through a Job List. There are, however, some general points worth re-emphasizing.

Busy, modern employees, with their shorter attention spans, tend to abhor long, unnecessary or dull meetings. Since, if you hold a Work Management Meeting, it is the one meeting that you need all of your direct reports to attend, you need to run it efficiently. So, for instance, you will: pay attention to the order in which the various items are covered; make sure that the meeting starts and ends on time; clarify when an item is open for discussion, as opposed to when you are *informing* them about non-negotiable decisions; ensure that appropriate amounts of air time are allocated to topics and to individuals.

Your team must also feel that the frequency of the meetings is right. While some teams find a weekly Work Management Meeting is required, generally a monthly meeting seems to suit many circumstances. Fortnightly meetings can become a chore and, in the case of complex jobs, may be too soon for meaningful updates to be worthwhile. On the other hand, if you wait longer than a month then it does not seem to provide the right degree of control and information exchange necessary. One factor affecting choice is the amount of progress feasible on a job within the review period. Ask yourself: What length of time is sensible before reviewing a typical job again?

During these meetings, and in much else that goes on in departments, it is the manager who sets the climate and the performance benchmark. As a manager, you are always being watched to see how you behave and react. The most effective way to disseminate best practice in almost all things is through example: recall the ancient wisdom, 'to preach, and use words if you must.' Staff look to what their manager expects by way of performance and behaviour, and tend to fall in line with those standards. So when reviewing jobs, your focus should be on looking for progress and finding solutions, not immediately trying to seek out and destroy "the culprit" when things have gone awry.

Too much focus on the negative alienates people, increases the chances they will hide things, and generally makes them less cooperative and harder to manage. Once a solution to a problem has been found, you can think of ways of helping the individual who got it wrong, thus reducing the likelihood of a recurrence and assisting with their development.

When you are unhappy with progress on a job, and you are not facing an emergency, it is generally best to avoid the temptation to issue instructions too quickly. Instead, summarize the problem and ask what could be done to bring the situation back on track. There are many reasons for doing this, and three in particular:

(1) If people are forever being "spoon-fed" and given the answers, it does not help them to think for themselves and develop.
(2) If managers always issue detailed instructions, then they implicitly take ownership of the job, and if their solutions do not work, then people can always hide behind the fact that the boss made the decision.
(3) If managers issue detailed instructions too soon, at best they get compliance. You get people's *commitment* when it is they who devise the plan and formulate the next steps.

If no-one in the team makes a satisfactory proposal or suggestion, then you can defer the discussion, make suggestions, or ask what you can do to help. You should give credit and positive feedback when you can, thanking people for their contributions. But do not overdo your praise when it is unwarranted. Staff rapidly lose respect for those whom they feel praise them inappropriately. Your praise then becomes a debased currency, or what they call in the computer world a "nonrecoverable error."

Although the length of the Work Management Meeting can vary, setting aside up to 2 hrs. generally seems to work best. Self-evidently, if the full 2 hrs. are not needed, you can always close the meeting as soon as all of the jobs have been reviewed.

3.2.2.4 Should All Jobs Carried Out by My Team Be Included on the Work Management List?

For inclusion on the Work Management List, we tend to define a job as a significant task, typically taking more than 2 hrs. to complete. Smaller, less important tasks, or jobs of limited interest to the team as a whole, can be kept on a separate action list, and followed through on an individual basis.

Although the manager must retain overall control of the Job List and add the items as work comes in, in the case of a high performing team, they can allow members of staff to place their jobs on the list with little or no discussion, unless a new job is of a size or degree of difficulty that it requires a debate. However, it is more usual for a manager to have some involvement in defining the scope and timescale of most jobs, and review their impact on an individual's existing priorities. When dealing with less experienced staff, or those whose performance is below standard, it is always wise for managers to retain responsibility for putting jobs onto the Work Management List, following discussion.

However, it is in everyone's interests for team members to inform their manager of any work they have taken on, or are proposing to take on, so that their jobs can be added to the Job List. From the individual's point of view, if their work is not listed, they may not get the credit for it later on. In addition, they may find they become overloaded in comparison with their colleagues, leading to an imbalance of work across a department. This can apply particularly in cases where more senior managers violate the chain of command by bypassing the Departmental Manager, and allocate work direct (see Fig. 3.6).

3.2.2.5 How Does the Work Management System Link to Organizational Project Management Systems?

Many managers operate within matrix and other structures in which staff may report to others for some elements of their activity. What should a manager do when members of their team are working on projects which are project managed from elsewhere in their organizations?

As discussed in the previous section, if you are responsible for managing an individual's work, and especially if you are a "functional" manager within a matrix structure, then the relevant parts of any project *must* be reviewed as part of your Work Management System. There are at least three reasons for this:

Bypassing: the bane of some people's lives
(How a Work Management System can help when the boss
bypasses the chain of command)

We know from our coaching and consulting work that many managers get extraordinarily hot under the collar when they are "bypassed" (by which we mean a more senior manager ignores the manager in the middle and goes direct to team members to discuss or allocate work).

We have some sympathy with the view that bypassing can sometimes make it more difficult for managers to control the activities of their staff. As against this, bypassing can give these staff useful exposure at more senior levels and also render senior management less remote. This is one reason why "skip-level interviews" have been instigated in some organizations. Such interviews give staff an opportunity to engage with more senior management. For their part, senior managers sometimes want to bypass so they can keep in direct touch with what is going on and perhaps get to understand any issues first hand.

The reality is that bypassing seems such a common occurrence that no matter how uncomfortable some of us may be with the practice, it is unlikely to disappear. If senior managers want to bypass, they will do so no matter what others may think.

If you have managers reporting to you and you want to avoid these managers' direct reports bypassing their boss (the US expression is "making an end run") you can act as follows. When these direct reports come to you, simply ask them if they have discussed the issue with their boss.

If you are the "manager in the middle", then your best advice is to use the sort of Work Management System described in this section. You (or your staff) can simply add to your list any jobs allocated by the more senior manager. You can then review them along with the other jobs. As a result, you: (1) retain control over the activities and workload of the members of your team; (2) are suitably informed about all of their work; and (3) have all of the information at hand should, for instance, someone in your team become overloaded as a result of these extra jobs, and you subsequently need to meet your boss to discuss workload and priorities.

Fig. 3.6 Bypassing: the bane of some people's lives

(1) You are responsible for quality and standards in your area. In order to meet this responsibility you need up to date knowledge of what is happening on the project, and you need to know, and as necessary agree, what technical advice or guidance is being given by your technical expert.

(2) When some of your team are working partially or wholly on projects, then you need an up to date understanding of the progress of the project, given its implications for workload in your area.

(3) Any organizational project has implications for "departmental memory", and this knowledge needs to be shared with the other members of your team. Reviewing the progress of the work enables this to happen, with the additional benefit that should your expert on the project team need to be replaced, then a number of potential backups will have developed some knowledge of what is happening on the project.

3.2.2.6 What About Micromanagement? Is It Ever Appropriate? Will People Feel I Don't Trust Them?

Micromanagement rarely gets a round of applause from those on the receiving end. Managers get accused of being control freaks, and staff resent the feeling that they are not trusted. So it is worth examining whether micromanagement is ever necessary. Richard Neustadt (1990) spent 30 years studying and advising US Presidents. He concluded that at times even Presidents have to micromanage: they *must* delve into the details when a situation could cause them maximum embarrassment, and "the crown jewels are at stake."

What applies to the holder of one of the biggest jobs in the Western world, similarly applies to managers in most other organizations. At times, managers may have to micromanage, for instance:

- A Project Manager gets repeatedly quizzed by senior management as regards the progress of a critical project which has fallen behind schedule
- A Head of Mortgages is constantly challenged by a hostile media to defend a bank's policies regarding impaired loans
- A University Dean is worried about the possible dire consequences of falling student applications for next year's degree courses
- A Sales Manager outsources a new product launch but starts to become concerned about the quality and experience of some of the consultants working on the project.

In situations such as these, failing to delve into the details is foolish. The managers involved must be: (1) satisfied that any plans, tactics or actions continue to be fit for purpose and will deliver what is required to time, cost and quality; (2) sufficiently close to what is going on so that remedial action can be taken; (3) sufficiently up to date so as to be able to respond to any questions "off the cuff."

If your Work Management System is operating effectively, then you are reviewing people's work at the right intervals, and there is little reason for delving further into the detail of routine projects. So how do you tell if you *are* guilty of unnecessary micromanagement?

Ask yourself the following:

- Am I constantly looking for detailed briefings for no real reason?
- Am I getting over involved in the tiny decisions when the staff are both willing and able to handle these without me?
- Do staff show signs of resenting my involvement or feeling infantilized?
- Do I try to micromanage everything, not just the "crown jewels" issues?
- Am I interfering for selfish reasons rather than because my expertise is actually needed (e.g. because I enjoy doing certain tasks, am bored, or am trying to show them, 'who is the boss?')
- Have I become a control freak, too focused on the *means* (i.e. being inflexible or over prescriptive about the way things get done) whilst perhaps losing sight of the *ends* (i.e. the actual results required)?
- Could this be a sign that there are too many managers in the structure?

If, having answered these questions, you decide that micromanagement is still required, then it will help if you communicate your reasons to staff:

- Explain why an assignment might require a short leash (the rationale for doing so may not be so obvious to them). Your reasons could include: this is a critical project; matters could go awry and we may need time to make contingency plans; some deadlines have already been missed and there is a need for some focus; the project requires as much experience as we can bring to bear; the company faces a reputational risk; you personally have to be absolutely up to date with the details because you are constantly being quizzed and might have to defend the team; our Director is under pressure from the Board on a particular issue; you have been told to get personally involved
- Emphasize that you are bringing an extra resource to the situation (you) and that your involvement will help ensure rapid action if required (e.g. allocating other resources or smoothing out issues with another function at your level). It is helpful if you are able to demonstrate that you are actually adding some value
- Reassure them that this is not a prelude to your becoming a "helicopter manager", hovering over every issue. You have neither the time, nor the inclination.

Micromanagement may be a necessary means to achieving an important goal. Nevertheless you should think carefully before micromanaging. If you have thought it through and are still in doubt, remember that whilst few managers get fired for micromanaging "crown jewels" issues, quite a few managers can get fired for not doing so.

3.2.2.7 Work Management Systems: Six Specific Benefits for Managers

- *You know the status of any work underway*
- *You keep people focused on what matters*

- *You are up to speed on the current workload in your area*
- *You delegate with confidence*
- *You can deal quickly with any "rotting rhinos"*
- *You balance workload amongst staff and better manage flexible working*

As discussed above, the team review approach to Work Management has a number of advantages, and on balance it is probably the best approach for most managers. However, even if you only conduct one-on-one reviews of jobs with your staff, your Work Management System still brings a number of benefits. We would highlight six in particular.

First Benefit: You Know the Status of Any Work Underway
Regularly going through the list of jobs with your staff enables you to monitor progress on each task. You are less likely to be confronted with an unexpected surprise. When your boss or anyone else asks questions about any work in your area, you have the facts readily available. At a minimum, you know the status of a job when it was most recently reviewed, and you also know the planned next steps. With this information at hand, you demonstrate your professionalism, and incidentally, it means you are less likely to be bypassed by an impatient senior management.

Regular review meetings also mean you can find out as much detail as necessary about what people are actually doing. You can ask to have explained to you anything that is not clear. What could be quite difficult in the course of a normally hectic working day becomes perfectly natural during a review meeting. Because you know that at a specific time you will review all of the work of your staff, unless something unexpected arises you do not have to remember to chase up particular jobs on an ad hoc basis. This saves large amounts of time for everyone, much more time in fact than is spent preparing for and conducting a regular review meeting.

Second Benefit: You Keep People Focused on What Matters
You are able continuously to reinforce current priorities and standards, and warn staff in advance about any possible developments which could affect what they are doing. If priorities change, then you are able to communicate these changes quickly. You are also in a position quickly to take any action you feel is necessary, such as allocating extra resources.

Because you keep following through on what is important, people take it more seriously, and as a result it is more likely to get done. You avoid the dangers implied by the Eisenhower quotation at the beginning of the chapter, that, "the uninspected inevitably deteriorates."

Third Benefit: You Are up to Speed on Current Workload in Your Area
Some managers live in constant fear of that most vexing of questions: "If we take on this next job, what will be the consequences?" A Work Management System provides the information you need about workload so that you are able quickly to weigh the consequences of extra work for any existing projects. If you have to

request extra resources or delay certain projects you have all of the data you need. You know: what work is underway and for whom; who is doing it; how it is progressing; how long it is likely to take.

Fourth Benefit: You Delegate with Confidence

Failing to delegate overloads the manager and frustrates the staff. Some managers find it difficult to delegate because they fear losing control. Your Work Management System enables you to delegate with confidence because you have no need to fret about the status of jobs. It obviates the need continually to pester your staff to focus on the important jobs, and it provides an early warning system of any potential problems, enabling them to be tackled as necessary. If it transpires that you need to get more closely involved in some issues then you can do so. In the meantime, you can be assured that the work is proceeding and that you are kept abreast of any changes.

*"Word is, Arnie, the Chairman **himself** is very keen to meet the manager in charge of our pylon design team"*

Fifth Benefit: You Can Deal Quickly with Any "Rotting Rhinos"

You learn quickly about problems with any of the jobs in your area, and you can take action accordingly. Sometimes people want to hide their difficulties from their

The power of Work Management Systems

Just in time

Appointed to his first supervisory job in his mid-twenties, within a couple of years David was promoted to lead a team of ten professionals. Nothing prepared him for what happened next. Within weeks he was overwhelmed. Swamped by information, emails and the need to attend a whole series of meetings, he found that people, and especially his department's principal internal customer, were constantly emailing and ringing up asking about the progress of various jobs. Previously he had been able to hold this information in his head. Now he could no longer rely on his memory, and he began to feel things were falling apart.

He set up a Work Management System. Initially he called a weekly meeting to review everyone's jobs. Within a couple of months, and once he felt that he had a better handle on operations, these meetings were scaled back to fortnightly. After six months he was still finding difficulties responding to questions from his principal internal customer. Despite the risks, he decided to invite this customer to attend that part of the Work Review Meeting set aside for reviewing their particular jobs. David not only saved time in subsequent briefings, the customer appreciated the opportunity to contribute to discussions and give their feedback.

The reluctant manager

We had been asked to improve the performance of a service department. We had recommended to a group of engineers that they should take the initiative by presenting their team leader with a list of their current jobs, together with a request to review them. The team leader came to us and said, "I sit with my team, we have no barriers, I know exactly what they are doing, even who they are talking to on the 'phone." However, he nonetheless agreed to a trial of a Work Management System, including a monthly team review meeting. After the first meeting he came to us and held his hands up. He was amazed to discover that he had been quite unaware of about a third of what his team were doing. The monthly meetings continued.

A demoralized lawyer puts the year into perspective

We were working with a manager who had introduced a Work Management System. When she came to conduct one lawyer's end of year performance appraisal, he opened the meeting saying that he had had, "a very frustrating year." When she showed him the list of jobs he had achieved in the previous twelve months it raised his spirits visibly. He was astounded at the amount of work he had actually done: he had had a very good year, just a rather frustrating last few weeks.

Fig. 3.7 The power of Work Management Systems

manager. They do not want to admit failure or publicize problems in front of their colleagues. Ideally they want to fix any problems by themselves. However, without proper monitoring, if they try to do so and fail, by the time their manager finds out, what started as a small local difficulty has expanded into a major crisis. Being forced to review each job regularly ensures that any "rotting rhinos", as one of our clients once described such problems, are put on the table and addressed before it is too late.

Sixth Benefit: You Balance Workload Amongst Staff and Better Manage Flexible Working

With a Work Management System you learn about work balance within your department—who is stretched, and who might need help. Knowing what people are doing day by day is especially important when you see these employees only periodically, such as is the case with part-time workers, those working from home or those employed on contracts. As these modes of working have become more and more common, it has become ever more necessary to develop an approach which monitors their performance and outputs.

One Director complained to us: "We have so many people working from home now, how can we be sure that they are working on what we want? In fact, how can we be sure they are working at all? It would take us many months to find out." Your Work Management System addresses this dilemma.

3.2.2.8 Work Management Systems: Four Benefits for Those Being Managed

- *You have more freedom to organize your work*
- *You get help with your work*
- *You do not get isolated in the organization*
- *You gain recognition for your contribution, and protection against the possibility of a farcical performance appraisal*

Many people are apprehensive when their manager introduces a Work Management System. They are afraid that it will add to their burdens, that their freedoms will be curtailed, and that they will be open to regular criticism, negative appraisals, and micromanagement.

In fact, a well functioning Work Management System has precisely the opposite effects. Once they have experienced the process, people come to appreciate its benefits, to the extent that they even look forward to the regular review meetings. Most people find that the meetings are helpful in their work, and they enhance their satisfaction and contribution.

Some of the main advantages of a Work Management System for those being managed are discussed below.

First Benefit: You Have More Freedom to Organize Your Work

Because your goals, priorities, workload are continually clarified, between review meetings you have the freedom to organize your work in the manner that suits you best. Since your work is monitored and reviewed regularly, your manager never feels out of control. As a result, you are less likely to be micromanaged, or to have to deal with the ad hoc "nagging" attentions of an anxious boss under pressure from above.

Proper monitoring and control increases the chances that an organization will perform. And when a department produces work of quality, delivers what it has promised, and keeps to its agreed budgets, all members of the team have more latitude, freedom and independence from unhelpful senior level interference (Neil 1996).

Second Benefit: You Get Help with Your Work

Regular review meetings are invariably of practical assistance in thinking through any jobs you are working on. If you are momentarily in trouble and want help, you have the opportunity to highlight the fact. You get a chance to draw on your manager's resources—their expertise, experience, knowledge of the organization—as well as their ability to influence at higher levels. Knotty organizational problems are often more easily dealt with by more senior people discussing the issues at their level. And if you need advice, guidance or even additional hands-on help, you can present your case during the meeting.

In the case of *team* reviews, these provide you with the opportunity to use the resources of your colleagues for information, brainstorming and for testing your ideas. Since you know what everyone else in the team is working on, you can also discuss any mutually relevant issues direct.

Third Benefit: You Don't Get Isolated in the Organization

Regular reviews of priorities and progress ensure that your work remains relevant and focused on what your organization requires. You are kept abreast of any important developments, and you obtain the up to date intelligence and information you require to perform effectively.

The process gives you the opportunity to educate your manager, and as a result the organization, about the problems and issues as you see them. Your manager has an up to date understanding of what you are doing, and a deeper appreciation of the day-to-day challenges you face. Managers are therefore in a position to remove some of the barriers and roadblocks on your behalf (we will discuss this in more detail in Chap. 5). They are always well-placed to brief anyone who asks about the status of any work you are doing, and they can represent you, or defend you if need be, to the rest of the organization.

Fourth Benefit: You Get Recognized for Your Contribution, and Protection Against the Possibility of a Farcical Performance Appraisal

In some circumstances you can feel very open to managerial whim when your annual performance is reviewed. At worst you end up getting appraised on your last month's work and the biggest three errors you have made in the year. This is because when they conduct appraisals, some managers rely all too often on their memories and impressions, or on incomplete, partial or the most recent information.

Similarly, few of us can remember in detail what we have done in the course of a year's work. This applies especially when we work primarily alone, or as our department's sole representative on a larger organizational project, or when we work some of the time from home.

Over the course of a performance year, a Work Management System provides the dossier of factual information about your activities and achievements. When your work is discussed and progress checked, your workload and contributions get recognized and recorded. This enables reviews for salary and development to be based on an accurate knowledge of your contribution. You also benefit from a more structured approach to coaching and feedback, which could otherwise tend to be impressionistic.

Lack of an adequate Work Management System can lead to an over concentration on metrics, which can leave people resentful and undervalued, with consequences for future relationships and motivation. We have some anecdotal evidence that an over reliance on metrics can sometimes lead to a culture of bullying, as staff are driven to comply with the measures.

> **Remember**
> - Work Management is a cooperative process benefitting both managers and the people they are managing
> - At its simplest it is a list of tasks people are working on, and a regular review meeting
> - Team reviews are generally best
> - The advantages for *managers* include: monitoring what is important; identifying problems quickly; and being in a position to take action and address the issues
> - The advantages for *those being managed* include: you can get on with your work; you obtain the support you need; your contribution is recorded; and there is an on going record of what you have done

3.3 Technique Number Three: Use Informal Methods and Management by Walking Around ("Walk the Patch")

In this section we will consider more informal methods of control, including what is sometimes described as MBWA "management by walking around" or "walking the patch." We will cover:

- *Walking the patch and how it helps*
- *Unobtrusive measures*

In addition to the more 'formal approaches' involving metrics and Work Management, there are a number of less formal methods which can also help managers gather the information they need in order to assist in keeping control.

3.3.1   Walking the Patch

Walking the patch is a well-known tried and tested approach. It is one way of anticipating the bulldozers heading your way, and becoming aware of any flesh eating spiders that might be hiding around the corners. It recognizes the inadequacy of trying to manage solely from the confines of your office. The more senior you are, and the larger your organization, the greater the tendency to lose touch with staff at lower levels and those on the front line, thus limiting your sources of information. This is particularly likely to be an issue when staff are geographically dispersed, as pointed out by Goffee and Jones (2006).

"He who does not mix with the crowd knows nothing", runs the Spanish proverb. Being seen by the staff, asking and answering their questions, showing an interest, listening, observing and understanding their perspectives can all help to provide an independent check on what is going on, and generally improve communications with those on the front line and elsewhere. You do not need to be an extrovert to do this. Your intention is to be visible and keep in touch, not to behave as a cast member at a theme park. When you walk the patch it helps you to keep in touch with the rumour factory, gives you a chance to head off any issues at the pass, and provides an independent check on what you are being told by those in your immediate circle.

It is often useful to walk the patch at different times. This ensures you establish contact with those who work flexible hours or different shifts, as the case may be. Some managers make a point of periodically arriving very early in the morning to give them a chance to network with certain staff. In some organizations some of the most useful information is only available outside of normal working hours, for instance early evening, which is when people circulate or drop into each other's offices.

The sensible course is to work out those networks you need to be part of and take the appropriate action. In some organizations there are certain people who are worth talking to as regular sources of information. In one large firm, a senior manager told us that he made a point of having informal chats with the security staff as well as the Chief Executive's chauffeur. Chauffeurs are an underestimated potential source of information. Tony Blair's former Chief of Staff Jonathan Powell pointed out that when considering which ministers were performing well, rather than seeking the advice of civil servants or well-placed politicians, he "sometimes thought it would be better to ask the government car service, as ministers' drivers usually had a far better assessment of them than Permanent Secretaries" (2010, pp. 148–149). Being effective implies making sure that you develop your own networks of information.

For more senior managers, meeting people in person and hearing their opinions direct can offset one particular worry: trying to understand what is going on through the filter of the management structure or other intermediaries. History is replete with examples of the dangers for kings and others in authority when they rely too much on the information of courtiers. If you walk the patch regularly, the fact that you are visible means that people will be much more likely to share useful information and insights with you.

"Still have faith in the 'hands-off' approach, Arnie?"

Some Chief Executives and Directors have sought to formalize their contacts by conducting periodic "fireside chats" with groups of staff based at different locations. These sorts of meetings provide an opportunity for an exchange of views, and valuable information and perspectives can be shared. During a time of major restructuring, one Chief Executive held a series of "brown bag" informal lunches so that he could meet all of the staff and listen to their concerns.

Some managers regularize these sorts of contacts and put them on a more formal basis. We worked with one Director who would hold monthly "birthday lunches" with groups of staff. Each staff member whose birthday fell in the given month would be invited to the lunch. In this way, the Director ensured that at the absolute minimum, he got to meet all of the 90 people in his Directorate over the course of a year. Recognizing employees' birthdays is taken a stage further in one US firm whose President writes a personal greeting in a birthday or anniversary card, which, when possible, he hand delivers. He explained:

The process forces me to go out and keep meeting members of staff. If you are an introvert like me, you will have a tendency to sit in your office and work. Without this discipline, there is always the chance that I would get involved in other issues and never get to meet the staff day-to-day. As President you are also Chief Morale Officer. You need to be visible, and

> **Social media, Blogs, Twitter, Facebook, Opinion Surveys and other feedback**
>
> Modern methods of communication allow managers to "walk the patch" electronically as well as literally. Traditionally many organizations have made use of employee opinion or climate surveys as a way of taking the pulse before any fever begins. Some organizations encourage blogs which enable people to express their views. Other firms provide a place on the company Intranet where staff can express their views about issues of concern. While the information and views expressed will not always be to everyone's liking, they do provide an opportunity for top management and others to understand the depth of feelings on certain issues, and be in a position to take action to address a wrong or correct any misunderstandings.
>
> It is always useful for a manager to take the temperature by consulting some half a dozen individuals who for various reasons are a good barometer of current climate. Typically these individuals will be at different levels and locations and together will enable you to cover most of the important areas of the organization. In organizations with a staff forum, works councils or unions, we have often found their representatives to be an important and underused source of information and counsel. In most instances, they have been voted into their roles precisely because they are well networked and are alive to people's concerns.

Fig. 3.8 Social media, Blogs, Twitter, Facebook, Opinion Surveys and other feedback

show you care. I try to find out from their boss something positive someone has done, and I then reference it. It gives you a context for talking to people and you can catch up with what they are doing.

One French CEO makes a point at regular intervals of joining the weekly meetings of one of her organization's working teams in the role of participant observer, explaining that the idea was based on the *"explication de texte"* (close reading) approach used in French schools. Pupils analyze in great depth a short extract from the literary text being studied. The assumption underlying the approach is that sampling a small section of a work, and studying it in great depth, sheds light on the whole.

Some senior managers make sure that from time to time they "walk the patch" with staff in customer-facing roles. This sometimes happens within predominantly sales or marketing led businesses, and the senior managers can take this even further by personally retaining account management responsibilities for important clients. It is flattering for the clients concerned but this is not the principal reason: these senior managers consider that this direct exposure to the marketplace helps them retain their 'feel' for the emerging issues in the business, sharpens their decision-making, and helps them to empathize with the problems of the staff.

> **Remember**
> Walking the patch helps managers:
>
> - Keep in touch with staff when they are actually at work rather than just when they attend meetings
> - Communicate about the work being done
> - Elucidate the issues around the job
> - Gain more of an understanding of the work, especially important when it falls outside their own professional fields

3.3.2 "Unobtrusive" and Other Measures

"Unobtrusive measures" is the label social scientists use to denote sets of indicators which typically do not actively intrude on, or interfere with, what is being measured or assessed (Webb et al. 2000). The measures are neither obvious, nor do they get in the way. For instance, when Charlie Chaplin's movies were first released, cinema managements reported that after a 2-week run, it was necessary to tighten the bolts in the cinema seats. The audience laughed so much that they had caused the bolts to become loosened (Robinson 2001). Similarly, it has been said that Dr. Crippen was first suspected of a crime not because of his wife's disappearance, but because of an unobtrusive measure: her jewellery was being worn by another woman (Gottlieb 1995).

> Managers should develop their own set of unobtrusive measures as quick indicators of potential problems

Imaginatively employed, unobtrusive measures provide very useful information. Business school professors have been known to count the number of participant name badges on display as an indicator of participant engagement in their sessions. One of our spouses assesses the quality of restaurants in an unfamiliar location by the state of the curtains. She considers that if the latter are clean and well cared for, this will reflect the quality of the establishment.

Chinese jade dealers traditionally used pupil dilation as a means of assessing customer interest in particular stones, and it has also been cited as an indicator of physical attraction or positive regard. When English referee David Elleray (2004) would be considering whether to administer a red card to a player following a foul, the fact that several of the player's team-mates ran forward shouting, "It's a yellow", would convince him. Since players rarely suggest anyone should receive a card at all, their reaction simply confirmed to Elleray that the offence merited a red card.

Questions to consider in developing unobtrusive measures

Are the staff suitably engaged in the work?

- Around the coffee machine people talk about work as well as their social lives
- They come to work early or do not rush off immediately at finishing time
- They show evidence of thinking, reading and talking about work topics outside official working hours
- They are pleased to present their subject or train others
- They usually know what those in similar roles to themselves in other organizations are doing
- They can tell you what competitors are doing
- Staff bring ideas that are not totally self promoting
- People learn from their errors and tend not to repeat them
- Any complaints focus on issues that can be addressed rather than problems that cannot be solved or irritants about working conditions
- They are not always looking for excuses to be out of the office

Do they work well together/with others?

- They take the initiative to form ad hoc teams to work on problems
- They hold meetings among themselves to discuss issues and decide actions
- They resolve issues among themselves rather than seeking your arbitration
- They do not "mischief make" or tell tales
- They answer each other's phones and deputize for others when necessary
- They network well with staff from other functions or departments
- They meet socially outside work hours
- There are strong friendships amongst team members
- Feedback from customers is positive

With whom do they network?

- Who networks with whom around the water cooler, over lunch, coffee?
- Who is in which network?

Do they work well with you?

- They tell you what is going on and watch your back for you
- They ask your advice and help where appropriate
- They offer advice and help where appropriate
- They neither resist unnecessarily nor creep to you
- They bring notes and backup information in support of their conclusions
- They respond to requests from you without constant follow-up
- Conversation groups do not break up as you approach
- Job advertisements are not part of their routine reading

Fig. 3.9 Questions to consider in developing unobtrusive measures

One client engaged in acquisitions always attempts to obtain access to the target's premises at different times of the day. They read company noticeboards, inspect staff work spaces, view any cartoons on display, in fact analyze anything which might give possible clues about the firm. They then follow up on these clues in more formal sessions with the target.

We recommend that managers should develop and refine their own unobtrusive measures to help with monitoring the progress of work as well as providing useful information about the team and how things are progressing. Some ideas for consideration in developing measures can be found in Fig. 3.9.

Remember
- Control is central to effective management
- There is no single solution to the problem of control, but three techniques which should be used together
- The three techniques can be used to build a collaborative management approach
- Control brings considerable benefits to *those being managed* as well as to their managers

References

Elleray, D. (2004). *The man in the middle: The autobiography.* London: Time Warner.

Fox, L. (2003). *Enron: The rise and fall.* Hoboken, NJ: Wiley.

Goffee, R., & Jones, G. (2006). *Why should anyone be led by you?* Boston, MA: Harvard Business School Press.

Gottlieb, S. (1995). *Hitchcock on Hitchcock.* Berkeley, CA: Faber and Faber/University of California Press.

Hargadon, A. (2003). *How breakthroughs happen.* Boston, MA: Harvard Business School Press.

Hubbard, D. (2007). *How to measure anything: Finding the value of intangibles in business.* Hoboken, NJ: Wiley.

Kaplan, R. S., & Norton, D. P. (1996). *The balanced scorecard: Translating strategy into action.* Boston, MA: Harvard Business School Press.

Leeson, N. (1996). *Rogue trader.* London: Little, Brown and Company.

McNulty, A. (1993a, November). Benchmarking: How to launch a project and get results. *Croner Employer's Briefing.*

McNulty, A. (1993b, November). Benchmarking: What is it and is it right for you? *Croner Employer's Briefing.*

Merton, R. (1968). *Social theory and social structure.* New York: Free Press.

Neil, A. (1996). *Full disclosure.* London: Pan Books.

Neustadt, R. (1990). *Presidential power and the modern presidents.* New York: Free Press.

Pfeffer, J. (1992). *Managing with power: Politics and influence in organizations.* Boston, MA: Harvard Business School Press.

Powell, J. (2010). *The new Machiavelli: How to wield power in the modern world.* London: Vintage Books.

Price, B., & Jaffe, D. (2008). *The best service is no service: How to liberate your customers from customer service, keep them happy, and control costs.* San Francisco, CA: Jossey Bass.

Reichheld, F. F. (2011). *The ultimate question 2.0: How net promoter companies thrive in a customer-driven world*. Boston, MA: Harvard Business Press.

Robinson, D. (2001). *Chaplin: His life and art*. Harmondsworth: Penguin.

Schon, D. A. (2001). *Displacement of concepts*. London: Routledge.

Watson, T. J. (1994). *In search of management: Culture, chaos and control in managerial work*. London: Routledge.

Webb, E. J., Campbell, D. T., Schwartz, R. D., & Sechrest, L. (2000). *Unobtrusive measures: Nonreactive research in the social sciences*. Chicago, IL: Rand McNally.

Weber, M. (1968). *Economy and society*. New York: Bedminster.

The Second Ingredient: Establish Expectations

4

To know that which lies before us in daily life is the prime wisdom

John Milton

If we could first know where we are, and whither we are tending, we could then better judge what to do, and how to do it

Abraham Lincoln

All the evil in this world is brought about by persons who are always up and doing, but do not know when they ought to be up nor what they ought to be doing

J. B. Priestley

The way you see people is the way you treat them, and the way you treat them is what they become

Jon Wolfgang von Goethe

SHARING AND AGREEING EXPECTATIONS BRINGS FOCUS AND CLARITY, ENABLING BOTH MANAGERS AND STAFF TO SUCCEED
The second ingredient to *Management by Permission* involves establishing expectations. To work together effectively, managers and staff need to know what to expect of one another. When this process works, it increases the likelihood that both parties' expectations will be met subsequently.

Applying the three control techniques from the previous chapter will go some way towards communicating what a manager expects. To complete the process, as well as give staff the opportunity to share their own expectations and concerns, most managers will also need periodically to meet each member of their teams "one-on-one." This chapter focuses on how to prepare for and handle such meetings, which are often also required as part of organizations' performance management systems.

© Springer International Publishing Switzerland 2016   63
T. McNulty, R. Marks, *Management by Permission*, Management for Professionals,
DOI 10.1007/978-3-319-25247-6_4

The chapter:

- **Starts by reminding managers of three important implications arising from the fact of dealing with human beings**
- **Highlights the basic information that all managers should know about each of their direct reports**
- **Outlines a three step process for first clarifying, and then discussing, expectations as part of a one-on-one meeting:**

  (1) the all-important preparation which managers should carry out *beforehand*
  (2) what managers need to do *during* a meeting
  (3) what should happen *after*

- **Provides checklists to help ensure all of the important areas are covered**
- **Recommends how to tackle successfully some of the main pitfalls involved**
- **Suggests ways of better understanding people's unstated expectations (their "psychological contracts")**
- **Explains how managers can improve their listening skills.**

A manager was describing one of her team members to us. "He drives me crazy", she said. "He spends far too much time out in the field firefighting, and not enough time here in the office supervising the staff." We asked: "What was his reaction when you told him?" "Well, I haven't told him yet", came the reply.

Few of us are mind readers, yet some managers act as if they expect their staff to be. To manage effectively in the modern world: *(1) managers must make clear, and staff must understand, what is expected of them; and (2) managers in turn need to understand as much as they can about the expectations of their staff.*

But while making expectations clear sounds simple in theory, experience suggests that it can be far from straightforward in practice. Certainly the performance management and appraisal schemes which exist in many of our organizations do not always solve the problem. We continue to meet large numbers of people in these organizations who are still uncertain about precisely what is expected of them. This chapter suggests how to address this gap.

Sharing and agreeing expectations does not imply that everything is negotiable, far from it. Managers are entitled to expect that certain tasks are done, and sometimes in very specific ways. But most modern employees also expect some say in what they do and how they do it, and at the very least they want to feel their views have been heard and taken into consideration.

Not all managers will need to follow what is set out in this chapter in all its detail: managers start from different places in terms of how well expectations have been shared and agreed with the various members of their teams. There is obviously a difference between sharing expectations with a time-served employee who has worked with you for many years, and a recent recruit inexperienced in the ways of your organization. However, most managers will benefit from reviewing the ideas we discuss, and considering what could usefully be applied in their own situations.

From the point of view of those being managed, the process of sharing expectations should help you to know where you stand, as well as give you an opportunity to consider your own expectations, and articulate some of what you might want. Reading this chapter should help you to prepare to do so, in advance of any discussion with your manager.

4.1   Never Forget You Are Dealing with Human Beings

This section discusses three important facts about dealing with human beings at work:

- *Their behaviour is strongly influenced by their lives outside work*
- *People are different and respond and behave in different ways*
- *In problems of relationships the manager is also part of the equation*

We were carrying out what we call a, "taking the temperature" assignment within one organization. The process involves us holding in-depth meetings with staff at various levels to obtain views about 'what is going well' as well as to pinpoint any areas for change. As we were updating the Chief Executive on progress, we alluded to a slight problem we had had in trying to schedule a meeting with one of his management team. The Director concerned had been difficult and unresponsive when we had initially tried to contact him. When we finally got to see him, he had behaved somewhat eccentrically. "Well, he's peculiar", said the Chief Executive, adding after a pause, "and another human being, just like the rest of us."

While it seems almost embarrassing to labour such an obvious point, we sometimes forget that in managing and working with others, *we are dealing with human beings*. And there are no perfect human beings in this life. People can be complex, moody and difficult, as well as positive, constructive and enthusiastic. Our work colleagues are not robots, and this fact of dealing with people has a number of important implications. For managers, there are three in particular.

4.1.1   Fact Number One: It Is "Whole Persons" Who Come to Work

First and foremost, while people may be employed for their ability to perform particular roles and tasks in their professional lives—as engineers, consultants, lawyers or whatever—nonetheless, as Chester Barnard (1938) pointed out many years ago, *it is "whole persons" who come to work*. Every day, these employees potentially bring with them a panoply of fears, emotions, pressures and private life concerns, any one of which can affect their behaviour and performance.

There can be any number of difficulties and worries in someone's private life. As Dr Johnson put it rather elegantly, "we judge the happiness and misery of life differently at different times, according to the state of our changeable frame" (Boswell 2008). Some people may be under financial pressures. Personal relationships may be coming to an end. Your staff may feel depressed or stressed for a whole host of reasons. Their state of health may be a concern; they may be adapting to a new culture; close relatives can become ill; worries about ageing parents can begin to weigh heavily. For those with dependent children, it can be tough trying to balance responsibilities for childcare when both partners have careers. When employees cross the workplace threshold, they are not always able to check in this baggage at the door, and the state of the baggage on a given day often affects how they perform.

Some managers have little sympathy with people's private life problems: they consider that life is tough for everyone at times, and we all have to find a way to cope. Yet even if you hold this view, as a manager you still have to deal with the consequences of how people's problems affect them at work. In practice, no-one performs as you might expect or require all of the time; sometimes the batteries are low. There will be moments when people's personal priorities, problems and moods preoccupy them to the detriment of their jobs, and at times like these, they may well make mistakes or underperform.

One consequence is that, provided it is not too damaging, as a manager you might have to put up with some immature or poor behaviour from time to time. So for instance, you ask someone to carry out a task by a particular deadline. For once they become uncooperative or even hostile. Rather than starting disciplinary procedures, you might just have to return to them a couple of hours later and quietly address the same issue again. In the meantime, they will have had a chance to think it over and they may well be in a better mood. If they are not, you must address the same issue with them again tomorrow, and again the day after, until it is finally sorted out. You may have to accept that not everyone will jump the first time you stand them in front of the fence.

The key to solving these sorts of difficulties is to remain calm and rational, and not to take things personally and allow yourself to react emotionally, or perceive their behaviour as an affront to your status, or whatever. Making allowances is part of what any manager gets paid for, and your team is unlikely to be entirely composed of latter-day Mother Teresas. What matters is whether people have the capabilities and the willingness to do their jobs, and whether, notwithstanding the occasional hiccup, they perform to the required standard. And remember that when some people are being especially difficult over work related matters they are sometimes acting the part of the canary in the mine, warning you of something wrong.

4.1.2   Fact Number Two: All Human Beings Are Different

"Every cripple has his own way of walking", noted the writer Brendan Behan. When a Dublin zookeeper was once asked to account for his outstanding success in the difficult task of lion breeding, he replied, "Understanding lions." Pressed to explain further, he added, "every lion is different" (Wisdom 1965). It is the same with people. We are not all cut from the same piece of cloth. We are driven in different ways, and we each have our own styles, backgrounds and goals. Some of us have awkwardness woven into the fabric of our characters. People can vary in temperament, ambitions and beliefs, and our teams invariably comprise a range of different nationalities and cultural experiences. Not everyone is motivated by what motivates us, and managers need to be careful about projecting their own values and aspirations onto others.

Our experiences and history have marked us all in different ways. We all tend to be a mix of the rational and the emotional. For example, some individuals can hold surprisingly fixed and dogmatic views on the most unlikely of subjects. Once you know what these subjects are, they are best avoided. A display of flippancy on their pet subject can lead some people to sulk for months. Individuals have been known to hold workplace grudges for years, and the more intelligent they are, the more they seem to apply their brains to rationalizing their emotional reactions in order to justify themselves.

People sometimes carry deep scars from their life experiences, and these scars can manifest themselves at strange times and in strange ways. You may never get to the bottom of why colleagues can behave the way they do. Long memories about real or imagined slights or insults may resurface many years later. For example, you have had a smooth working relationship with someone over a number of years. One day, out of the blue, something you say or do provokes a disproportionate reaction. It is like shaking a bottle of tomato ketchup: nothing happens for ages, and all of a sudden the ketchup is all over the place, and it is hard to get it all back into the container. At times, it is as well to expect the unexpected.

In working with others we cannot always make accurate guesses about what goes on in people's minds. We will not always learn to recognize how they see the world, the triggers which annoy them, or even their priorities in life. What works for one person will not work for everybody, and managers must be prepared to adapt their approaches accordingly.

By way of a practical example, some staff can become irritable if you disturb them when they are hard at work early in the mornings. Perhaps it is because they have learned that they are at their most productive during these hours and want to use this time to get their most important work done. Others prefer to be left alone immediately after they have returned from a long meeting. They want to be left in peace for 15 mins. whilst they draw breath, collect their thoughts, review their notes and add any action items to their "to do" list. Some people prefer to be briefed verbally; others prefer information in writing (and, by the way, you should inform anyone reporting to you which of the two you prefer). It is for the manager to observe the signs and signals, note people's reactions, and act accordingly. People's background and training may offer clues as to how they want information: many engineers like models; many accountants prefer numbers and tabulations. In other words, cut with the grain.

People often send clues about how they wish to be treated, and we should be alive to these. Few employees offer as much help as one project manager we knew, who placed a pie diagram, with a movable arrow at its centre, adjacent to his desk. A label at the top of the diagram read, "Adrian is . . .", and in the ten sections of the pie, he had written descriptions of his varying moods: "happy", "annoyed", "occupied", "approachable." He would move the arrow depending on his current state of mind.

While some people like Adrian can be almost Garboesque in their occasional desire to be left alone, others want more regular contact and reassurance. One manager complained to us that his Director treated him, "like a library book." He added: "He takes me down from the shelf when he wants to know something, and he puts me back when he's finished. In between you don't even get a 'hello' from him." This individual craved more recognition and attention than he was getting from the Director. Yet when one of us discussed this with the Director concerned, we discovered that he was in fact entirely happy with the manager's performance, and felt that he was paying him a compliment by leaving him alone to get on with his work, rather than wasting his time on social niceties. This leads us into the third important fact concerning human beings at work.

4.1.3 Fact Number Three: The Manager Too Is Part of the Equation

Because they themselves are also participants in a two-way exchange involving another human being, managers have to take their share of the responsibility for their relationships with others. The behaviour of the manager affects that of the employee, and vice versa. This interplay can work very well, but it can also lead to friction.

Whenever stress levels increase, relationship difficulties between managers and their staff become more common. Previously, we alluded to the increasing diversity of the workforce in many organizations. Some people find it easier than others to relate to those from different cultures, or those with different backgrounds and interests to their own. To take a simple example, the common tendency of some managers to be forever employing sporting analogies or references does not always go down well with those who have little or no interest in sport.

Workplace relationships are not always sweetness and light. There will be times when you argue and there will be times when there is tension. Sometimes managers and staff quite simply do not like each other. You can end up working with people who in other circumstances you might cross the road to avoid. In one sense this ought to be an irrelevance. What matters is how people perform, not whether you share their work habits, interests, beliefs, values or even lunchtime eating preferences. Yet we fallible human beings often seem to find it hard to put to one side our feelings and reactions towards others.

However if we are to manage effectively, we must try to control some of these emotions. Few of us have the freedom to choose all of the members of our teams, and even when you can, you should avoid selecting only those whom you like, or are always easy to work with. You will not get on with everybody. There are people you will not like and there are people who will not like you. The chemistry will not always be right and some personalities will inevitably clash. If you have to work with the people you dislike, and most of us need to do so from time to time, then perhaps we should grit our teeth, and as a politician once put it, make up our minds to, "bestow a benevolent neutrality" upon those whom we simply cannot abide.

At times like these, treating people with respect, consideration and understanding—what some people call old-fashioned "good manners"—can help us maintain relatively harmonious relations with others even when the personal chemistry is not right.

Remember
- In managing and working with others, you are dealing with human beings, with the moods, imperfections and peculiarities that accompany their strengths
- At times, people can behave unpredictably
- Often, the greater the level of professional expertise, the more idiosyncratic the behaviour
- Getting emotional yourself rarely helps, rather, read the clues that people send you, and work out how to respond
- Treating people with respect and consideration (old-fashioned "good manners") can help get you through when you don't personally like individuals

---

4.2   Do the Basics First: Get to Know Your People (If You Don't Already)

In this section we:

- *List out the basic "facts" managers should ideally know about each of their direct reports*
- *Discuss other sources of potentially useful information*
- *Highlight the two key questions all managers should be able to answer about each of their direct reports*

4.2.1   People: The Basic Facts

The inscription found at the Greek temple of Apollo advised: "Know thyself." It is sound advice. It follows that managers also need to know their people, and in this section we suggest what managers ought to know, as well as some ways of finding out.

As a general rule, the better that you know people, the better placed you are to manage them. As a first step, there are a number of simple fact based questions that all managers should be able to answer about each of their direct reports (see Fig. 4.1).

Basic facts managers should know about each of their direct reports

- Qualifications
- Professional interests
- Experience
- Level of expertise in their field/other fields
- Previous posts held
- Length of time in current role
- Length of service in the organization
- Recent annual performance ratings
- Recent career, salary and bonus progression

Fig. 4.1 Basic facts managers should know about each of their direct reports

We suggest that managers should now pause and consider the extent to which they can answer each of the questions in Fig. 4.1 about the members of their own immediate teams.

Most of this information is readily available, although not all managers bother to obtain it and consider what it might mean. Yet taken together, these basic facts will often give more insight into people, and tell you more about what you need to know, than all of the opinions, untested assumptions, hearsay, half-truths and speculations about individuals' motives and personalities which often circulate in organizations. If you do not know all of the answers to the questions, you should obtain them as soon as possible.

Even if you have managed someone for some length of time, collating together this basic information may highlight issues you had not fully appreciated. You may spot patterns you had not seen, or be able to make inferences that can lead you to ask questions, take action and even avoid potential problems.

For instance, in examining one individual's career record, you may notice that he has tended to move jobs every four or five years. If he is now in his fifth year in his current post, might he soon be seeking a career move, a job change or a new challenge? Similarly, it can be helpful to consider any patterns in a person's recent performance data. If after a number of years of high performance people suddenly underperform, then what might be the reasons, and can you help? Also you should consider how an individual's performance ratings compare against those of other colleagues, and whether as a consequence some people might feel particularly unsatisfied with their current level of remuneration, or with a recent bonus.

Simple information such as length of service in an organization can shed light on the strength of people's organizational networks. Long service employees are more likely to be well-connected, and any opinions they share with you may well carry significant weight in that they reflect the views of an important or sizable group of colleagues. Also, when considering how to react towards certain events in your department or organization, remember that others may well take their cue from the attitudes of these employees.

If nothing else, when you have these basic facts at hand, you can refer to them selectively in any discussions with those concerned. In doing so, you demonstrate an informed, interested and professional approach. Most people respond positively to professionalism in others and it will do you no harm in helping to secure the active cooperation and engagement of your staff.

4.2.2   Going Beyond the Basic Facts About People

Of course, 'knowing your people' goes beyond knowing the basic facts, and managers vary widely in terms of how much else they know about those who work for them. Some managers develop quite close personal relationships with certain members of their teams. They can, for instance, reel off details about these individuals' family backgrounds, hobbies and outside interests. Through working together, people can get to know each other really well, to the point where either party can finish the other's sentences.

It is certainly true that close relationships can sometimes help managers in better understanding people, their motivations, and their likely reactions. Some managers argue that a close connection between themselves and their people usually leads to a happier and more productive workplace. Such managers sometimes feel that building personal relations makes them more approachable, with the added benefit that they often obtain useful information about which they might otherwise remain in ignorance.

However, there can be problems with these sorts of relationships in the workplace. Occasionally they can get in the way of difficult work decisions, and if managers appear closer to some staff than others, it can lead to cliques, jealousies and accusations of favouritism. Inevitably in some cases the very fact of establishing close relationships with some of your staff leads directly to more difficult relationships with others. Some people feel that an enemy's friend cannot be their friend.

Team members do not always get on well together. Scratch the "surface bonhomie" which exists within some teams and you sometimes find extreme personal dislikes seething there. Furthermore, no matter what the individual manager might want, some people place a strict dividing line between their professional and private lives. Certain individuals routinely share personal matters; others most decidedly do not, and they like to keep a distance between themselves and their work colleagues. Their right to do so should be respected.

Those who want to maintain their personal privacy usually consider attempts to delve into nonwork matters a gross intrusion. They will resist revealing personal information just for the sake of it. However, most people will, in our experience, generally tell their managers what they feel they need them to know. So, for instance, if individuals have some domestic or other constraint that could affect their work, they will often share it ("I need to leave on time on Thursdays. My partner attends a course and I need to take care of the children.").

It is also as well to remember that in a more sceptical world, many people are much more suspicious of others' motives, and they will resent it strongly if they feel a manager or anyone else is attempting to build a relationship in order better to manipulate or control them.

There are no hard and fast rules in these matters. How well you get to know your staff as people, and the sort of relationships you build with them is a matter of your respective personalities, preferences, and work circumstances. As in most areas of management, individual managers have to find their own approaches, and establish what works for them in a given situation. But do not fall into the trap of trying to build personal relationships as your major tool in managing people: it invariably fails.

4.2.3   Other Sources of Information About People

It is useful to supplement your own observations about people with the views and feedback of others. In some organizations, HR may have access to the results of personality, aptitude, psychometric and other test data. Similarly, managers may be able to review with the individuals concerned the implications of any available "360-degree" data. In any case it is usually possible to learn about someone's press or reputation in an organization quite quickly, including perceptions about their level of professional expertise, strengths, and any perceived deficiencies. Feedback on these matters is of most value from those who have worked directly with the people concerned. Your own manager may also have views, and useful insights can be forthcoming from trusted work colleagues who also deal with your staff on a regular basis. It is sometimes through third parties that managers get to hear about matters that could be affecting individuals' behaviour, or their performance at work.

Many managers commission formal customer or client surveys. These can help in obtaining systematic feedback on a department or team, as well as provide insights into how some individuals are perceived, especially when these individuals are in customer-facing roles. If you plan to ask for formal feedback from customers and others, it is good practice to let your staff know that you are doing so. It usually gets back to them anyway, and can cause resentment if they feel you have been seeking information about them 'behind their backs.' When conducting any customer survey, it is generally sensible to frame your questions impersonally (e.g. "What sort of service are you getting from us? How well are we meeting your needs? How could we improve?") Where you can, always try to obtain specific examples and evidence in support of any opinions being expressed. And before reaching any definitive conclusions, remember to weigh the various opinions quite carefully. When giving feedback, people can vary in their motives and agendas, and how they perceive others often reflects something about themselves or their own situations.

4.2.4   In Conclusion: The Two Key Questions Any Manager Must Be Able to Answer

So, you have assembled the basic facts and information about your staff. You have developed a suitable working relationship with them, based on your respective preferences and personalities. And you have gathered some information on how they are perceived by others. You should now be in a position to answer the two key questions that all managers should be able to answer about their direct reports: *What are they willing to do? What are they able to do?* (Hersey and Blanchard 1989).

4.2.4.1 Willingness

Willingness means that you need to know what your direct reports are, and are not, prepared to do in a work context. How hard will they work? If they are given certain responsibilities, based on their track record, can they be relied upon to deliver? Are they of a mind to put in the time, energy and discretionary effort required? Always? Or only under certain conditions? To take an obvious example, there's no point a manager expecting someone to work at a time or in a manner that would mean contravening deeply held religious or ethical principles.

4.2.4.2 Ability

Ability concerns their overall capabilities. What skills and competencies do they have? What jobs and tasks have they been trained to do and are able to do? What are their strengths? Again, managers' expectations need to be realistic, and there is little point expecting an individual to a carry out an unfamiliar task in an optimum manner without the proper knowledge, training or support. Chapter 6 of this book deals with how to prepare and implement a development plan so as to address any shortfalls in training, skills or experience.

Once you have answered these questions you are now ready to begin to formulate what you can *realistically expect* of each member of your team. This is discussed in the following section.

Remember
- For managers, there are many sources of readily available information about people
- Your staff may feel slighted if you do not take the trouble to find out basic facts about them
- They may well consider your lack of knowledge reflects a lack of professionalism on your part
- Close workplace relationships can be a double-edged sword
- You must respect people's desire for privacy about their private lives
- Before formulating what you can realistically expect of your staff, you must be able to answer two key questions:
  - What are they willing to do?
  - What are they capable of doing?

4.3   Establishing Expectations

In this section we will:

- *Discuss why most managers need to hold the occasional 'sharing expectations' meeting with each of their direct reports*
- *Present an overview of the three phases involved in any such meeting or meetings (before, during, and after)*
- *Consider how managers can best prepare so that all the important bases are covered*
- *Provide some tips on how to handle the meetings themselves*
- *Set down what needs to be done after the meetings*

4.3.1   If You're Happy and You Know It . . .

The old saw of, 'if it ain't broke, don't fix it', certainly applies to agreeing expectations. If your Work Management System (Chap. 3) is satisfactory, the organization's objectives are being achieved, and you are getting what you want from staff without too many problems, then you probably have no need to go through the in-depth process set out here.

Nevertheless, the occasional short meeting with each member of your team is still useful, if only to say, "keep doing what you're doing" or to make sure that all is also well from their point of view. To manage effectively requires being knowledgeable about people's concerns and issues and these often only become apparent in the course of a one-on-one meeting. Even when a Work Management System is working well, some people can misinterpret events or a manager's intentions. A periodic person-to-person discussion means that any misunderstandings can be nipped in the bud, making it less likely that anyone will put two and two together and make twenty-two.

Even if someone has worked for you for years, we still think it is important to make time to meet for the occasional one-on-one session. It enables both parties to draw breath and review their expectations away from the hustle and bustle of day-to-day activity. In any case, in most organizations, and especially larger ones, there is usually a requirement for managers and staff to meet together two or three times a year as part of the formal performance management and appraisal arrangements.

The approach we suggest in this chapter, with its stress on the importance of an on going Work Management System, the need to do some fact gathering on your staff, and the requirement for detailed preparation, may go beyond what is required in most situations (and it certainly goes beyond what is prescribed in most organizations' performance planning and appraisal management systems). It is for the individual manager to select those elements which will best dovetail with what is required in their own circumstances, and in order to meet the requirements within their own organizations.

4.4 The Three Phases of Establishing Expectations: Before, During, and After

Managers start from a variety of different places in terms of how well their direct reports understand what is expected. However, apart from those cases in which individuals have just started to work for a new manager, the *tabla rasa* or clean slate rarely exists. Job descriptions, performance targets and objectives are likely to exist in some form, with staff often working to a performance plan or set of expectations which may have been established a long time ago. Even if they have never been the subject of a formal discussion, mutual expectations will have been set in some way.

At its simplest, the process we recommend for establishing expectations involves: arranging a meeting with a member of your staff; sharing with them what you want; listening to their responses; and agreeing a way forward. What has been agreed then gets implemented. Life, however, is rarely that simple. Often people may have had some bad experiences in the past with these sorts of discussions. In many organizations, the process is associated with assessment, rewards and promotions and it can put people on edge. At their worst, these discussions can almost turn into a type of "Mexican standoff", with each party waiting for the other to make the first move.

Figure 4.2 sets out an overview of the three step process involved in establishing expectations. It highlights the key tasks at each phase, and each step is discussed and described below, under the three separate headings. Although most managers will not necessarily need to prepare to the level of detail set out here, what follows can be a useful checklist to help ensure all the bases are covered. Following what we suggest, in particular with regard to the preparation phase, will greatly improve the chances of success.

4.4.1 Before the Meeting: Prepare

There are three main tasks to be carried out in advance of any meeting (Fig. 4.2). Having assessed an individual's overall willingness and ability to carry out assignments, you then need to begin to develop your list of specific expectations of them. There are six areas which need to be considered, and each of these is now discussed.

PHASE	PRINCIPAL TASKS
BEFORE THE MEETING: PREPARE	(1) Clarify for yourself what you expect from each team member, given their willingness and ability. Consider: 1. Their current performance: what they need to do more of, less of, stop and start doing 2. The overall organizational strategy 3. Your department's current and future role, goals, responsibilities, targets, projects and initiatives 4. The needs of your own boss/manager 5. Your own priorities 6. The priorities of the individual members of your team (2) Develop an initial list of your expectations. Consider each individual's likely expectations, concerns and reactions, and your responses
DURING THE MEETING: SHARE AND DISCUSS	Meet and discuss your list • State what is non-negotiable • Ensure objectives people can control/ influence • Listen to people's expectations, concerns and issues • Agree the next steps
AFTER THE MEETING: FOLLOW THROUGH	• Revise your list accordingly and confirm agreement, as required • Provide them with a copy of any written agreements • Revise job description if necessary • Monitor and review, adding items as required to the Work Management List • What are the likely challenges involved and how can you help? (this is also dealt with in the next chapter)

Fig. 4.2 Overview of three step process and key tasks at each phase

4.4.1.1 Their Current Performance: What They Need to Do: More of, Less of, Start Doing, Stop Doing

Considering how people are currently performing in their roles is the best start point for clarifying expectations. Jobs with clearly defined outputs and performance expectations may require less preparation time (and less discussion time). Notwithstanding, most managers could usefully ask themselves some basic questions:

- How have things been going?
- What has gone well and less well?
- Have they been meeting the required standards of performance? Are you disappointed in some areas?
- Do some expectations seem to be unclear?
- Are there any particular problems or issues?
- Is there anything you have been avoiding saying, which needs saying now?

The answers to the questions should help pinpoint areas for improvement. Some people find working through the, "do more of . . .; do less of . . .; start doing . . .; stop doing . . ." approach to be a useful way of framing their thinking.

A common complaint from some people is that they feel overloaded much of the time. Since we are all limited to 24-hr. days, one particular area to highlight would be any unnecessary or redundant activities. It can be a useful exercise to pinpoint the extent to which some staff are continuing with tasks which have now outlived their usefulness: people collecting data in particular ways because they have always done so; time spent developing reports which were required for a previous manager or era and which people no longer read. In organizations, much more time gets wasted on redundant activities than is generally realized.

4.4.1.2 The Overall Organization Strategy

Current strategy and other internal documents usually contain comprehensive information about an organization's overall plans, targets, and mission, as well as important contextual and other background material. Organizations vary in the extent to which they will allow managers at all levels access to some of these documents—they may contain sensitive or commercially confidential information. If you are unable to consult the relevant materials direct, then in practice most people can almost always find out everything of significance to their departments by asking for information from their own managers.

If you are working to an annual strategy document, then it is important to check from time to time whether there have been any alterations to the planned strategies. For any number of reasons, changes in emphasis or significant revisions can happen subtly and these are not always announced with a great fanfare.

Materials describing an organization's values and culture are also sometimes available. Some of these documents give useful insights as to house style, business values and ethics, and "the way we do things around here." At times they provide useful guidance as regards standards and expected behaviour. Other publications can sometimes be quite general and almost indistinguishable from what can be found in any organization. The worst kind of documents can be viewed quite cynically by staff (Watson 1994) and are seen as little more than "corporate graffiti" (Robertson 1995), with their truisms and platitudes which no-one takes seriously and which bear little relation to how business is actually conducted, or members of staff are treated.

4.4.1.3 Current/Future Departmental Goals, Targets, Projects, or Initiatives

Specific departmental requirements are typically set out in the more detailed business planning and other documents relating to particular functions and business areas. Published policies and procedures can also be a useful guide to what might be required, and these can also indicate activities requiring attention. Many organizations also allocate and publish "targets", "key performance indicators" or "critical success factors" for specific departments or functions. An organization's balanced scorecard or dashboard is also worth consulting since it may well highlight issues requiring input from your department (Kaplan and Norton 1996).

Often ignored, sometimes much maligned, and in many places unfashionable, job descriptions or role profiles can be an important building block in any discussion about expectations. Unfortunately many available job descriptions are not always up to date. Worse, they may have been developed as little more than defensive documents designed to help achieve a pay grade or points in a job evaluation scheme. The result can be voluminous documents, containing endless accountabilities and long-winded descriptions of job context, with a consequent loss of focus on what a jobholder is expected to deliver.

If the current job descriptions are poor or too wordy, it is fairly easy to develop new ones, and it is usually best to do so in conjunction with the jobholders themselves. All that is required in most cases is to define between eight and ten principal accountabilities or "key result areas" which comprise the main elements of the job. The descriptions do not need to be extensive or long-winded. A series of simple one sentence statements— such as, "Run the department in line with agreed professional standards"—will suffice in most cases (see Fig. 4.3). If desired, a short "person specification" can be added, setting out the qualifications, skills, experiences, professional requirements and

---

Simple job description for a marketing manager

1. Design and deliver effective sales and marketing campaigns
2. Maintain awareness of marketplace changes; formulate and implement responses
3. Recommend, secure agreement to and carry out fit for purpose branding strategy
4. Lead, build and develop a sales and marketing team
5. Direct and control relevant outsourced contracts within assigned area of responsibility
6. Build and maintain relationships with senior management team colleagues
7. Build and maintain external relationships

Fig. 4.3 Simple job description for a marketing manager

competencies needed for the role. The latter can be of help in considering performance standards as well as people's development needs (Fig. 4.4).

In deciding what is required of each jobholder, self-evidently the manager of a unit or department needs to be satisfied that, taken together, all of the objectives and responsibilities assigned to a department will be met. In most departments, responsibilities and targets are shared out amongst the members of the team. Whilst the targets themselves may well be non-negotiable as far as the team overall is concerned, there may be considerable scope for debate about 'who on the team will do what.' This is one issue to which the manager should give some thought in advance of any individual discussions.

Is there any point to job descriptions?

Whilst not absolutely necessary to clarify what is expected – most managers can set out most of what they want in half a dozen bullet points – short, up to date job descriptions, setting out the main purpose of the job and its principal accountabilities, do bring a number of advantages:

- When individual job descriptions and targets are taken together, it enables a manager to check that all of the team's responsibilities and goals are covered. It reduces the risk that any important activities could fall by the wayside, and enables the manager to verify that there are no unintended conflicts generated amongst team members through unnecessary or unplanned duplication

- Unlike annual targets, which can become dated or less relevant should circumstances change (e.g. the loss of a major customer), job descriptions enable the ready definition of a "patch" or set of responsibilities which each jobholder owns, and from which they cannot walk away, regardless of changing circumstances

- They clarify each jobholder's expected area of contribution, thus reducing the risk of individuals competing with their colleagues for work, or refusing to take on certain tasks because they 'thought they were someone else's job.' A set of accountabilities defined for each individual can also be shared with all of the members of a department or team, so that everyone knows the others' responsibilities. We often recommend such sharing as a simple yet valuable part of any teambuilding programme

- They can prove useful in those circumstances in which it is difficult to agree precise objectives. For instance, you may not always be able to define specific sales objectives relating to a given group of customers, since their circumstances may change. However you make an individual accountable for maximizing the returns from a given group of accounts, and for taking any necessary remedial action in the light of unexpected changes. Setting too precise objectives in changing circumstances is not dissimilar to trying to forecast the weather – the further into the future, the harder it is to forecast accurately.

Fig. 4.4 Is there any point to job descriptions?

In considering what else is required, bear in mind that your group or function will also need to continue to develop its knowledge and capability in the field. This can be achieved through individual development actions (discussed in detail in Chap. 6), benchmarking and research, with the relevant tasks allocated, progressed and recorded (Chap. 3 describes how this can be captured as part of the Work Management System).

As we will discuss in the next chapter, organizational initiatives—typically those tasks or projects driven by other functions or descending from on high, such as a "quality initiative" or a centrally driven "change programme"—vary in number and priority. In agreeing expectations with staff, it is important that relevant initiatives affecting the department are addressed. Sometimes one or several team members may take ownership for implementing a given initiative within a department.

4.4.1.4 The Needs of Your Own Boss/Manager

In addition to the specific jobs and objectives that they allocate, scratch the surface and you will find that most of those who manage us also have their particular hobby horses or "hot buttons." Often these reflect personal priorities or biases and they must be taken into account in establishing departmental targets. Some managers have particular standards or approaches they wish to see adopted in some aspects of the work. Earlier in this chapter we recommended finding out about the qualifications, experience and background of the individual members of your team. Similarly it can be useful to understand your own manager's background and previous roles: for example, knowing that your boss has an accounting background will affect the way you present financial or other information, as well as enabling you to anticipate the sorts of questions which may be asked. This is especially the case when your manager formerly worked in your Department: it can explain why they wish to stress or emphasize particular aspects of the work, or require tasks to be carried out in a particular manner.

Very often senior managers want tasks carrying out in a particular way for no other reason than that is the way they want them done. For example, a director may be familiar with a particular project management approach because he likes the reports it generates and the discipline it brings. He has worked with the approach for many years, has confidence in it, and as a consequence wants all projects in his area to follow this methodology, even if other approaches could deliver a similar or arguably better result. As discussed earlier in this chapter, managers are human beings as well, with their own particular biases, and they are entitled to insist that some things are done their way.

In preparing to discuss expectations with your staff, in addition to what your own manager *wants*, you should take into account their *needs*. There may be some issues which require you or your staff to watch your boss's back for him or her (Fig. 4.5).

4.4.1.5 Your Own Priorities

You may have your own particular objectives or priorities for your team or for certain members of the team. Sometimes within a team, some members will form their own little "clique", and this can be detrimental to the team overall. So you may decide to ring some changes and reallocate some tasks or reporting relationships.

Helping the boss to perform

In one organization, a senior director in an international firm on the acquisition trail mandated a monthly two hour meeting on the status of the project pipeline. The timing of the meeting was set for the last Friday of the month. This was in order that he would be fully briefed immediately prior to that month's Board meeting on the following Monday. One of the members of the Board was an acquisitions expert, and the Director wanted to be au fait with all of the issues because he knew he would be closely quizzed at the meeting. For various reasons his choice of Friday was not the best timing from the point of view of the staff, but it met his need. Doing what is required to give bosses what they need to be effective at their level may not always suit our own desires. "It is your job to make the boss perform", said Peter Drucker. Ensuring your boss is able to perform effectively at his or her level is never a waste of time.

Fig. 4.5   Helping the boss to perform

Changing circumstances in organizations often require deeply ingrained habits to be revisited and reviewed. For example, you may want some individuals to improve information sharing across the department, or you may wish someone to take the lead on reviewing an on going project. Similarly, you might want an employee to take responsibility for some particular processes or events.

"And now we come to your fifth Number 1 priority, Arnie"

4.4.1.6 The Priorities of Staff

It is worth thinking in advance about any particular issues individuals are likely to raise. For instance, you might have heard on the grapevine that someone might want responsibility for a particular project or assignment. You should also ask yourself what might be worrying people currently, both at work and possibly outside. For instance, when individuals dig their heels in over how stretching a target should be, it is worth knowing whether receiving a full bonus or high performance rating is simply an issue of pride and status, or whether it is a financial imperative given that they are struggling with a heavy mortgage or debt.

Asking someone, "how should you be managed in order to get the best out of you?" is a very powerful question which can elicit some very useful answers.

It is also important to get some insight into people's "psychological" or "implicit" contracts. Researchers first highlighted these some years ago and there have been numerous studies since (Gouldner 1954; Levinson et al. 1966; Lorsch 1979; Guest and Conway 1997; Anderson and Schalk 1998; Guest 1998). While formal contracts of employment are legal documents concerned with issues such as pay and work hours, psychological contracts reflect the often *unexpressed, informal agreements and understandings* which exist between individuals and their employers. Some examples would be: travel arrangements; or expectations about the appropriateness of 'going direct' to certain individuals within a hierarchy. Managers interfere with these informal contracts at their peril, as a newly appointed university dean discovered when he tried to impose a system of electronic diaries on a team of academics accustomed to the freedom to come and go as they pleased.

"I am afraid, Mr Blenkinsop, that the new travel policy does not include a choice of airline"

In some cases these tacit agreements, customs and practices have evolved over many years, to the extent that employees have gradually come to consider them almost as "rights" and part of their "package." For example, someone leaves

---

How simple changes can unwittingly affect the psychological contracts of employees

For several years a Manufacturing Director had attended his company's monthly Board meetings. His presence was required for one topic only, a one hour agenda item during which he presented the monthly operating statistics, and responded to questions. On the retirement of his manager, the Chief Operating Officer, a replacement was appointed. This new COO decided that henceforth, he would present the statistics himself, based on information provided by the Manufacturing Director.

Initially irritated by the change, it was only after a couple of months under the new arrangements that the Manufacturing Director came to realize the full implications. Because his name had been removed from the circulation list for the monthly pack of Board papers, he was now deprived of an important source of information. He no longer had the benefit of hearing the reactions of Board members to his presentation first hand, and as a consequence was less confident in his ability to prepare the monthly materials in a way which would meet their concerns. In addition, since he no longer had the opportunity to engage with Board members each month, an important network had been destroyed.

He also noticed that his non attendance had begun to change the relationship between himself and a number of his colleagues. Board members had stopped contacting him prior to the meetings, and other colleagues had stopped seeking him out as a potential source of information. As well as feeling less able to do his job, the Manufacturing Director felt he had effectively been demoted. The decision by the new COO had essentially changed the Manufacturing Director's "psychological contract" with his employer.

Fig. 4.6 How simple changes can unwittingly affect the psychological contracts of employees

promptly on Thursdays because they have to look after children, and suddenly a new manager decides to hold a weekly meeting on Thursday afternoons.

Understanding someone's psychological contract can be difficult, and some of its elements may be unknown to the individual concerned (see Fig. 4.6, for example). The full significance of the Manufacturing Director's attendance at the Board meeting only became apparent once the arrangement had changed. But even when people are aware of how a change could affect their psychological contracts, they may be embarrassed to speak openly about it.

When managers get resistance from a member of staff, and try to understand the reasons behind it, it is often because a suggested action would violate someone's psychological contract: perhaps handing over a certain project to someone else could incur a loss of face or status (these sorts of issues have great importance in some cultures, and for some people).

So how can managers get to understand and take into account the psychological contracts of their staff? Some of the following suggestions may help:

- Observe people's behaviour at work. Pay close attention to their reactions to any changes, and what happens as soon as any changes occur

- Wherever you can, consult people in advance about any significant changes, or at the very least consider the possible effects of any change before it is introduced
- Ask yourself how any change could potentially affect people's status, network, sources of information, authority, or how they and their teams might be perceived by others
- When changes are made, review the situation again after a month or so to see if there have been any unintended consequences which have affected people's psychological contracts. As Richard Hooker pointed out centuries ago, "Change is not made without inconvenience, even from worse to better"
- Consider discussing the concept of psychological contracts openly with staff, trying to tease out any expectations. When people are treated as adults, with whom it is possible to have a mature exchange of ideas, they invariably respond positively. It is often possible for managers to make changes which will achieve a desired effect without inadvertently or unnecessarily changing people's psychological contracts.

4.4.1.7 Develop an Initial Discussion List of Your Expectations for Each Team Member

A useful pre meeting discipline for managers is to develop a preliminary list of what they expect from each of their direct reports. This helps to focus any discussion and the resulting list can be shared during one, or as necessary, more meetings. Managers already familiar with their priorities and requirements may be able to develop their lists of expectations with little effort. Figure 4.7 is an example of one manager's preliminary list for discussion.

Manager's preliminary list for sharing and discussion

1. Deliver:
    a. responsibilities as set out in job description
    b. sales targets as agreed on bonus plan
    c. all tasks as set out on Work Management List

2. Lead Corporate Quality initiative

3. Provide full support in implementing departmental decisions, once views on issues have been taken into account

4. Share information and expertise (including organizational history) with all members of the team

5. Train and coach Paula and Maurice in own professional field

6. Monitor and review expense sheets in the Department and make sure that these are all completed prior to month end

Fig. 4.7 Manager's preliminary list for sharing and discussion

In developing such a list, consider the six factors in Fig. 4.2, as well as how you will respond should individuals disagree with some of the items (although do not fall into the trap of thinking you have to answer unexpected questions immediately—you can always say you want more time to think before you answer). It is particularly important that, before discussing expectations with them, you are clear in your own mind about the "non-negotiable" issues, those goals or performance standards which you will insist on. People may be less deferential, and individuals more assertive and demanding in terms of what they want to do, but this does not mean that they can be allowed to negotiate everything. If necessary, this needs to be said. *Management by Permission* is hard-nosed consensual management.

The *first two* items in Fig. 4.7 are self-explanatory. In this example, the manager is happy that the existing job description is an adequate depiction of someone's current role. *Item 1b)* reflects targets already defined and agreed as part of the company's bonus scheme. *Item 1c)* reinforces that the jobholder is responsible for any jobs allocated to them on the Work Management List. *Item two* concerns a company initiative in the area of quality for which the manager would like the employee to take departmental responsibility.

Item three raises a potentially awkward issue which had begun to cause difficulties in the Department. The manager wanted to make sure of the individual's commitment to implement decisions even when they did not necessarily agree with them. As part of the *quid pro quo—Management by Permission* implies that 'deals' of this nature will increasingly need to be done—he is committing that this staff member will be consulted about issues where they have some concerns, and he will make sure their views are heard.

Items four and five are related in that the employee concerned was an experienced individual who was being asked to pass his knowledge and expertise onto others. The manager had noticed that this individual had been taking two of the members of staff—Maurice and Paula—under his wing. Adding it to the list shows the individual that the manager has noticed and also gives them formal credit and recognition for their action in developing others.

The final item on monitoring expense sheets is one of life's little chores—those unpleasant tasks which are to be found in almost all jobs. These tasks are often administrative in nature, are usually uninteresting, few people enjoy doing them, and most of us tend to put them off. They are jobs such as completing the weekly call plans, writing up reports after meetings with customers, following company protocols and procedures for procurement requisitioning. Often these tasks get delayed, avoided or ignored. Some of these tasks are pure "grunt" activities and are often put in place to meet the requirements of monitoring and control.

It is as well to be specific about these less than pleasant tasks from the outset. Even the most enjoyable of jobs invariably involve some routine tasks. The truth is we might all prefer to be writing our elegant software modelling the world economy, or thinking up interesting new product ideas. However, we still have to complete our attendance records and monitor people's travel expenses. If you have any part-time workers reporting to you, you should consider whether they too could take responsibility for some of this routine work. Their part-time status is often a real benefit, and it is unfair to allocate these activities exclusively to the full-time employees.

Managers sometimes ask us whether they should ask their staff to prepare their own "wish lists" in advance of a meeting. Generally we advise against this. If both the manager and the individual come to the meeting with their own lists, then it can set up the meeting as if it is to be a negotiation. That can result in entrenched positions, people wanting to save face, and create unnecessary conflict.

Remember
- The Work Management System is a key tool in defining and refining expectations
- Setting and refining expectations is an on going process, over and above any formal organizational performance management system
- Use the checklist in Fig. 4.2 to help think through what is expected
- In the majority of cases a periodic one-on-one meeting is necessary
- Staff should be given a chance to have their say, but some matters are non-negotiable
- In advance of any meeting, time spent by the manager in preparation will repay tenfold

4.4.2   During the Meeting: Share and Discuss

The basics of handling a one-on-one meeting—such as agreeing a time in advance, setting aside as long as is necessary, and making sure you are not disturbed—need not detain us here. Most managers will understand these basics and if not, they are available in any relevant textbook or through a quick Internet search.

Figure 4.2 sets out the four key points to bear in mind when you meet to go through your list. Each is discussed below.

4.4.2.1 State What Is Non-negotiable

We have already alluded to this subject. Some matters are simply not up for negotiation. You need to be clear when you are opening up a topic for debate, as opposed to when you are simply explaining what has to be done, by whom and by when. For instance, an essential aspect of any clear working arrangement is how much discretion individuals may have, and when they must refer upwards. Similarly, certain projects need to be delivered by a certain time, in a certain way, despite what individuals may think, and certain tasks need to be carried out by certain individuals.

In addition to defining "what" is required, some thought should also be given to "how" some activities need to be delivered. For instance, you might require individuals to behave in particular ways in some circumstances. When explaining "how" you want something done, you are more likely to secure someone's active cooperation if you also explain "why" you want it done, as in the following two examples:

I know these two departments can be difficult. We need to be polite and helpful. We need their cooperation and it does not help if we get their backs up.

On this, I would like the results emailed to me, on a spreadsheet and categorized under the following headings. . . . I need this format as we now have to collate the results with data from departments X, Y and Z.

4.4.2.2 Ensure Objectives People Can Control/Influence

Whatever goals or activities you agree, you must be on your guard against setting overambitious targets. To look at some people's objectives, you would think they were trying single-handedly to solve world famine. Of course it makes sense to be appropriately ambitious, and "stretch targets" work as motivational factors for some people. However, there can be a fine line between what is stretching and what is impossible. If the targets become too hard, people get frustrated, they often abandon the chase prematurely, and they do worse than they might have done had no objectives been set.

Sports psychologists often advise their clients to focus on factors they can control, and to forget the rest. Figure 4.8 builds on this by presenting three concentric circles, labelled in turn *control*, *influence* and *impotence*, the idea being that you should prioritize from the centre outwards. It can be a helpful reminder in target setting of the importance of stressing that which people can *control* or at least *influence*, rather than goals which, whilst desirable, people cannot do very much about. Only when we have developed plans and taken action to address what we can control should we turn our attention to what we can influence, where self-evidently our chances of success are reduced. We should completely ignore those areas in which our attempts to address a situation merely expose our *impotence*.

Fig. 4.8 Control, Influence, Impotence

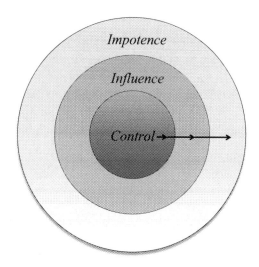

4.4.2.3 Listen to People's Expectations, Concerns and Issues

In the previous chapter we said that if we had to select one piece of *general advice* for managers, it would be to keep matters in their areas under control. If we had to select only one *specific skill* for most managers to acquire in order to improve their effectiveness, we would choose "listening."

In all our years as management and organizational consultants we have heard numerous complaints from people about their managers not listening. We have yet to hear a single complaint about any manager listening too much. When practised effectively, listening is one of the most powerful yet underestimated tools at the manager's disposal. It can solve problems, build relationships, take the heat out of difficult situations, and help set the climate in which people will allow you to manage them. It is also very useful when discussing and agreeing expectations: it helps you to see matters from the other person's point of view.

Many of us believe that we listen much better than we actually do, and proper listening certainly requires attention and practice. When conversing with others, the temptation for most of us is to listen by halves, mentally preparing our own responses which we will launch into as soon as the other person has stopped speaking. For managers, this habit is especially dangerous in that they can jump to conclusions before hearing all of the evidence, or worse still, provide an answer before the question is clear. Unless you are careful, you run the risk of forcing a discussion down a track which will either lead nowhere, or into a blind alley of misunderstanding or even resentment.

So what do we mean by effective listening? It starts by encouraging people to talk. Some people need to know that you want to hear what they want to say. You convey this with phrases such as: "Can you tell me about this?"; "What are your views on this?", or, "How did all this start?", "What exactly did happen?", or "What's your perspective on that? I would like to hear your views."

Once they have started to speak some people also need encouragement to continue. They need to know that you are still interested, and nods and verbal acknowledgement may well be all that is needed. Sometimes a more direct approach is required, such as, "Tell me more about that", or "That's interesting. Go on", or "What happened then?" In the initial stages certainly, the aim is to keep the information flow going, not to drive it in any particular direction. For instance, try to avoid questions which interrupt the flow (e.g. "Was that Thursday or Friday?") You can return to these sorts of details later.

There is one test of the really effective listener: it is the 'listening with understanding' technique. *You need to be able to summarize what a speaker has said to that person's entire satisfaction.* You understand their views, ideas, feelings and opinions on a topic so well, that you are able to restate their position precisely (Rogers 1991). When someone is happy that you have fully understood their position, you can then begin to work with them to devise a solution or agree a course of action, confident that you have understood all of the facts as they see them, before jumping to any conclusions prematurely.

Help in mastering this technique can be found in Fig. 4.9.

How to listen with understanding

As part of management seminars, we often give executives the opportunity to practise this summarizing technique as part of a thirty-minute group discussion. We ask the group members first to agree a topic for debate, and then to institute the following rule:

"People can express their views on the topic only after they have first restated the ideas and feelings of the previous speaker accurately, and to that previous speaker's satisfaction."

In other words before presenting their own individual points of view, each person must first achieve the other speaker's frame of reference, and understand that speaker's thoughts and feelings so well that they are able to summarize them satisfactorily. This does not mean acting like a parrot or a recording device: you must summarize the content in words which satisfy the speaker that you have truly understood.

To help with this exercise, which managers invariably find difficult and exhausting, we suggest that in trying to summarize, they make use of some of the following or similar opening phrases:

"So can I just try to summarize? What you're saying is ..."
"Just let me recap. What I'm hearing is ..."
"Let me just make sure that I've got this right ...."
"Can I clarify I understand what you are saying .... Is that it?"

Most managers practising this technique (and you don't need to attend a seminar in order to learn it) are astounded by the results.

Fig. 4.9 How to listen with understanding

We are never too worried that managers will overuse this "listening and understanding" approach once back at work. Firstly it is hard to listen, to the exclusion of all else, for extended periods. Secondly most managers always have an opportunity to interject their views at some point in any interaction with others.

We do recommend that when you are engaged in discussions with colleagues, either as part of clarifying expectations, or more generally in fact gathering or problem-solving, it can often be helpful to let them know that you are trying to focus initially on listening and rephrasing. One reason for doing so is that occasionally some people can interpret listening with understanding as 'mimicking' or playing games, and they will object to it as a manipulative technique.

By starting with phrases such as: "I need to check I have understood you properly, can I just try to summarize what I think I have heard?"—in other words letting them know what you are trying to do—the dangers of annoying others are greatly reduced. Letting people know what you are trying to do is another greatly underestimated technique in management.

"Perhaps, Arnie, I should have been a little more specific in the matter of acceptable dress"

Four Advantages of Listening with Understanding

Why is listening with understanding such an important management skill?

Firstly, when we listen with understanding, we demonstrate to the other person that we have not only understood their point of view, we are also taking their opinions seriously. Often people get frustrated because they feel their ideas are dismissed before they are even properly grasped. By listening effectively, we demonstrate that even if we subsequently disagree with someone, at the very least they will know that it was after having understood them. We have shown them that we are able to see things from their point of view before we try to explain to them what we think. We are much more likely to secure their active cooperation on other matters because we have done them the courtesy of understanding and acknowledging their point of view. As an aside, this technique can also be beneficial when trying to deal with difficulties within families or in private life relationships. We know this because countless managers have reported this back to us, in many cases some years after they first learned the technique.

Secondly, when people go through phases of unhappiness or frustration, talking to someone who knows how to listen can be most beneficial. Allowing people to vent their frustrations or voice their complaints to a listening ear also seems to remove the heat from situations and help individuals to feel better. For us, this has often been a surprising by-product of carrying out in-depth interviews with staff as part of consulting assignments. People report that they feel better having had the opportunity to express their views and have these listened to. On one occasion, following a programme of interviews with the Board of one organization, when we returned to see the Chairman the following week, he greeted us with the words: "I don't know what you've done to them. They are all really happy." What we had done, for the most part, was simply to listen.

Thirdly, listening with understanding can be especially useful in solving difficult problems in that it ensures that the problem is correctly understood and defined before anyone, including you, tries to solve it: without effective listening, we may be tempted to assume we understand the problem before we have all of the relevant facts. This can lead to the dangers of tackling the *symptoms* of a problem rather than dealing with its *causes*. This stress on problem identification is not to ignore that some managers may well know the solution to a similar problem which may have occurred previously. It is simply to state that it is wise to be careful about jumping to conclusions before a problem has been fully understood. When you listen properly you are better able to spot the flaws in an argument, the source of an error, or some fact which people have misunderstood or of which they are unaware.

Fourthly, when dealing with an emotionally charged situation or trying to solve a difficult problem, and a listener keeps on summarizing in a nonjudgmental way, as the speaker hears the summary played back to them, with each successive restating, they often further expand and build upon what they have already said. Indeed on many occasions they continue to do so, to the point that they discover that they have actually solved their problem, or at least found a workable action plan. Hearing a summary has the effect of helping them to clarify, examine and critique their own arguments and opinions. Since they have developed the solutions themselves, rather than having them imposed, they are much more likely to implement them, since they personally "own" them.

With the possible exception of those emergencies requiring immediate action, using effective listening to ensure that a problem is fully understood rarely exacerbates the situation. Once understanding has been achieved, one can easily revert to the standard problem-solving and other techniques which one may have otherwise used earlier (Fig. 4.10).

Try getting people to summarize what you have said

If you don't believe that people sometimes fail to listen to each other, the next time you issue detailed instructions or try to explain something to someone, try the following. Finish your explanation, and then say to the person: "Just so that I know that I have communicated effectively, can you summarize for me your understanding of what I have just said?" The results may well be quite shocking. Frequently, our messages will have been misunderstood; somehow we will have miscommunicated; perhaps our listeners have only been half listening to us, or perhaps bringing their own current biases to what they hear.

Hearing a person's summary of what you thought you said enables you to correct any possible misunderstandings immediately. It can save a great deal of time in future.

Fig. 4.10 Try getting people to summarize what you have said

Tips for Dealing with Contentious Issues

When discussing expectations, there will often be differences of opinion, and sometimes positions can become quite entrenched. Where there are areas of contention, having listened and demonstrated by rephrasing that you have understood their point of view, as far as possible you should take people through your thinking process, explaining your rationale. You may well need to return to the discussion on a separate occasion. There is no immutable law of nature which says that disagreements have to be addressed in one meeting. Several meetings may be necessary and desirable, and you may well want to consider holding these meetings in different settings. Often individuals will share issues and concerns over a coffee or lunch which they would not tell you in a more formal organizational setting, or during the discussion in your office half an hour previously.

What sorts of areas are likely to be contentious? Sometimes, responsibility for particular activities can be a source of great tension within teams. Problems can occur when more than one individual believes they are looking after, or should look after, a given area or activity. Individuals may have a variety of agendas—some hidden, some not so hidden—for wishing to take responsibility for some matters. Some roles are considered "high status." Being put in charge of a new activity or product can be seen as consolidating someone's position, giving them exposure to top management, or providing the opportunity to develop their expertise on an exciting new technology. At a more mundane level, responsibility for a certain product can perhaps give someone a chance to make monthly visits to a factory near their brother-in-law's home town, fitting in a game of golf in the process, or to fulfil a lifelong ambition to visit a particular overseas territory.

No matter how well you know your people or talk to others who might be able to provide insight, it can sometimes be very difficult to uncover the real reasons for someone's entrenched position, strongly expressed preferences or apparent intransigence. Their rationale might be understandable if you knew all the facts. We recall one instance of a manager in an international firm insisting on taking account management responsibilities for a customer in a particular country. It later transpired that he had bought a property in the country in question, and it suited him to make periodic visits there.

If you find yourself having to sort out these types of disputes as a manager, make sure that you have not created conflict unknowingly. Job descriptions and performance targets should be unambiguous, and bring clarity to the areas under discussion. We have heard some managers argue for overlapping some roles and activities, and in some cases they have set up internal competitions amongst team members. In our experience, the possible benefits rarely seem worth the costs in terms of tension, stress and damaged relationships. Often the result is the members of your team being kept in a state of permanent tension to little useful purpose. Many employees deeply resent being treated in this manner.

"All packed and ready to go, then Arnie tells them that from next year they're on hourly contracts"

4.4.2.4 Agree the Next Steps

At the close of the meeting, you should agree the next steps. At its simplest this could be an undertaking to prepare a revised set of expectations which you will send back to the individual.

As a result of the discussions, you may wish to talk to others and/or gather further information prior to finalizing any one individual's goals. For instance, you might want to review work balance across the team. It makes no sense having some people overloaded, whilst others have too little to do.

Again, there is no rule of nature that forces managers to make immediate decisions about every issue. In the overarching interests of everyone, you may well wish to consider expectations "in the round" and make some revisions to preliminary agreements based on information received later. People are much more prepared to accept changes if the reasons for the changes are explained.

Remember
- Not everything is negotiable
- In setting objectives, don't try to solve world famine
- Setting impossible targets and overloading people with work gives the perfect excuse for failing at everything
- If possible, tell people the reasons for decisions: when someone knows 'why?' they are more likely to cooperate
- Many of us spend too much time on "transmit", and too little on "receive"—effective listening is one of the best instruments in the manager's tool kit
- At the end of the meeting, clarify "what next"

Example of an agreement following discussion

What the organization expects:

1. Deliver responsibilities as set out in job description.
2. Increase sales in key accounts by 20%.
3. Deliver assigned tasks, including those on the Work Management List.
4. Share information, expertise (including organizational history) with all members of the team.
5. Provide full support in implementing decisions, once views on issues have been taken into account.
6. Train and coach colleagues in own professional field.

What the job holder expects:

1. Full account to be taken of my views on professional matters in my field, prior to decisions being taken and implemented.
2. Represent the company at the Annual Benchmarking Conference.
3. Be able to make at least two overseas benchmarking visits per year to gather information about international trends and best practices in my field.

Fig. 4.11 Example of an agreement following discussion

4.4.3   After the Meeting: Follow Through

The main task once the meeting is over is for the manager to write down the main points and agreements arising from the discussion, after which these are sent to the staff member concerned for review. Sometimes further discussions will take place before the agreement is finalized. As appropriate, any agreements may be recorded on the relevant organizational performance management forms.

The example in Fig. 4.11 is based on a format we implemented in one SME which did not have its own prescribed performance management form. The format used matters less than the fact of having had the discussion, and then recording in writing what has been agreed.

Sometimes people wish to include development actions as part of the written agreement. While it is certainly possible to do so, our experience suggests that these should form part of a separate discussion. Development is an important subject in its own right. Individuals may need to discuss development planning in the context of possible future career moves, as well as their current roles, and the ground needs to be properly prepared (see Chap. 6).

Whilst it is important to set down any agreements, given the dynamic nature of many jobs in modern organizations, no agreements can be fixed and final in all their detail. If the situation becomes very dynamic you may need to be prepared to meet again and revisit your list of expectations. In any case, refining and shaping expectations is often a continuous process: sometimes in organizations the goalposts *do* turn into hanging baskets. As matters evolve—new projects, new hires, employee resignations—the regular Work Management Meeting with the team will provide sufficient opportunity for updates, and as necessary any reallocation of responsibilities. Similarly, the regularly updated Work Management List will enable individual achievements to be recorded year on year.

This latter list deals with one of the principal objections voiced against performance appraisal systems, encapsulated in the words of one individual who told us: "The trouble with this system is that I only ever get assessed on my last month's work, and my two biggest errors throughout the year." The truth is, that without a Work Management System, with its regular contacts, information sharing and record-keeping, performance management and appraisal can become highly contentious and difficult to handle.

A final task after meeting is to decide whether any changes need to be made to an individual's job description. As discussed, all that is required is a simple format (see Fig. 4.3) defining, in eight or so statements or principal accountabilities, an individual's "patch"—those areas of responsibility which are theirs and from which they cannot walk away.

4.4.3.1 Some Agreements Will Not Be Written Down

Whilst ideally both parties should articulate and then document their expectations, some agreements will not be written down. For example, individuals sometimes may have personal constraints in their lives—a working spouse for instance—which require them to arrive late on a particular day, given the need to drop children at school. In such circumstances, the manager may agree to allow an individual to arrive half an hour later, provided that he makes up the time on another occasion. Such arrangements are quite common in organizations and are usually best left 'informal' to prevent the creation of precedents, and to stop a current privilege from turning into a right.

These verbal agreements and arrangements will not disturb other employees provided that they are communicated appropriately, are seen to be two-way, and a price is seen to be paid for the flexibility. So if someone leaves an hour early each Wednesday, others should be aware that they are compensating by coming in half an hour earlier on Thursday and Friday mornings. However, you cannot contravene company rules, and managers should agree only what they can deliver within their delegated authority. At times, some people do bend the rules; if they do, they must be prepared for the consequences.

Remember

- Both yourself and those you manage are complex human beings with histories and outside lives that impinge on behaviour at work and your expectations of each other
- Unless expectations are made explicit we will infer them in the light of our individual experience and beliefs; these assumptions may be wildly inaccurate
- Various elements in management play a role in setting expectations— regular contacts, a Work Management System
- Working through the process set out above will address many of the problems associated with performance management and appraisal
- What most people expect from their managers above all else is that they are competent, effective and they deal with them professionally

References

Anderson, N., & Schalk, R. (1998). The psychological contract in retrospect and prospect. *Journal of Organizational Behavior, 19*, 637–647.

Barnard, C. I. (1938). *Functions of the executive*. Cambridge, MA: Harvard University Press.

Boswell, J. (2008). *The life of Samuel Johnson*. New York: Oxford University Press.

Gouldner, A. W. (1954). *Patterns of industrial bureaucracy*. New York: Free Press.

Guest, D. E. (1998). Is the psychological contract worth taking seriously? *Journal of Organizational Behavior, 19*, 649–664.

Guest, D. E., & Conway, N. (1997). *Employee motivation and the psychological contract* (Issues in people management, Vol. 21). London: IPD.

Hersey, P., & Blanchard, K. H. (1989). *The management of organizational behavior*. Englewood Cliffs, NJ: Prentice-Hall.

Kaplan, R. S., & Norton, D. P. (1996). *The balanced scorecard: Translating strategy into action*. Boston, MA: Harvard Business School Press.

Levinson, H., Price, C., Munden, K., Mandel, H., & Solley, C. (1966). *Men, management, and mental health*. Cambridge, MA: Harvard University Press.

Lorsch, J. W. (1979, March–April). Making behavioral science more useful. *Harvard Business Review*, 171–180.

Robertson, T. S. (1995, March). Corporate Graffiti. *Business Strategy Review, 6*(1), 27–44.

Rogers, C. (1991, November). Barriers and gateways to communication. *Harvard Business Review*.

Watson, T. J. (1994). *In search of management: Culture, chaos and control in managerial work*. London: Routledge.

Wisdom, J. (1965). *Paradox and discovery*. Oxford: Basil Blackwell.

The Third Ingredient: Run Interference

5

*Most of what we call management consists of making it
difficult for people to get their work done*

Peter Drucker

*Create all the happiness you are able to create; remove all
the misery you are able to remove. Every day will allow you,
will invite you to add something to the pleasure of others, or
to diminish something of their pains.*

Jeremy Bentham

*They keep releasing these new company 'values' and
'mission' statements. It's like listening to an opera. The
music's nice, but I can't understand the words*

Middle Manager

*I've just had another email from our in-house Sales
Prevention Team*

Marketing Manager

**BY ACTING AS A SHIELD AND WORKING TO REMOVE ANY
BOULDERS FROM THE RACETRACK, MANAGERS HELP TO CREATE
THE ENVIRONMENT IN WHICH THEIR STAFF CAN PERFORM**
The third ingredient for managing effectively is to help run interference for
your staff. In American football, running interference describes how certain
players block opposing players, thus preventing them from tackling the player
with the ball.
For the manager, running interference can involve:

- helping to anticipate or remove any 'boulders' falling on people's
  racetracks
- coaching people to cope with organizational barriers
- acting as an "umbrella", shielding individuals from what could hamper
  their effective performance

© Springer International Publishing Switzerland 2016
T. McNulty, R. Marks, *Management by Permission*, Management for Professionals,
DOI 10.1007/978-3-319-25247-6_5

Although running interference has received scant attention in the management literature, managers need to make it part of their business. It can make a real difference to both productivity and morale. The chapter focuses on some of the ways in which managers can help provide the necessary organization, air cover and assistance so that people can get on with what they need to do.

Having described how organizations can conspire to drive people away from their work, we:

- provide an *organization checklist* highlighting issues managers must address to set the right context for people to perform, and help anticipate and avoid disruptions
- help identify the worst *manager imposed barriers* and suggest possible remedies
- pinpoint some common *organizational barriers* and advise what managers can do to mitigate some of the worst effects
- highlight some significant *self-imposed barriers* which individuals can put in the way of their own performance, and propose some solutions

"Where are you going?" asked his manager. "Day two of the 'Customer Satisfaction' course", replied the engineer. "What was the first day like?" "Oh the usual stuff", came the answer, "compulsory swimming lessons for those of us who can already walk on water."

There are many ways in which people can get diverted from their work, and in truth, it is rarely funny. A sheep-dip of mandatory training seminars foisted onto all employees, when some of them already consider themselves experts on the subjects in question, is but one example. Whenever people feel patronized in this or in other ways, it wastes their time, pulls them away from their work, and can foster cynicism.

Such diversions are a much greater problem in organizations than is generally realized. Like horses that need to run with blinkers (or "blinders" in the US), employees tend to perform to their best, and provide the most value to their organizations, when they focus on the important tasks in front of their eyes, rather than on the many distractions competing for attention within their peripheral vision. They need to work on their priorities, and not get derailed by self-inflicted wounds, annoying management communications, energy sapping politics, or any one of the myriad of other potential disruptions which can occur in modern organizations.

5.1   Modern Organizations: A World of Distraction

A visitor from an alien planet, placed in a modern organization for a short period, could be forgiven for concluding that much of what goes on appears purposefully designed to disrupt, upset, divert and derail people, and generally prevent them from doing what they were hired to do.

Many of these diversionary wounds are self-inflicted: the constant checking of emails; repeated texting; responding to mobile phones; wasting time on the

Internet. Services and equipment designed to make our lives easier and improve our efficiency now provide yet further sources of distraction. Many people seem to find it hard to put their communication gadgets to one side, and resist the almost pathological desire to be constantly in touch.

As if these self-inflicted problems were not enough, our organizations have taken up the cudgel with a vengeance. They provide other forms of distraction and irritation which can cause a loss of focus for many a long hour. Whilst there are many culprits—and a number of them, along with some suggested solutions will be discussed in this chapter—in our experience two of the most common are: *time-wasting emails*, and the often well intended, but all too frequently crass, *management and organizational communications*.

Ready access to *email* has, since the 1990s, spawned legions of one and two fingered typists, able to dash off written communications to large numbers of people at the click of a button. Copies of missives are sent to all and sundry, often as part of a defensive or political manoeuvre. As a result, some staff receive hundreds of emails per day. They face a stark choice: become email slaves and never get any work done; or ignore much of what is sent with the risk that people can later say: "but I copied you in."

Whilst email has undoubtedly helped in communicating consistent information quickly to large numbers of people, it has also led to problems. As some have learned to their cost, when the blood is rushing to the head is not always the best time to hit the "send" button. Ill-considered emails, sent in moments of emotion, pique, tiredness or frustration, can threaten careers. More often, they simply upset their recipients, who in turn waste their own and others' time and energy discussing the content of these missives or concocting replies. The replies in turn lead to further correspondence and the cycle is then repeated as each participant feels obliged to have the last word, putting their views on record. In the meantime, no work is getting done.

Some of the least appropriate of these emails are subsequently forwarded to others. If particularly ill-judged, they can find their way outside the organization. Sometimes staff get to see them again in the media or on the web. Corporate leaders as well as their firms have even been held up to international ridicule as a result of some email correspondence.

Whilst many *management and organizational communications* try to be well meaning, they often appear as condescending, content free or asinine. The worst examples waste time, lower morale, say very little at considerable length, and can leave employees thinking that their leaders are either contemptuous of them or have little regard for their intelligence.

Examples of communications which can be poorly crafted can include: corporate mission, culture and/or "values" statements; business performance updates; and announcements relating to organization changes. To be clear: there is nothing intrinsically wrong with periodic communications from on high. Indeed, setting out organizational strategies, guiding principles and important information updates can be very helpful. People want to know what their organization stands for, what it is trying to achieve, and to be kept informed about any significant changes in personnel or structure. And whenever possible (and it is not always), the people at the top should communicate their rationale for certain decisions: what might appear strange or unfathomable can seem much less so once the full facts are known.

Particular difficulties arise when certain statements: (1) preach or espouse behaviours and values which are not seen to be practised; (2) contain misleading spin or half-truths; and/or (3) employ excessive or vacuous business jargon and clichés.

Employees are not fools and do not appreciate being treated as such. They know when the preaching is not being practised or when people's behaviour does not match their public utterances. If there is a top-down drive on controlling costs, whilst at the same time resources are squandered on unnecessary luxuries or perceived "perks" for some members of staff, then the leadership of the organization loses credibility.

Similarly, people rarely respond well to spin. They have their organizational networks and can, and usually do, check the veracity of what they are being told. Once they find attempts to mislead on one subject, then statements from the same source on other topics will lack credibility. People tell us they get especially irritated when a misleading spin is subsequently put onto information they themselves have provided.

Many people tolerate management jargon—or "mid-Atlantic guru speak" as one of our clients put it—about as well as nature tolerates a vacuum. While jargon can have a useful purpose in enabling experts in technical and professional fields to talk to one another with precise meanings, this is rarely the case with the jargon usually spouted in organizational communications.

The parade of hackneyed phrases and management mantras which often pervade the corporate scene leaves most people cold. Dipping into the business cliché drawer and pulling out today's and yesterday's fashions rarely impresses. Readers of this book will each have their own particular bêtes noires. Common irritants include: the hoary old chestnuts such as stressing the importance of 'our people as our most important asset' (whilst employees know from experience that a business downturn will lead to a reduction in headcount); various examples of homespun folk wisdom and business clichés (often little more than the thinly disguised sound and sparks of personal axes being ground); and the mutual back-slapping 'we're all in this together' ethos which is supposed to exemplify the culture in some places, yet which leaves little impression other than a sense of hollow, false bonhomie.

While some people find fashionable business jargon little more than a source of amusement and fun, others find it deeply irritating and bogus. What writers consider to be shrewd observations, recipients can view as platitudinous piffle. Bluntly, most staff are less worried by who might have moved their cheese (Johnson 1998) than by cheesy evangelism masquerading as penetrating insights.

"There is less to Blenkinsop's presentation than meets the eye"

Remember
- Most people perform best when they can focus without constant diversions
- Running interference—protecting individuals from disruption in order that they can get on with their important work—is part of the manager's job
- Never underestimate the time-wasting and potential misinterpretation resulting from email indiscipline and annoying organizational communications
- People can, and do, check the information they receive
- Never treat people as fools or insult their intelligence

5.2   Running Interference: Get Your Organization Right First

This section

- *Explains how to design a fit for purpose organization which will help anticipate and avoid many of the impediments to people's work*
- *Introduces an Organizational checklist highlighting the eight important areas to be tackled when designing an organization*

- *Discusses each of the eight elements in turn and describes the main pitfalls to be avoided*
- *Describes various techniques for:*
  - *dealing with role conflict within and between departments*
  - *improving working relationships between dissenting individuals*
  - *helping to get some useful insights into an organization's culture*

For the manager, the most important first step in running interference is to optimize those elements of organization affecting your team. Getting these organizational building blocks right will head off at the pass much of what subsequently disrupts people and their work. It will also save a great deal of time and help deal with the organizational politics which often result from a lack of clarity.

When considering organization, some managers believe that getting the structure chart right is the main issue. However, structure is only one of a number of elements to effective organization. Whether you are running an SME, managing a department, or are the head of a large firm, you need to do your best to make sure that the various elements which make up organization are fit for purpose, properly aligned, and work together in concert.

The Organization checklist in Fig. 5.1 identifies the eight most important areas, each of which is discussed in turn below.

Every manager's situation is different, and you must consider what is required and what actions need to be taken in each of the eight areas. As is the case with many aspects of organizational life, you cannot exert *control* over all of these elements, although you can bring your *influence* to bear in almost all areas. Wherever you have concerns, you need to find a way of compensating for any potential weaknesses so as to minimize their effects.

If you can satisfactorily deal with most of the questions raised under each of the eight headings, then most of the potential barriers faced by your staff will disappear.

5.2.1   Strategy/Vision/Mission/Tactics

As argued in the previous chapter, being clear about the mission, vision and strategy of an organization or department is a prerequisite to defining anyone's objectives. Yet whenever we hold individual discussions with the members of any organization or team, it is remarkable how often there is a divergence of opinion about some aspects of what their firm, business or unit is trying to do, and the tactics to be employed.

Sometimes this is because neither the strategy nor mission were ever properly agreed, nor were they clearly articulated. Occasionally we discover that the strategy *was* clear but it has become outdated: the marketplace or technology has moved on, and a firm's products or services have not kept pace. We have met some managers who told us that they had doubts or concerns about a strategy from the very beginning, but rather than voice these doubts, they went along with the majority. The consensus about the best way forward was only skin-deep. One consequence is

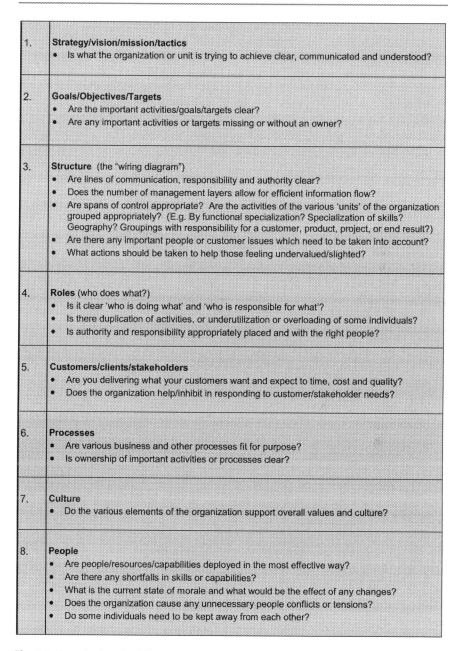

1.	**Strategy/vision/mission/tactics** • Is what the organization or unit is trying to achieve clear, communicated and understood?
2.	**Goals/Objectives/Targets** • Are the important activities/goals/targets clear? • Are any important activities or targets missing or without an owner?
3.	**Structure** (the "wiring diagram") • Are lines of communication, responsibility and authority clear? • Does the number of management layers allow for efficient information flow? • Are spans of control appropriate? Are the activities of the various 'units' of the organization grouped appropriately? (E.g. By functional specialization? Specialization of skills? Geography? Groupings with responsibility for a customer, product, project, or end result?) • Are there any important people or customer issues which need to be taken into account? • What actions should be taken to help those feeling undervalued/slighted?
4.	**Roles** (who does what?) • Is it clear 'who is doing what' and 'who is responsible for what'? • Is there duplication of activities, or underutilization or overloading of some individuals? • Is authority and responsibility appropriately placed and with the right people?
5.	**Customers/clients/stakeholders** • Are you delivering what your customers want and expect to time, cost and quality? • Does the organization help/inhibit in responding to customer/stakeholder needs?
6.	**Processes** • Are various business and other processes fit for purpose? • Is ownership of important activities or processes clear?
7.	**Culture** • Do the various elements of the organization support overall values and culture?
8.	**People** • Are people/resources/capabilities deployed in the most effective way? • Are there any shortfalls in skills or capabilities? • What is the current state of morale and what would be the effect of any changes? • Does the organization cause any unnecessary people conflicts or tensions? • Do some individuals need to be kept away from each other?

Fig. 5.1 Organization checklist

that an organization's or a team's strategy is not always really "owned" by some of the very individuals whose activities and support are key to its achievement.

The net result can be people working to slightly different agendas, leading to arguments, misunderstandings, wasted time and disruption.

On the assumption that your team or unit *does* have a clear strategy and mission (and if it does not, then you and your team need to develop and articulate them) you should initially try to 'smoke out' any disagreements within your own group. One simple way is to ask people to write down the top five priorities for the team or organization, as the case may be. Posting the results and checking for consistency can be very revealing and provide a useful basis for a team discussion about priorities.

Whilst it is preferable if the members of your own team agree with the strategy, provided they are still working towards it, it does not necessarily matter if they disagree with some aspects of it. What you do not need are individuals engaged in guerrilla warfare trying to undermine the overall plans.

It is as well periodically, and in conjunction with your team, to revisit the strategy to test everyone's continuing commitment as well as to assess whether anything might have changed. Some of your products might be guaranteed for life, but this does not necessarily apply to your strategy. In a dynamic market or situation, it may need to evolve rapidly to meet changing circumstances.

5.2.2 Goals/Objectives/Targets

A clear vision and strategy must translate into a set of goals, each with an owner. Self-evidently, taken together, the goals need to encompass the entire strategy. It is important to check that this is in fact the case. Again, any divergence of opinion about goals needs to be flushed out. Within some teams it is necessary to root out activities which may have been important at one time but are no longer required.

Even when the strategy and goals of the organization are clear and agreed, it is worthwhile testing for functional or departmental goals in opposition. For example, Software Development's desire to invest in new research facilities could clash with the Finance Department's aim to reduce short-term borrowing at the bank. Similarly, Marketing want to delight customers by meeting every technical need, and as a consequence, increase product variety, whilst Manufacturing's concept of delighting customers involves reducing costs, which is helped by reducing the product range.

Often these sorts of conflicts can only be addressed at more senior levels in the organization. Some business commentators laud the power of "creative tension" in these circumstances. If the differences are allowed to remain unresolved then in reality the 'creativity' is often quite thin on the ground, while the 'tension' persists to no useful purpose. The result is diversion and wasted time and effort. There is a tendency sometimes for departments in a dispute also to engage in "Mexican standoffs": each party knows their position, they think they know the position of the other, but the conflicts are never resolved. If you find yourself in this situation, then you need to address the conflict with the people involved.

5.2.3 Structure

The majority of senior executives and managers alike do generally try to design their structures in order best to answer the sorts of questions raised under the "structure" heading in Fig. 5.1. Nevertheless, a number of compromises are usually lurking behind most organization charts. Be aware that most of the time, if you are anticipating the "ideal" structure, whether for your own team, or for your organization as a whole, you are waiting for Godot. It is not going to happen.

In developing your organization chart, in the majority of circumstances a host of factors needs to be taken into account. Whilst detailed organization design falls beyond the scope of this book, the following five points are probably the most important ones to remember:

(1) The need for compromise away from your "ideal" is almost inevitable. Certain individuals or situations will need to be accommodated. People can get extraordinarily hot under the collar about: what a particular chart might imply regarding their status; the precise placing and height of boxes on a chart; job titles (their own and others'); to whom people report; and whether reporting lines are "dotted" or "solid." Provided you feel that your structure is workable, and you can limit the possible negative effects of any of the compromises, there is little point being too precious about all aspects of the design. However, you may need to explain in person to some individuals the rationale behind certain decisions.

(2) People often agonize over spans of control (or how many direct reports each manager should have). While opinions vary, in our experience the right span of control is what enables a manager competently to carry out the four management tasks we have distilled for this book, viz., control, clarifying expectations, running interference and development. So for example, how many direct reports is it practicable for a manager to have, given the requirement for in-depth discussions about individual performance and development targets, and subsequent follow-up?

(3) Be wary of choosing a structure based on current fashions or because you have been told that other organizations in your industry or field are successfully using it. One firm had a disastrous experience having introduced a matrix organization which had to be abandoned after three months. After the event, one of the managers involved told us:

A matrix structure was imposed on us from on high because we were told that is how our main competitor was organized. But they had always been organized in that way. Their senior staff were well used to dealing with more than one boss, and they had a number of processes for driving things forward and making sure nothing ever fell through the cracks.

We had none of that. What the matrix structure did in here was to pull out the last few rivets which had been holding this place together.

What made matters worse was that when some of the local managers subsequently investigated the competitor's structure in more detail, they found that its matrix only applied at the senior management level. Lower down in that organization they had never operated in that way; functional managers had always "line managed" their staff. The company had caused a major disruption to its operations to spend three months mimicking a structure which had never existed in that form.

(4) Unless you are the Chief Executive responsible for overall organization design, in most cases your own structure forms part of a larger structure and it will need to be adapted accordingly, and as circumstances change. By way of an example, when a newly appointed Chief Executive takes responsibility for an underperforming organization, or one with which they are unfamiliar, they will often redesign the structure so as to maintain closer and tighter control of all aspects of operations. Often the result is a corporate centre with increased powers. Such a development would be likely to have implications for your own area.

These sorts of changes can be tiresome for those involved, especially if any of the departments affected have been performing well, but it is as well to accept that whenever a new boss arrives, all bets are usually off in any case. No matter how well we might have performed in the past, everyone starts from a clean slate and we all have to earn our spurs afresh. Chief Executives will generally tend to allow greater devolution and freedom once people have proved that they can be trusted, which generally means by delivering what they say they will deliver.

(5) Irrespective of developments in the wider organization, it makes sense to keep your structure under periodic review with a view to possible changes. The solution to one organizational problem often spawns the next, containing within 'the seeds of its own destruction', and left alone, your structure can tend to become the solution to yesterday's problems. Make sure it helps solve problems rather than being the source of them (Greiner 1998). Whenever there are significant changes to the context in which you are working, then spend some time considering the implications for your team. As was argued in Chap. 2, many decisions in organizations are made for reasons of which you may be only vaguely aware. Rather than trying to take every one of these decisions apart, your energies would be much better focused on working out how best to respond, and this may necessitate a change in structure. As always, whenever you make any change, it is wise to examine its effects later on for any unintended consequences which may have resulted.

5.2.4 Roles

As discussed in the previous chapter, "roles" refers to primarily to "who will do what." Once you have communicated to individuals what you expect of them, it can be very useful for team members to share openly what they expect from each other, as well as what they will need from each other in order to meet their respective objectives.

Sometimes on-going disagreements about 'who is responsible for what' can be a source of difficulties within teams. Unintended overlaps, duplication and even gaps can also be points of contention. These need to be surfaced and addressed. Many of the personal conflicts and personality clashes which occur between individuals do so because of unresolved or unstated disputes about roles. Once these are sorted out many of the interpersonal problems disappear.

Overlap and duplication are typical points of contention, and as a general rule, making one person accountable for a given activity does seem to reduce the potential for conflict as well as save time. For whatever reason, if a manager does not feel it is appropriate to make one person accountable for a particular task, then joint accountabilities are sometimes feasible. However, an excessive use of them can hamper effective working and lead to frustrations. Certainly these "dual key" arrangements, wherein both parties have to agree before any action can be taken, might help to facilitate greater quality in decisions. However, they are rarely the most effective when rapid decisions are required. Both parties are not always instantly available to discuss the next steps, and time can be wasted constantly awaiting another's agreement to proceed with a given course of action.

Role conflicts become harder to deal with when there are disputes *between* departments which in turn report to different managers, or as is sometimes the case, when functional departments operate at different organizational levels. One example of the latter would be an engineering or IT department in a large firm which has teams working centrally, as well as at business unit and operational level.

If the parties involved cannot resolve their differences, and the intervention of more senior managers does not work, then various approaches can be adopted.

For one organization we developed a set of "Ten Golden Rules" setting out the relationships between line managers and internal service providers. There had been some major turf wars and relationship difficulties between some of the parties. To reinforce the importance of working together, Rule Number One stated, "We are all on the same side." Once the new working arrangements were established and understood, the interpersonal difficulties receded.

For several firms we have facilitated so-called "Responsibility Charting" exercises (Beckhard and Pritchard 1992). Typically these involve a meeting amongst the parties concerned, during which they agree a way forward, with reference to the sort of "table" to be found in Fig. 5.2. The issues or responsibilities to be determined are listed out in the left-hand column, with names or functions, as appropriate, listed across the top. The parties involved work together and agree who takes responsibility for what, and the conditions under which, for example, individuals need to consult or inform (see the key at the bottom of the table).

Issue	Corporate Engineering	Business Engineering	Site Engineering
Engineering policy	R	S	S
Customer liaison	S	R	I
External research contracts	R	S	I
Minor product modifications	I	A	R
Factory cost savings	I	I	R
Developing high potential staff	R	S	S

KEY (use for completing each column)

R = responsible
A = approval (right to veto)
S = support - has to provide resources towards the action (without necessarily being in agreement)
I = must be informed or consulted (but no right to veto)
- = no relevance for this item

Fig. 5.2 Responsibility charting

Following discussions, a completed chart setting out what has been agreed is issued to relevant parties, who subsequently implement what they have agreed.

Although time consuming, and provided debate is conducted in an appropriately mature manner (as philosopher David Hume put it: "Truth springs from argument amongst friends"), the approach has the advantage that those involved are given an opportunity to contribute to discussions and have their opinions aired. As a result, people are generally more committed to making their agreed solutions work, even if they do not get everything they want.

5.2.5   Customers/Stakeholders

As customers, most of us will have had the experience of departments, and occasionally entire businesses, seemingly organize themselves around the requirements and convenience of their staff rather than serving clients. Jack Welch neatly encapsulated this attitude when he took over GE. He remarked to the effect that many of the senior staff seemed to have their faces towards the Chief Executive, whilst their rear ends were directed at the customer.

This state of affairs can arise irrespective of whether a group or unit is supporting an internal customer, an external one, or relevant stakeholders. In checking whether your organization and services are appropriately positioned so as to respond to the needs of these various parties, it is also worth examining the responsibility for and ownership of client relations. No matter what may be agreed within your organization, your customers may wish for a different arrangement.

5.2.6 Processes

We are using "processes" in this context in its very broad sense to mean the many and various activities which can be involved in ensuring the smooth functioning of the organization, and in helping to achieve certain tasks. Most organizations seem quite adept in identifying their core business and management processes (e.g. supply chain activities, marketing, strategic planning, business development, project management, performance management, succession planning). However, almost all processes need to be revisited from time to time to check that they are still meeting their objectives, and that they have evolved to meet changing circumstances.

It is also worth reviewing periodically that your list of current processes is complete, and that those you have are both necessary and fit for purpose. Avoid inventing cures when there is no disease (Fig. 5.3).

5.2.7 Culture

Over time, certain values, core beliefs and particular 'ways of doing things' tend to evolve within groups, departments and organizations. These elements can become embedded as part of a particular culture or house style, and they can exert a strong

How organizations can invent cures when there is no disease

In one firm a thirty minute morning briefing meeting was piloted at each manufacturing facility. The manager of each unit within the factory outlined the day's activities and targets, set aside some time for individuals to suggest any ideas, and answered any questions. After a short period top management felt that the sessions had proved so successful as an aid to communication and teambuilding, that they decided to mandate the process within every department in the firm.

Unfortunately, the approach was entirely unsuited to some of the more technical areas, where project lead times could be counted in months and sometimes years. After many weeks of frustration and wasted time, the staff in these areas finally rebelled and refused en masse to attend the meetings. They argued that daily meetings were pulling them away from their important work, and that their old system of fortnightly meetings was much more appropriate for their requirements. Senior managers were called in to mediate. After several more weeks of wasted time and unnecessary conflict, the mandatory daily meetings were quietly dropped.

Fig. 5.3 How organizations can invent cures when there is no disease

influence on behaviour and decision-making. For example, some firms make their hiring decisions in part based on the extent to which individuals' values and attitudes seem to be in line with those identified as desirable within an organization's culture.

Whilst some attitudes and behaviours can be viewed positively in that they can bring people together and help get the work of the organization done, sometimes they can be dysfunctional. The very characteristics which might have accounted for an organization's traditional success, may now be preventing it from responding quickly to changes in its market or circumstances. For example, a take it or leave it, "eat what you kill" philosophy could well have helped to build revenue during the early days of a start-up. However, once first mover advantage has passed, attitudes towards customers will need to change as the firm finds itself competing against cheaper alternatives appearing in the marketplace.

"I can never remember if Fridays are Arnie's 'Team Spirit' or 'Individual Ethos' days"

In considering your organization, it is important to be aware of both the positive and negative aspects of a particular culture. In some instances you will want to "cut with the grain" by ensuring that any decisions you make are consistent with the prevailing culture; in other cases you might wish to seek to change or challenge some aspects of the culture, should this be required.

As described at the beginning of this chapter, poor communication practices and disciplines, especially with regard to email, can be a major source of irritation and disruption. While managers can do precious little to prevent annoying communications from outside their team, cultural norms relating to email usage within a team can be addressed.

In one firm, a team developed a set of guiding principles to govern the use of emails. The aim was to improve efficiency, limit unnecessary conflicts and prevent misunderstandings. The principles covered items such as: limiting email length (long emails, even if read, are not always assimilated); considering whether an email was the best form of communication (why not discuss the issues in person?); banning the sending of emails when writers were in an emotional frame of mind; and reducing the number of "copies for information."

A fun and useful way to obtain insight into the values and culture of a team, group or organization is to ask them to compose an "organizational blasphemy"—a phrase or slogan so alien to what the team, group or organization represents that people squirm in their seats when they hear it (McNulty 1998). Examples of blasphemies would be:

> *Four-star restaurant: "If we run out of veal, use lean pork. No-one will notice"*
> *Bespoke tailor: "So what if the stitches fall out when they get it home. We've made our money, haven't we?"*

Individuals take it in turns to read out their blasphemies, each of which is posted on a flipchart. Typically in reviewing the list there will be several common themes which will tend to give some insight into how people perceive their group or organization, and what they feel is important. There may well be some blasphemies which differ markedly from the others, and it can be fruitful to explore what this might mean. Similarly it can be useful to consider how the blasphemies of a particular group or team might differ from those of the wider organization to which everyone belongs, and further examine the implications for how one team might relate to other parts of the organization.

5.2.8 People

Regarding team composition you need to ask yourself constantly whether you have all of the skills, know-how and technical capability you need in your team in order to deliver your strategy. Where are the gaps? Do you need to recruit new blood and/or develop existing people in order to fill these gaps? Do your people have the right values and attitudes?

With regard to poor relationships between team members, most difficulties are generally the result of issues not being dealt with in the other key areas of organization. For the most part, if people are all working towards a common strategy, with goals, roles and processes all agreed, relationship difficulties and conflicts between individuals are reduced.

Nevertheless, personal chemistry between some team members can sometimes get in the way, as can their different working styles. You will need to be alive to the warning signs, many of which can be subtle: do some people avoid looking at one another during meetings? Do some ignore others when they speak? As a manager you cannot demand that people like each other, but you can insist that they establish a constructive working relationship which ensures that the work gets done.

When dealing with "personality clashes", low-key interventions can often work. Sometimes simply mentioning to the individuals concerned that you have noticed a problem can get them to sort matters out. If a more direct approach is required, you might consider setting a deadline for the warring factions to report back jointly with their solution. In line with the "listening" advice from the previous chapter, it usually helps if people can be persuaded to agree a ground rule whereby each must first listen and then summarize the other's viewpoints before expressing their own.

If the conflicts persist, we have seen some managers further increase the pressure along the lines of, 'if the two of you don't sort it out, then I'll give you a solution neither of you may like.' The latter has been known to produce results, although if the parties concerned have been fighting like ferrets in a sack, there is sometimes the risk that their fundamental differences are never addressed, the conflict simply goes underground, and resentments resurface later on other issues and in other ways.

An alternative approach involves what has been termed "role negotiation" (Harrison 1972), although the term itself is a probably a misnomer. This process involves the parties in dispute meeting together to discuss their differences. Through bargaining, they arrive at a series of agreements whereby each will change aspects of their current behaviour in order to obtain something from the other party. One of the assumptions behind the approach is that people are more likely to keep to agreements they themselves have reached.

Individuals prepare in advance by completing a one-page form (see the sample worksheet in Fig. 5.4), which they subsequently share and discuss during their meeting. Roger Harrison (1972), the innovator of this approach, advocates that any subsequent agreements should always be written down, although we have found that this last step is not always necessary.

Remember
- Each manager is responsible for getting the elements of their organization right as best they can
- Getting these elements right is the first step in running interference
- Organization is never simply the structure: it comprises a number of important aspects, all of which need to work in concert
- The cause of most relationship difficulties between people is ambiguity or disagreements about aspects of organization, in particular, strategy, goals and roles
- Most relationship conflicts disappear once people agree strategy, tactics and 'who is doing what?'
- Review the eight elements of organization periodically: circumstances can, and often do, change

Resolving issues between people: worked example of one person's worksheet

1. **If you were to do the following things more or better, it would help me to increase my own effectiveness:**

   - Make sure I am kept better informed about decisions made when you visit customers
   - Set an example on controlling costs
   - Fight harder with our Director to get our plans approved once we have agreed them

2. **If you were to do the following things less, or were to stop doing them, it would help me to increase my own effectiveness:**

   - Acting as a judge and jury on project expenditure
   - Checking up frequently on small details of work with my team, without letting me know
   - Asking for so many progress reports

3. **The following things, which you have been doing, have helped me to increase my effectiveness, and I hope you will continue to do them:**

   - Passing on product information during Work Management Meetings
   - Making yourself available whenever I need to talk to you

Fig. 5.4 Resolving issues between people: worked example of one person's worksheet

5.3   Identifying and Dealing with Manager Imposed Roadblocks

This section:

- *Identifies a number of barriers which managers sometimes inadvertently put on the racetrack*
- *Makes a number of practical suggestions with regard to how these barriers can be sidestepped or removed*
- *Highlights the important role of Work Management in identifying any roadblocks*
- *Discusses some of the ways in which you can work with your team to identify any boulders on the runway*

In spite of Drucker's somewhat tongue in cheek comment quoted at the beginning of the chapter, few managers put barriers in the way of staff on purpose. It generally happens unknowingly. So, once you have sorted out as best you can the aforementioned organizational elements, how can you identify anything you might be doing (or not doing) which could be causing problems?

Figure 5.5 lists out some manager imposed boulders. It is not an exclusive list: rather, it reflects some of the more common barriers which have emerged during our consulting work and research. It is worth reviewing the list and considering whether you might be the source of any problems. More detailed explanatory comments are to be found below on some of the items.

5.3.1 Poor Communications/Information Sharing

In some organizations information seems to have turned into a form of currency, to be hoarded or sometimes traded in exchange for other information or favours of various sorts. This state of affairs has arisen because: certain information is sensitive; problems may have been caused owing to information having been misused or leaked; or you may work in a culture in which some managers see information as power, and use it accordingly. Sometimes people play games with information (and in talking to others, often employing the irritating cliché: "If I told you, I'd have to shoot you").

It is true that some people cannot be trusted with information: they like to be those with the news and as a result become a sort of "one person public address system." As was said about one individual we knew: the one way of ensuring that information would be widely circulated would be to inform them in strictest confidence.

What information is made generally available, and to whom, is a matter of circumstances and judgement. However, with regard to manager and staff relationships, if people need information in order to do their jobs, then it should be provided to them. To withhold it in such circumstances can cause inefficiency, frustration and ultimately resentment. Bluntly, if some of your staff cannot be trusted to handle sensitive information appropriately, then this raises a deeper question about their suitability for their roles, and that will need to be tackled. As one of our clients put it: "We may have to release their talent elsewhere."

5.3.2 Wasting People's Time/Poor Management Disciplines

The items highlighted in Fig. 5.5 under this heading will be familiar to most people. Unless you are your organization's foremost technical expert in a given field (and if so, there is presumably a strong reason why you are as yet unable to pass this mantle onto others) taking technical work away from your staff can stall their development and often frustrates them. It is especially annoying when managers find it difficult to admit (especially to themselves) that their "technical" expertise has become of a rather mature vintage.

Common examples of manager imposed boulders

Poor communications/information sharing
- Failing to clarify the goals of a project or what is expected of an individual
- Failing to provide the up to date information which people need to do jobs
- Assuming some information is not to be shared and withholding it

Wasting people's time/poor time management
- Excessive socializing in meetings (you or others)
- Calling meetings because you enjoy them, or to emphasize your status
- Taking "technical" work from others because you enjoy doing it
- Holding forth at length on your pet subjects
- Delaying decisions, or being unavailable when required

Poor use of team working/task forces
- Imposing a team approach unnecessarily
- Allowing teams to become ends in themselves

Overcontrolling/Disempowering
- Starving people of the resources or authority to do the job
- Ignoring suggestions without explaining your reasons, or listening selectively
- Imposing excessive bureaucracy, reporting or micromanagement
- Insisting that contacts with selected others are made only through you
- Forcing staff to work on your chosen solution rather than on the problem itself
- Forcing the latest gimmick or technique irrespective of its suitability

Actions which demotivate
- Being perceived as rewarding everyone equally irrespective of performance
- Imposing policies affecting everyone instead of dealing with rule breakers
- Allowing lack of transparency in decision-making
- Failing to give credit where it is due

Poor work allocation
- Failing to delegate
- Allowing poor work balance (some people overworked, others underused)

People issues
- Failing to fix broken relationships or handle politics at your level
- Allowing interpersonal difficulties between team members to fester
- Failing to deal with poor performance or being seen as having "favourites"

Fig. 5.5 Common examples of manager imposed boulders

Poor meeting disciplines are a common problem, and it is not just the standard complaints about inadequate or missing agendas, poor time management during the meeting, and non-existent or sub-standard minutes and no actions issued afterwards. In one firm, a recently divorced manager arranged early evening team meetings as a replacement social activity. While many of his colleagues felt great personal sympathy towards him, it was not acceptable to impose this practice upon those *not* returning to an empty house, and they rightly rebelled.

5.3.3   Inappropriate Use of Teams or Task Forces

"It is only the provisional which lasts" runs the French expression. Whilst ad hoc task forces can be an important ingredient in getting things done, they can be overused in some organizations and by some managers. Teams and task forces are a means to an end, not ends in themselves. Neither are they always the solution, irrespective of the problem. Whenever and wherever they are employed, their terms of reference must be clear, and their activities kept under review to ensure they continue to meet the purposes for which they were intended.

Task forces can sometimes become somewhat "clubby", with some members wanting to keep the team together, owing to an enjoyable working atmosphere and camaraderie. Such an atmosphere is not necessarily a problem (unless the "club" excludes certain individuals who need to belong) but it should not deflect from the fact that once task forces have achieved their goals they should be disbanded. The temptation to search around for fresh tasks for the team should be resisted. A different project almost always needs a fresh team, if only to give others an opportunity.

*"Now, off the top of your heads, how do we as a team **feel** about the definition of a liquidity ratio?"*

5.3.4 Actions Which Demotivate

There are many ways in which managers can demotivate their staff, and most of us have been on the receiving end of bad experiences in this regard. Many managers turn these negative experiences around, and use them so as to inform 'what not to do' when dealing with their own teams.

In terms of what seems to demotivate in modern organizations, we hear four fairly consistent complaints:

The *first* is when managers *tolerate or fail to deal with those members of staff who are breaking or stretching the rules, or performing poorly.* This is especially galling when such individuals are seen to receive the same (or in some cases greater) financial and other rewards as those who are continuing to perform diligently and to standard.

It is certainly true that in many contexts it can be difficult and time-consuming for a manager to address poor performance or tackle those who ignore certain rules. The situation is not always straightforward and the issues rarely clear cut. In smaller organizations some of the individuals concerned can hold key client relationships or are perhaps central to delivering products, services or current projects. In larger organizations, managers do not always feel that their employer will support them if they try to undertake firm action: they are told to try and 'sort matters out' in a low-key way.

These sorts of situations can be amongst the most taxing problems that any manager can face. Despite the possible pitfalls, the issues need to be addressed. Tolerating poor performance and rewarding people irrespective of their behaviour can have a toxic effect on the morale of the rest of the team, and may well contaminate the performance of an entire business or unit.

A quiet word with the individuals concerned can sometimes work, and no further action may be needed. Surprisingly, some people may be unaware of the extent to which their behaviour is deemed unacceptable, or even the fact that it has been noticed. When you raise your concerns with someone, you need to be sure that you have first marshalled your facts and evidence. Following initial discussion, the typical next steps will include: recording any actions; writing to individuals as appropriate; monitoring; following through; and holding further meetings as necessary. As in most cases, acting professionally will usually see you through. In larger firms HR Departments can advise as to the appropriate steps to follow to get matters back on track. Many organizations have formal procedures for dealing with these sorts of situations, and there will be occasions when people will have to move on.

A *second* issue, which links to the first one, is *a tendency for managers sometimes to introduce restrictive or draconian policies affecting everyone, rather than deal directly with those few individuals who are apparently taking advantage of, or abusing, a system.* The new policies often end up causing major inconvenience to the vast majority who were completely innocent of any abuse. This causes real ill-will. Two examples follow.

In one international firm two individuals booked overseas travel without first clearing it with their Director. The result? A policy was instigated which required the company's travel agent to refuse all requests for flight tickets and hotel reservations until they had received the appropriate form signed by the Director concerned. Individuals planning to travel overseas at weekends were now obliged to wait until the relevant forms had been signed, which was invariably dependent upon the Director's availability. Travel at short notice, which was often required to meet client needs, became a nightmare, with individuals sometimes having to wait until late on a Friday evening before being able to confirm their preferred weekend flights (which were sometimes fully booked by this time) and in addition they were occasionally unable to obtain reservations in those hotels adjacent to the client's offices (meaning daily taxi trips, and greater costs and inconvenience whilst working abroad).

In another firm, individuals had traditionally been trusted to charge reasonable expenses whilst "on the road." This had worked for a number of years until three individuals began putting in excessive claims. As a consequence, a policy was instigated whereby everyone was limited to a maximum *per diem* rate irrespective of circumstances, and this was bitterly resented by those who had never abused the system.

A *third* area relates to *the need for transparency*, where possible. Morale drops when people are no longer confident that existing rules and guidelines are applied in a fair and consistent way to everyone. Typical areas affected are promotions, as well as various rewards and benefits. Managers need to be aware of the effect on the wider team of rumours and innuendo as regards "special deals" for certain individuals or groups. Wherever possible, you should aim to be as transparent as you can about matters such as: expected performance standards; criteria for promotions; and the rationale for allocating work to particular individuals.

The *fourth* area which is often mentioned by staff concerns *the failure on the part of managers to provide appropriate recognition for a job well done and for quality work*. The issue is not so much the financial or other rewards, it is more to do with visibility, and the acknowledgement that a certain individual carried out a certain task. This should not be overdone—as we have pointed out elsewhere, if you praise people to excess or when it is not deserved, your praise becomes a debased currency. Nonetheless, people take umbrage whenever they feel managers or others fail to give credit where it is due, and they can become quite angry when others take the credit for what they perceive to have been their ideas or achievements.

5.3.5 People Issues

When the managers running different departments do not get on, or are in dispute, it frequently causes problems for their respective staff at lower levels. If you are the manager in this situation, do not allow any damaged relationships with colleagues to remain unfixed, nor permit conflicts with other functions to remain unresolved.

You do not have to like everyone, however you do need to resolve your differences such that work is not affected adversely.

As we argued earlier in the chapter, most of the difficulties in relationships are caused by ambiguity or disagreements about strategies, goals, processes, and accountabilities. If you find that you are clashing with another manager or department you might want to start by checking whether you have differing views about ways forward, especially in these aforementioned areas.

When in one international firm we sat down with two individuals to discuss a "personality clash over hiring policy", we discovered that the real issue was a disagreement between the different parties about the need or otherwise for a uniform business strategy across subsidiaries. While most country organizations were focusing on large accounts, several of the smaller country operations were seeking to reduce their exposure and risk by marketing to a much wider range of potential clients, including some smaller customers. The result was considerable shrapnel flying around about the types of individual to be hired. It was only resolved once the strategy for certain countries was formally changed to allow this approach and take into account the circumstances in some of the local subsidiaries. As soon as the recruitment policy was amended, the interpersonal grit disappeared.

However, disputes may not always be that straightforward. Conflicts over organizational goals can be particularly difficult to address in small firms when the partners or owners see a different direction for their business, or when the aims of the institutions involved are social, charitable, religious, ethical or political. Smaller firms may well need to be hived off into different divisions; in extreme cases the founders may need to go their separate ways. In larger organizations, disagreements may need to be elevated to more senior levels, although that can sometimes throw sparks on dry tinder and lead to solutions no-one may want.

Before escalating any disputes, your own manager has a right to expect that you will try and solve the problems at your level. To this end, the techniques we have described earlier—such as: Effective listening (Fig. 4.9); Responsibility charting (Fig. 5.2); and Resolving issues (Fig. 5.4)—should help to a significant extent, even if only to pinpoint the real causes of the difficulties. These techniques can be especially useful in smaller organizations where people are very often emotionally attached to particular products or markets, and debates are not always conducted as rationally as would ideally be the case.

5.4 Identifying and Removing Any Barriers

As far as day-to-day working goes, one of your key processes is the Work Management System described in Chap. 3. It is your advanced guard. Keeping in touch with your people and their work through regular contacts should help you uncover many of the obstacles to their performance. As you listen to frequent updates on people's work, you will be able to get some insight into whether you might be the cause of certain difficulties, and be in a position to take action.

Provided team members are prepared to address the issues constructively, you could also share Fig. 5.5 with them, using it as a way of identifying any roadblocks.

> Having addressed the eight fundamental elements of organization, your Work Management System is your advanced guard in running interference

During Work Management Meetings involving the whole team, it is important to observe the body language: if you sense that certain people are uncomfortable, or seemingly reluctant to speak out on some issues, you may need to follow up with them later. It is also worth listening out for any relevant jocular comments or cynical remarks. Jokes can often be coded messages about items which are bothering people. "There is no such thing as just a joke" (Watson 1994). And as George Bernard Shaw put it: "When a thing is funny, search it carefully for a hidden truth."

Away from Work Management Meetings, you can also quiz people directly about anything which may be hampering their performance. Simply asking how things are going will often elicit important information and give clues as to any roadblocks or irritants. More generally, for each member of your team, you should know the conditions under which each of them performs to their best.

As has already been pointed out, "how can you best be managed?" can be a very useful and powerful question to ask of a person. The answers often contain very useful insights, and will frequently highlight what they see as barriers, although you will not necessarily learn everything you need to know. People are not always the best judges of the conditions under which they do their best work. Managers need to observe people in particular situations and note the reactions. Doing whatever you can to ensure the conditions are right for people to perform is never a wasted effort.

For example, some very gifted, high performing individuals in their fields nonetheless handle the cut and thrust of organizational politics very badly. They lack the patience and diplomatic finesse necessary to handling some relationships, and as a consequence they need to be protected from this. There are occasions when you will need to act as their lightning conductor. Take the heat; deal with the special interest groups; create the space they need in order to do their jobs; clear lines for them.

In one international organization a project manager responsible for a critical project was spending up to 3 hrs. every day wandering around the organization getting papers signed. His manager took away this responsibility and enabled the individual to get back to his engineering and planning work where he was at his happiest and most productive.

Sometimes you will have to protect your people by defending them and their contributions to others in the organization, and occasionally to senior management. This can be especially challenging when the person concerned tends to avoid the interpersonal niceties, or if they have already left a negative impression on a senior manager. A problem managers can face is when their own boss takes a dislike to a member of their team, and it can be quite difficult to defend an individual against the impression they have created, perhaps based on a very limited exposure.

"I really should have told you that Bob gets very touchy if you talk to his people before I've cleared it with him"

As you listen to any feedback coming from above, make sure you understand it, acknowledge it as required, and respond appropriately ("Yes, that's clearly a development need we will have to address and I will discuss it with him. He has been working hard on the Oasis project for the last nine months and it has been quite stressful given that the client changed project manager three times, and they keep changing what they want"). Bear in mind that without the sort of up to date evidence provided by your Work Management System, it can sometimes be difficult to protect and defend a team member adequately.

An interesting reversal of this problem is when you have to defend the actions of senior management to your team, for example, in the wake of some of the sorts of inappropriate communications which were discussed at the beginning of the chapter. As previously discussed, wasting effort on matters which you can neither control nor influence is pointless. So while you cannot prevent annoying communications from outside your area, you can exert some control and influence over how to react. For instance you can place the emphasis on the important *content* of a message rather than its form: "Yes I know that 'all staff' update contained quite a bit of jargon, but we do need to think about how we can get closer to some customers. They keep feeding back that we aren't always as responsive as we could be."

Try to avoid being cynical when irritating communications appear from elsewhere in your organization. Never forget that people often look to their managers as a guide to how to react or behave, and when the manager is over critical it can undermine people's confidence in the organization as well as affect attitudes and morale. As the Latin proverb puts it: "It is absurd for someone to rule others, who cannot rule himself."

5.4.1 The Role of Team Workshops

Many managers find it useful to supplement Work Management Meetings with the occasional off-site team meeting at which the team discuss broader strategies as well as identify barriers and roadblocks. Like ships returning to port, over time teams can tend to gather "barnacles" which can hamper progress. Run well, workshops can provide a useful opportunity to draw breath, take stock, and identify and scrape off any of the barnacles.

A typical barnacle is a process or reporting requirement which was mandated in the wake of a previous organizational crisis. Despite the crisis having long since passed, and the issue dealt with, the weekly bureaucratic form-filling remains. Unless they are rooted out, such activities can tend to persist long after they have outlived their usefulness.

In our experience these team get-togethers tend to be at their most effective when: (1) they are focused on business issues and work-related matters; and (2) attendees are asked to carry out some simple preparatory work or reading beforehand.

For example, as their preparatory work, participants can identify: three things that are going well; three things that are going less well; and three barriers to performance. Responses can be tabulated in advance by a member of the team or external facilitator and the results used as a catalyst for discussion at the event itself. This approach has many advantages including: uncovering the strength of feeling on some issues; obtaining people's considered comments; and ensuring that the views of the less vociferous or less assertive members of the team are taken into account. When the issues of concern are tabled anonymously in this way, it can help bring a focus on the topics themselves, rather than on their source.

If you do hold an off-site workshop with your immediate team, make sure that you agree what will be communicated to the wider team or, as necessary, wider organization when everyone returns to work. Whenever we conduct workshops we always allocate 10 mins. at the end of the meeting in order to flipchart the agreed messages to be transmitted "back home." This helps to ensure consistency and keep under control any communication vacuum which might otherwise get filled with false rumours ("They had a secret off-site meeting. I am sure they were talking about closing that facility").

Teambuilding is a means to an end (such as improving an organization's performance) not an end in itself

Rather than a 1-day "strategy and barnacle busting" meeting, some managers like to hold residential "teambuilding" workshops, often lasting several days. Typically these are designed to help team members get to know one another better, cement relationships, uncover people's concerns, and carry out some action planning. Such events can work well, although there is sometimes a danger that they can become ends in themselves rather than a means to an end: having a close-knit team is not always the solution to every organizational problem, and not all individuals are comfortable with the atmosphere of forced bonhomie which can sometimes characterize these occasions.

While some individuals enjoy non work related simulations, team games and exercises (although sometimes they return to work wondering about the immediate relevance of such activities to their day-to-day situations), others do not appreciate being forced into unfamiliar situations or being asked to carry out tasks unrelated to their roles. This is especially the case when these individuals perform poorly on some of the workshop exercises. Some events can go disastrously awry, building resentment rather than relationships, sapping people's confidence, and leading to the subsequent lampooning of those who "failed" at a particular exercise. When this gets out of hand it does little for team atmosphere once people are back at work.

Before embarking on any type of teambuilding event managers should think carefully about what the individual members of their team will find acceptable. And they should certainly *never* allow an external facilitator to lead their team through any exercises without knowing in advance precisely what is involved. Not everyone appreciates being spattered with paintballs, or sitting in a circle, whilst holding hands and singing *Kum Ba Yah*.

Some firms engage outside consultants to carry out formal organization reviews. These can involve benchmarking (McNulty 1993a, b), analysis of existing processes, in-depth interviews with people at various levels, and fact gathering discussions with groups of staff. These assignments can help pinpoint areas for attention (including any barriers) and test the extent to which the organization's strategies are being effectively implemented. Workable action plans can then be agreed to address the issues and lance any growing boils. Many people appreciate the opportunity to share their opinions in this way and the involvement of trained outsiders can help send the message that management is taking people's views seriously, and is prepared to take the appropriate action (Fig. 5.6).

Again it is important to specify precisely the role and scope of the consultants' activities. These assignments are focused on helping the organization, and must not be allowed to turn into a consultant job creation scheme, nor a training ground for junior consultants.

Successfully taking the temperature in an organization

Following a number of changes within a financial services organization, in addition to launching a benchmarking exercise, a retail director commissioned outside consultants to hold a series of discussions with a sample of managers and staff within branches. All levels in the branch hierarchy were represented. A short discussion outline was sent out in advance so that all of the participants knew the sorts of areas to be covered during the discussions.

The outline included questions about: what was going well and less well; perceived barriers to performance; suggestions for improvements or changes. When the series of interviews began, it transpired that within a number of the branches many of those selected for interview had taken the initiative to hold preparatory discussions with small groups of colleagues. In some cases they had also prepared detailed written comments and were able to furnish examples of centrally imposed bureaucracy and other paperwork which they felt were getting in the way.

When the consultants reported back, the Director found there were many positives on which the organization could build, as well as a number of problems inadvertently affecting performance and morale. Many of the problems related to confusion about some elements of strategy, redundant processes, unnecessary duplication and excessive form filling.

He fixed the immediate issues and in addition instigated a "quick wins" programme. Staff were encouraged to send their gripes, concerns and issues to a central email address. All submissions were kept under constant review and a monthly report was sent to everyone within the Directorate highlighting any changes which were being instigated as a result of the feedback. This process proved so popular with staff that the monthly updates became a permanent feature in the organization, with staff also forwarding their 'good news' stories drawing attention to successful local innovations and initiatives.

Fig. 5.6 Successfully taking the temperature in an organization

Remember
- Managers can put a variety of barriers on the track without intending to
- Key culprits include:
  - withholding important information
  - allowing poor performers to "get away with it"
  - imposing unnecessary controls on those who do not require it
  - failing to fix damaged relationships with colleagues
- Use Work Management Meetings to help pinpoint any barriers
- Effective managers look after the interests of their people:
  - sometimes you are the lightning conductor
  - sometimes you are the protective shield
- Make use of consultants and team events as appropriate but always control the purpose and content of any exercises or events

5.5   Identifying and Dealing with Organization Imposed Roadblocks

This section:

- *Recommends how networking and "paying your tax" can help anticipate any barriers the organization puts in the way*
- *Explains how to handle "corporate micromanagement" when projects are under pressure*
- *Provides a foolproof method for dealing with organizational initiatives imposed from on high*

Why is it that some managers are seemingly so brilliant at: (1) anticipating issues which can appear unexpectedly from around corners; (2) running interference for their staff when organization wide initiatives and other roadblocks threaten to get in the way; and (3) providing the early warning system which enables their teams to prepare and respond?

One of their secrets is their organizational network.

In Chap. 3 we stressed the importance of walking the patch and networking within your own area of responsibility. To run interference effectively, your network needs to extend more widely, certainly within your own organization, and often outside as well.

A strong internal network provides a ready source of information about proposed changes. By learning about proposals and developments in advance, you are able to head off issues at the pass. It is your canary in the coalmine which warns you of a problem before it is too late to deal with it. You can anticipate potential difficulties and influence the situation as necessary. Your network also helps you to grease the wheels and often you can get things done more efficiently and effectively than would be possible through more formal organizational channels. You can test out ideas, adapt your proposals as required, and build support for any changes you are considering.

Two important questions are: (1) who should be in your network?; and (2) how can you build the relationships you need?

In terms of network membership, it should not be difficult to identify those who are important to you in your current role. One group of names will be obvious: those in service or support roles with whom you interact; your internal customers; and those to whom you provide services. Another group may be less obvious. Powerful and influential people often reside in some strange and surprising places in organizations, and many of them have negative power in that they can prevent or delay certain things from happening. Those in various facilities or services roles are often in this category. One of life's little ironies is that very often some of those we like or respect the least could well be those we need the most.

Certain individuals are well-known as being especially important in some organizations and it can be interesting to ask colleagues for their views. Who is influential? Who is listened to? Who has information? Who has negative power?

Questions to ask about key people in your organization network
1. What are these people like?
2. What makes them tick?
3. What are their objectives? Wants? Needs?
4. What are their responsibilities? Performance goals? Bonus targets?
5. What are they unable to compromise on?
6. What are their hot buttons? Hobby horses? Interests?
7. What pressures or constraints are on them?

Fig. 5.7 Questions to ask about key people in your organization network

Who needs to be influenced if I am to be effective? When running in-house seminars, whenever we ask for the names of key people with whom to network, it is often the same half a dozen names which appear on almost everyone's list.

Once you have identified your list, the next step is to prepare to network with them. Ideally you should to be able to answer a number of questions about these people. Figure 5.7 provides a list of some of the sorts of questions to consider.

When you require help, support and information from someone, it is obviously better to have built some relationship in advance rather than making a request the first time you meet. It is a mistake only ever to engage with colleagues when you want something. Human nature is such that colleagues are not always prepared to respond to others' needs for help immediately. Asking a favour out of the blue and late in the day can create resentment. Often people's objections to any change can be the result of not having been prewarned or consulted in advance.

The best networkers treat people with respect and tend to focus initially on building relationships. They tend to relate to people in a manner which assumes they might one day need their cooperation. Before approaching anyone, it is worth considering what they might conceivably need from you or your function, as well as thinking about how you could provide it. You can ask them directly what they might need and how you could help.

One highly successful networker we knew had developed what she called a "buckets of goodwill" concept in terms of relationships with colleagues. As favours were granted, she would imagine that the bucket was being emptied, and she would then start making refill plans.

5.5.1 "Paying Your Tax" on Account

Researchers have highlighted various techniques which increase the likelihood that others will do our bidding, and six universal principles of social influence have been distilled (Goldstein et al. 2007). One principal is the "norm of reciprocity" which states that we generally feel obliged to return any favours performed for us (Belmi and Pfeffer 2015). We have observed that, like it or not, some people often wish to extract a price for their cooperation. We call this "paying your tax", or, for those who prefer a sporting analogy, paying your green fees. This is an investment you make, in advance, which will help you subsequently if you need cooperation and information.

The price paid for cooperation differs according to individual. Some people want to know how you can help them and what you might provide (resources, information, advice, contacts, even an introduction into your own network). With others you might have to spend half an hour listening to their gripes, followed by their views on the latest developments in the world of keeping bees (or whatever their particular interest may be), or hearing about their weekend activities. Sometimes this tax paying has to be done outside normal work hours and often in informal settings away from the work environment.

If you believe that people do not sometimes extract such a price then perhaps consider whether you yourself sometimes unconsciously extract a price from others: when you are being entertaining with your stories and anecdotes, they actually feel they are paying their tax.

Developing an external network is also helpful. Relating to others facing similar problems to yourself gives a sense of perspective and at stressful moments can sometimes help in keeping you sane. You can test ideas on others as well as comparing and contrasting your experiences. Our "Executive Leadership Groups", which involve individuals from different organizations meeting periodically to exchange ideas and provide mutual advice and support, are one such network. It is also useful to keep up to date on emerging trends in your field and take the pulse of your marketplace. When there are changes afoot you can anticipate likely customer reactions and be ready to react appropriately. You also obtain information which in turn you may be able to use as currency (Fig. 5.8).

"Do you remember, Blenkinsop, when I asked for your help in sorting out that expenses issue?"

Playing your "blue chips" (as well as those of your boss)

In the world of casinos, "blue chips" are the high value counters. In the organizational world these blue chips represent the counters which we may wish to give to colleagues in order to get things done. All of us have a limited number of these. Our colleagues will often cooperate with us on some issues if we state that we feel strongly about them. However, these colleagues will allow us to play only so many blue chips. They will cut us some slack on some issues, but not on every issue. Use your blue chips on what matters.

At some point, all of us may need to ask our boss to play some of his or her blue chips for us. We might have reached an impasse with a colleague; someone is being unhelpful and their cooperation is vital to achieving one of our agreed goals. However it is a real mistake to waste your boss's blue chips on issues which in the last analysis are relatively unimportant, or issues which you could have sorted out yourself. Asking your boss to play them on political or emotional issues (e.g. you have fallen out with someone) may result in you not being forgiven by the boss nor the individual concerned.

Fig. 5.8 Playing your "blue chips" (as well as those of your boss)

5.5.2 Dealing with Corporate Micromanagement When Projects Are Under Pressure

Whenever high profile organizational or critical projects are underway, and especially when these are in trouble, there is a tendency for senior management to require constant reporting. Managers throughout the chain of command also want to be kept informed about progress and be satisfied that any problems are being addressed. However, the people tackling the problems also need uninterrupted time in order to solve them.

If you are the manager in this situation you need to get the balance right between giving senior management the comfort they require that the work is proceeding, whilst shielding those engaged on the project.

If your organization has a project reporting system or similar, then there will be various processes by which progress can be tracked, and these will typically include a number of set piece meetings at which there are opportunities for senior managers and others to ask questions. Make sure that these reporting processes are adhered to, and provide the key people working on the project with whatever support they need to complete any electronic updates, paperwork or prepare for meetings. For instance, you could provide hands-on help in assembling any presentation materials and checking that these are fit for purpose.

If there is no formal organizational system for tracking progress and keeping management informed, then work out what you need to do in order to keep them satisfied, whilst maximizing the time that key people can spend on the actual work.

You may decide to take personal responsibility for keeping senior management up to speed. The important task is to defend your staff against constant, unstructured ad hoc requests for information and updates from different sources. Few of us produce our best work when constantly interrupted by people asking ill-informed questions or raising points which have already been dealt with or previously answered elsewhere.

When senior management keep ferreting for information it is usually because they are not satisfied that matters are under control. You need to work out what information they need, and find a way of providing it. For instance, you could schedule a weekly progress update, at which all the key people would be present and at which you could take questions. As necessary, work constantly with the team, understanding the problems, jointly planning, directing actions, testing and challenging results, getting resources and generally removing any boulders from the track.

5.5.3 Defence Against the Dark Arts: Dealing with Organizational Initiatives

It can be a salutary exercise to ask employees in any organization to compile a list of programmes or initiatives currently underway. Whether you are a member of the senior management group, or an individual on the receiving end of some of these initiatives, we suggest you try it. Whenever we ask this question of executives or management teams, the result is usually an inordinately long list.

When the listed items are analyzed, they generally fall into at least three different camps.

The *first category* consists of functional and other centrally driven programmes or processes. Many of these, such as budgeting or strategic planning, take place on an annual basis, and are necessary for the smooth running and effective operation of the business. A fair number of initiatives of this type can also be required for statutory reasons, and are therefore mandatory. The activities may not always be popular with busy managers, but people must, and do comply because the activities are necessary.

A *second group* consists of legitimate attempts to drive forward current business priorities and the strategy. Some of these programmes are a response to short-term performance problems. Others may have been triggered by changes in the external environment or perhaps a crisis, such as a current PR problem the organization is facing. Again, these initiatives are invariably necessary and their objectives frequently laudable; sometimes the very survival of the business is at stake. Staff can have few grounds for complaint about the imposition of such initiatives, provided that the solutions and actions proposed make sense and deal effectively with the issues at hand. Again, people will generally comply.

It is with the *third category* that most of the problems seem to lie. This group consists of the periodic initiatives, techniques or fads instigated or imposed by different departments or individuals. Not all of the initiatives are equally important, and at worst, some can seem little more than the misguided efforts of certain people to elevate their own importance or that of their function. Some of the worst examples can seem little more than someone's solution in search of a problem, and can be both annoying and harmful when they are seen to constrain people's professional practices, insult their intelligence, or simply recycle old ideas (Watson 1994).

In larger organizations the number of initiatives can be overwhelming. Like the bubonic plague, they are set on world domination, and few departments would have time to meet all their other responsibilities if they were to respond to all of the initiatives as per their guidelines. Many of the techniques have memorable and exotic names, such as the "Bergonzi seven-point problem-solving approach", or the "Benoni planning protocol" (both figments of our imagination). They may well have validity in certain fields, and can indeed bring discipline and rigour to the activities of some departments. But their uniform application across an organization can be questionable when they are too general to help in some areas, and too specific or unsubtle for application in other fields where better tools may already exist.

When the techniques, as is sometimes the case, are presented in the form of memorable acronyms, such as CLUNK, SPOT, or SPASM, it can lead to widespread mockery and ridicule. Generally these acronyms do less for the credibility of the methods than their authors might imagine. And those introducing the techniques might feel slightly less self-satisfied were they to hear some of the alternative suggestions for the acronyms which sometimes gain currency at lower levels in organizations. By way of an example of what can happen, after some of its initial technical problems were reported, the "APT" (Advanced Passenger Train) became known in some UK circles as the "Albino Pachyderm Train" (Great White Elephant).

In the eyes of trained specialists, some of the proposed techniques are simplistic when compared against some of the highly sophisticated disciplines and methods they use day-to-day. When such techniques are mandated, some employees engage in malicious obedience, deliberately sabotaging attempts at getting them to conform. Others devise elaborate schemes which fool the organization into thinking they are using the approved methods whilst in fact cleverly avoiding doing so. When they get away with it they wear their achievement as a kind of badge of honour. All of this wastes time, which would be better spent on the real work of the organization. And as always, it is bad for morale when people begin to call into question the judgement and credibility of senior specialists from other functions or those leading the firm.

Not only do these programmes struggle for time and space on busy people's agendas, sometimes they are competing solutions for the same problem. Occasionally, new programmes are churned out before a previous solution has been fully implemented. And frequently, what started out as a means to an end becomes an end in itself, with individuals monitored as to whether they have completed someone's on line forms, rather than whether any problems actually got solved.

The real trouble is, once a couple of these sorts of initiatives have taken root in an organization, they can grow like thistles in a meadow. At middle management level, the effects can be quite insidious as the initiatives jostle and compete for priority, like a herd of anxious sheep trying to squeeze through a small gap in a fence.

Whatever their rationale, the net effect of too many initiatives can be to constipate an organization, with staff subjected to too many at once, and excessive demands placed on a number of key people whose expertise is required elsewhere. If you are a Chief Executive or a senior manager, be wary about how many are launched in your organization. If you are a middle manager, you need a strategy for coping. Sometimes, as was once said about psychotherapy, these techniques become the problem for which they purport to be the solution. It is dangerous for managers to allow these initiatives to be imposed on employees without some push back; staff will very soon become disillusioned if wrong-headed initiatives constantly get in the way of people's work.

It can be a challenge to provide staff with the right sort of air cover. Figure 5.9 sets out an approach for helping to decide what to do.

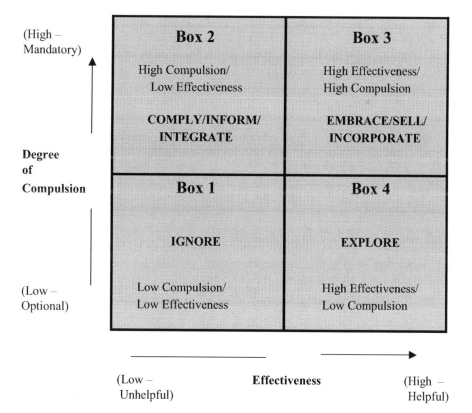

Fig. 5.9 Handling organizational initiatives

The matrix is based on the idea that the *degree of compulsion* attached to an initiative will vary depending on factors such as its source (e.g. CEO, customer, your boss, another function) and the rationale (e.g. legal requirement). Similarly, initiatives also vary according to their *effectiveness*. This gives four different stances which can be adopted, as follows.

Box 1: Optional/Unhelpful: IGNORE

If you pander to unhelpful and inappropriate techniques you risk losing the dressing room. By complying, you might think you are being politically astute and managing upwards. The staff, however, are likely to think that you are just being weak. Therefore, if the technique or techniques have not been mandated, and having examined their potential application in your area, you decide that they would be of no help in addressing any current or future problems, then they should be ignored.

Before finally rejecting the techniques, be mindful of the fact that few approaches have nothing at all to offer, even if they represent merely a review of some of the basics. If nothing else, they can add value in that they have forced you to revisit the rationale for your current practices, and reconsider their appropriateness.

When deciding to ignore a technique, you should be prepared to explain your rationale, in case you are asked. Depending on your organization, you may also wish to inform certain individuals about this decision, again, explaining your reasons. Describe to your boss the effects that compliance would have on your people. Make sure that the boss has a message to take upstairs if need be.

Box 2: Mandatory/Unhelpful: COMPLY

For the manager, this is the most challenging of the four situations. You have to comply with something which is ineffective or unhelpful. The difficult balance is how to avoid defending the indefensible, which wastes valuable time and likely loses you credibility with your own staff, without undermining the leadership of the organization.

Sometimes it is possible to question or challenge the timing and scope of these initiatives. Could, for instance, the objective be achieved in a different way, one which perhaps makes use of existing systems and procedures? In such cases, it can be helpful to discuss with the programme owners the rationale for their programmes, and attempt to uncover what they actually require, rather than what they seem to be asking for. For instance, if there is a request for information, sometimes it is possible to ask what is behind the request and the reason for it. As discussed previously, ideally you want to find a way of working on solving the problem, rather than being on the receiving end of another's sometimes inappropriate solution.

It is worth noting that the intention behind an instruction or proposed course of action is usually laudable even if the solution itself is inappropriate. In describing the situation to your own team, one approach is to acknowledge the underlying issues or concerns, and then focus on what these might mean for them. One manager told his team:

> Well, they're probably reacting to the loss of that big account and the downturn in the market. What it all means for us is that we need to make sure that our new development project comes in on time. In the meantime I am fixing a meeting with the Director to see if we can get them to change their reporting requirements and instead use our existing system.

If the techniques really are not useful—and there is usually *something* worthwhile in these techniques, if only a revision of the basics as per Box 1—then proceed as follows:

(1) Inform your management about the effects of using the technique or taking this action, specifically:

- What will happen (e.g. the reactions of staff)
- What will probably happen (e.g. the effects on morale)
- What could happen.

   Pushing back *can* work, provided that rational reasons are put forward and management is willing to listen. A refusal on your part to cooperate can be dangerous, but this needs to be balanced against the dangers of losing the respect of your team and affecting morale.

(2) If you are nonetheless required to proceed, examine the extent to which you can shield your people from the consequences. Also examine whether, and if so how, you can use your current systems to obtain the required result. Finally, before you expose your team to the technique, make sure you yourself have fully understood what is involved. It will not help your credibility with your team if you are forced into a course of action which makes you appear to be playing the manager's role in a re-run of an episode from *The Office*. Faced with a situation of having to implement a programme in his department, one manager of our acquaintance gathered his team together, announced, "I have been told to tell you this", and then proceeded to read out the details in a robotic voice not unlike that of a Dalek. We would not recommend others to emulate him, but we are certainly sympathetic.

(3) Inform your team what they are required to do. Explain that it is mandatory. Also explain what you have done (points (1) and (2) above).

As always, you should offer your best professional advice to your own manager, but not sulk if it is not acted on for reasons that cannot be shared with you. Where you have concerns by all means ask for the organizational background which is behind a particular decision—it is very easy for bosses to assume that everyone knows as much as they themselves do. However, remember that our bosses may have some information which is necessarily confidential to them, and that the rationale for some organizational decisions may be based on information of which you will be unaware at your level. The decisions may not be to your liking, but they may not be as misguided as they appear from your perspective.

Box 3: Mandatory/Helpful: EMBRACE
There are three questions for the manager:

- What are the big benefits for us?
- What must I do to get the staff on board?
- How quickly can we incorporate the approach into our current plans and systems?

Box 4: Optional/Helpful: EXPLORE
The main questions here are:

- What in this proposal is useful to us?
- Can we incorporate any relevant ideas into our current work?
- Can these initiatives be harnessed towards achieving our objectives?
- Are there things we need to do to make other people's lives easier?

Remember
- Build networks:
  - outside your immediate team
  - in the wider organization in which you work
  - within your field
- These networks will help you anticipate developments and run interference
- Some people extract a price for their cooperation, so be prepared to "pay your tax"
- Find ways of protecting your people so they can get on with their work
- Do benchmark, but get behind the rhetoric and don't fall foul of your organization's "corporate immune system"
- Harness any organization wide "initiatives" as best you can so as to help achieve your agreed goals

---

5.6   Protecting People from Self-inflicted Wounds

This section:

- *Emphasizes that people need protecting when their development needs could threaten their careers*
- *Highlights some dangerous situations and recommends what managers should do*

Benchmark to uncover best practices, but don't be a dedicated follower of fashion

When organizations succeed, people search for the recipe. Studies are launched, financial performance is analyzed, and journalists interview senior management and those familiar with the company. Opinions are expressed as to the reasons behind the success. Gradually some interesting ideas emerge. The organization seems to do some things differently, and it is these factors which are highlighted. Articles get written exemplifying the identified best practices, even leading in some cases to the development of new theories of management or organization. As a consequence, others begin to mimic the practices.

Little by little, however, problems can begin to emerge, and three in particular.

First of all, the mimicking firms do not have equal success. On one level, it is obvious. So many variables could possibly account for any organization's success, that it is very difficult to isolate those which really do make a difference. People who wear diamond studded tiepins rarely suffer from malnutrition, but shipping cargoes of diamond studded tiepins to an area affected by famine will not solve the hunger problem in the long term.

Secondly, on closer examination, practices lauded in the "model" organizations are not all they appear, or were never implemented as claimed. Many of the staff in the mimicking firms knew this only too well: their networks often extended into the model firms, and they knew how things were really done. To cite the old prairie song, these "Home on the Range" examples belong to an idealized world, 'where never is heard a discouraging word, and the skies are not cloudy all day.' They are the business equivalent of the happy families pictured on breakfast cereal boxes. The pictures of smiling children and doting parents do not always truly reflect early morning breakfast times in many of our families.

Thirdly, some organizations held up as role models are subsequently found to be wanting. Their practices were flawed, would only appear to work in a particular context, or, as has happened in some notable cases, it was later discovered that these organizations had been indulging in some other less than savoury practices.

It is laudable to seek out best practices and consider what could be adapted to your organization – indeed we advocate benchmarking as a catalyst to help in considering improvements. However, the process needs carrying out in a structured manner and with some care. Adopting "best international practice" is sometimes just being no worse than anyone else. Avoid the dangers of industrial tourism by thinking through your problems first. Start with your problems or concerns before looking at other people's solutions. This will help you improve your chances of selecting the right ingredients to copy and adapt, and not fall foul of your organization's corporate immune system, with the resulting rejection. Done badly, the results of benchmarking are like mimicking a rock star's drug habits because you think it will help you play the guitar like him. Drugs were never the ingredient; he performed in spite of them not because of them.

Fig. 5.10 Benchmark to uncover best practices, but don't be a dedicated follower of fashion

So far in this chapter we have focused on how organizations can sometimes put barriers in the way of individuals, preventing them from getting their work done. We have also suggested some ways in which managers can run interference and help these selfsame individuals perform in these circumstances.

This final section touches briefly on the dangers of certain *self-imposed* barriers. These can be actions that people take, or sometimes actions they fail to take. As well as hampering their effectiveness, at worst these sorts of barriers can limit organizational careers and even threaten people's employment. The individuals concerned are often unaware of their self-inflicted wounds. As a manager you need to be alive to them and provide protection when necessary.

The broader subject of identifying and addressing development needs is dealt with in-depth in the next chapter. However, unlike most development needs, which can generally be addressed in a controlled or low-key way, and often within a protected team environment, some self-imposed barriers can leave people very exposed.

To take a simple example: if you know that one of your team is due to attend an important meeting, perhaps involving a key customer, and that the situation is likely to stretch their diplomatic skills, then you need to address the situation. This could involve coaching them beforehand so that they prepare and perform appropriately, or perhaps even removing them from the situation altogether.

If such an individual has to attend, then consider what support they will need. When the meeting is imminent, a rehearsal is invariably sensible. If the individual concerned is making a presentation, then get them to run through their materials in advance, as well as do a 'dry run', possibly in front of your team.

The presenter should also prepare a set of possible questions and model answers in advance. With a little thought it is usually possible to anticipate any 'difficult' questions (and team members are often very adept at spotting the sorts of questions which could trip up their colleagues) and prepare appropriate answers. The need for very precise wording in answering some questions can be important. And it is noticeable that once people have brainstormed a list of questions and answers, they will often recognize the need for revisions to their presentation materials.

Thinking through questions and answers in advance is always a useful discipline, and not only for junior or less experienced people. And before any difficult meeting, it is always useful to ask: "what is the question I least want to be asked?" and then prepare your answer.

Important presentations are often nervous occasions and it can be tempting for people to go "off message" or start to waffle. Interestingly enough, many of the biggest errors are made once someone has delivered their materials: they are relieved that the hard part is over; they came through it; they breathe a sigh of relief, get over confident, are no longer on their guard, and suddenly they have made an unwise remark.

5.6.1   The Potential Dangers When Engaging with Senior Management

Some members of staff often crave the opportunity to engage with the senior management of their organizations. They find the idea of exposure to senior people or taking part in a presentation to them motivating and exciting, often believing that it is their chance to impress, make their mark, and gain the proper credit for their work. Given the opportunity, some individuals also want to, "tell it to them as it is", or in some way, "put management straight" on some aspects of the organization.

Such exposure can be dangerous for people's careers. In the case of junior staff, if they make a poor first impression on senior management, the situation is usually irretrievable. An invitation to be open about the problems of the organization or tell the CEO how they would improve the business could be an invitation to career suicide. Unless they have prepared well they are likely to respond with off the cuff remarks, ill thought through assertions, hearsay and rumour. It can be mission impossible and, as it says in the movie, they will self-destruct in 5 seconds. If you think people may get asked questions of this nature then ask them to formulate the three, sharp messages which they want to convey.

Ideally any messages to be conveyed will be seen to add some value, provide some insight, or will relate to issues which could realistically be addressed. Your aim in helping staff to prepare their messages is not to plant your own messages. It is simply to make sure that their messages do not cause them trouble.

Sometimes it can be possible to prewarn or prewire some of the senior staff in advance: "Surinder is great with customers and a real high potential but he can sometimes be a little unguarded in what he says. We are knocking off some of the rough edges but he's still got a way to go. It will be good for him to have this opportunity and I am sure he'll learn some lessons. Any feedback will be welcome." Sometimes people need protection from both senior management and themselves, in the overarching interests of the organization.

One danger sign is when the subject matter of a presentation relates to a particular senior manager's background or early career experience. Some senior managers like to feel that they are still experts on the topics under discussion, even if by current standards their knowledge might be seen as slightly dated. However, it seems to be human nature for people to wish to demonstrate their "expertise", even if they are blissfully unaware that the field might have moved on. It is also human nature for some junior staff sometimes to eschew the interpersonal niceties by responding abruptly or unthinkingly to questions or comments. We have seen situations in which the junior staff mistakenly believe that they are impressing seniors with a display of their up to date technical mastery, while the senior management are feeling patronized and becoming irate. Senior people are frequently much more thin-skinned and sensitive than they might appear, especially in the company of their peers. And they have long memories.

When helping people to prepare a presentation to your organization's senior management, the standard disciplines apply. The preparation must cover both the content of what is being presented, as well as the way people conduct themselves. You need to clarify beforehand what people are actually going to say, coach them on the effect their remarks are likely to have, and help them to modify or eliminate some of the content. If you know your people well, you will soon learn to spot the sorts of matchsticks over which they could trip. Without careful planning, their experience can be nasty, brutish and short.

5.6.2   How Much Protection Should the Manager Provide?

Running interference does *not* mean that managers should take it upon themselves to address every problem any member of their team might have, nor deal with every boulder which lands on the track. Ask questions which help people to devise solutions and think things through; be available as a source of advice and wise counsel; smooth the patch if necessary; but do not take a problem away if the individual is capable of solving it or the matter is not time critical. People often learn the most from the difficulties they face.

But do not leave people impossible tasks, and be alive to the issues that you alone can sort out. On occasion you will need to take personal charge of some issues because the individuals involved would find them too hard, or they are not in a position to deal with them.

Remember

- Disruptions and diversions are the bane of modern organizational life
- Barriers to performance can be caused by: organizations; managers; and the individuals themselves
- The role of the modern manager includes:
  - Getting the various elements of organization right so people can perform
  - Running interference so as to protect and shield people as necessary

---

References

Beckhard, R., & Pritchard, W. (1992). *Changing the essence: The art of creating and leading fundamental change in organizations.* San Francisco, CA: Jossey-Bass.

Belmi, P., & Pfeffer, J. (2015). How "organizations" can weaken the norm of reciprocity: The effects of attributions for favors and a calculative mindset. *Academy of Management Discoveries, 1*(1), 93–113.

Goldstein, N. J., Martin, S. J., & Cialdini, R. B. (2007). *Yes! 50 secrets from the science of persuasion.* London: Profile Books.

Greiner, L. E. (1998, May). Evolution and revolution as organizations grow. *Harvard Business Review.*

Harrison, R., (1972). When power conflicts trigger team spirit. *European Business,* 57–65.

Johnson, S. (1998). *Who moved my cheese? An amazing way to deal with change in your work and in your life.* New York: Random House.

McNulty, A. (1993a, November). Benchmarking: How to launch a project and get results. *Croner Employer's Briefing.*

McNulty, A. (1993b, November). Benchmarking: What is it and is it right for you? *Croner Employer's Briefing.*

McNulty, A. (1998). Organizational blasphemies: Clarifying values. In J. William Pfeiffer (Ed.), *The Pfeiffer library* (2nd ed., Vol. 14, pp. 9–12). San Diego, CA: Jossey-Bass/Pfeiffer.

Watson, T. J. (1994). *In search of management: Culture, chaos and control in managerial work.* London: Routledge.

The Fourth Ingredient: Develop the People

6

The young Alexander conquered India. Was he alone?

Berthold Brecht

I just realized that I let a twenty-year-old choose my wife and my career

Career Development Workshop Participant

Why should I care about future generations of management? What have they ever done for me?

Anon

Whenever we have a vacancy, all our international managers start playing the same game. In the States it's, 'Where's Waldo', in Germany it's, 'Where's Walter?', and in the UK it's, 'Where's Wally?' It all boils down to the same: no-one has trained adequate replacements

Regional Director

DEVELOPING YOUR STAFF NOW AND FOR THE FUTURE HELPS THEM PERFORM BETTER AND RETAINS THEM FOR LONGER

The fourth and final ingredient to effective management in the modern world is to develop your people. Modern employees tend to consider development as part of their informal contract of employment. If their development is not addressed or they see no opportunities for further growth, they can become disaffected, underperform, or leave.

Developing your people is also in your own interest. The more you help your staff to develop, the more valuable they become to your department and your organization. People who have been developed are better equipped to do their jobs, more capable, and generally perform better.

In this chapter we will show you how to:

- Identify and build on people's strengths
- Identify development needs and opportunities

© Springer International Publishing Switzerland 2016

T. McNulty, R. Marks, *Management by Permission*, Management for Professionals, DOI 10.1007/978-3-319-25247-6_6

- Work to eliminate those "disabling weaknesses" that prevent people from deploying their strengths
- Develop people in their current roles
- Help people develop towards new roles
- Achieve development at minimal cost

Although the chapter is mainly directed at managers wanting to know how to develop others, it can also be considered a useful guide to self-development.

"You have a choice of dentists today, Mr Blenkinsop. Mr Jones is high on emotional intelligence, but Ms Kominski knows what she's doing"

The 'Visit to the Dentist' cartoon was used as part of a client presentation. We had been asked to review a firm's approach for selecting and developing staff for some key international roles. They had already done useful work in defining the skills and "competencies" they believed necessary for success in the roles. However, after discussions with some of their managers, we had concerns. We felt there was too much emphasis on certain of the 'softer' skills (such as "teamwork" and "cooperation"), to the detriment of other important factors, such as technical skills, knowledge and international experience. Since our client sometimes used cartoons in their internal communications, we produced one of our own to stress the dangers of too narrow an approach to development and selection.

The cartoon also contains an important lesson for managers in other organizations: it is easy to become fashionably obsessed with just one aspect of people development, whilst ignoring the other elements. And that leads us to the key message of this chapter, and the last of the four ingredients: "*Make sure you develop your staff.*"

Developing your people is important for at least two reasons. First of all, more and more staff view development as part of their informal contract with their employer. If their development stalls, so does their motivation and commitment to you. We have met managers who are afraid that developing their people will make these staff more marketable. Our experience suggests that as a general rule, the more you develop people, the longer you keep them. Even if an employee's rewards do not fully keep pace with what they could obtain elsewhere, they will tend to remain where they are, at least for a while, so long as their employability or value is increasing. When they are engaged in interesting work which helps them grow, it takes much longer for them to get around to pursuing job opportunities elsewhere. What gets them posting their résumés on the Internet, searching job board sites, or responding to calls about their LinkedIn profiles, is the feeling that they are no longer developing in professional and market terms.

Enlightened self-interest is also behind the second reason for developing your staff. In other words, developing them also serves your own interests, since better trained employees are better equipped to do their jobs and deliver their targets. Your staff will be more capable, more up to date with the latest thinking in their fields, and as a consequence, of more value to you. They are less likely to stagnate in their roles. As Handy (2006) puts it rather bluntly, "once you stop learning you might as well stop living." If you continually help people to formulate and implement realistic development plans, you also have the opportunity to align their job and career interests with the changing needs of your organization. In some circumstances you might even avoid having your own promotion or career held up because there is no appropriate replacement for you.

This chapter provides some practical guidance in the two main tasks in people development:

(1) making sure staff have the competencies, technical skills and experience they need to perform effectively in their *current* roles; and (2) helping them prepare for possible *future* roles, based on a realistic assessment of their capabilities, interests, constraints and career aspirations. We suggest how managers can work in conjunction with their staff to achieve these two tasks. In doing so, we also show how, contrary to some people's expectations, some of the best development can be achieved at little or no cost.

> **Remember**
> - DEVELOPMENT IS A NECESSITY NOT A LUXURY
> - People see their development as part of their remuneration package
> - Effective development increases capability and motivation and also improves performance
> - A lack of development leads to stagnation and often causes people to look for other jobs elsewhere

6.1   Development in the Current Role

In this section we will show you how to:

- *Develop people in their present roles*
- *Help people analyze their own development needs*
- *Conduct a development review meeting*
- *Use Work Management Meetings to identify and progress development needs*
- *Produce an action plan using a menu of development actions*

For some people, such as those new to a job, or those who do not wish to move from their current position, development is focused entirely on their current role. Interestingly, those who are ambitious, or anxious to progress quickly in their careers, sometimes need to be reminded that their initial focus should also be on development in their current role.

An obvious first step for both the manager and the individual is to find out what support is available within their own organization with a view to taking advantage of it. The best schemes may even supersede what we suggest here. For example, in many firms the HR Department provides useful advice and guidance, enabling access to aptitude or other tests, identifying appropriate courses, as well as championing certain training and development initiatives. These can include seminars and courses, company wide coaching or mentoring programmes, as well as job or management rotation programmes. HR can also facilitate assignments to other parts of the organization. Sometimes they issue guidelines, questionnaires and forms which can help with career and personal development planning. Often this planning activity is linked to an organization's performance management or appraisal scheme, and in some cases HR will oversee the collection of data from development planning exercises as part of company wide succession management.

However, practices and attitudes towards development vary widely from employer to employer, and from time to time within the same organization. This is to the extent that in some organizations, and even at the most senior levels, development seems to be left to managerial or individual whim. Generally, it is the larger, more established employers who tend to be more structured in their approaches, although even in these cases there is always the chance that some of the more ambitious development schemes get shelved as soon as there are pressures on budgets. Furthermore, some organizations seem to be more concerned with the provision of training *courses* rather than of balanced, work based *development programmes*. Nevertheless, in some firms there are excellent development schemes for those wishing to pursue particular career paths, together with formal reviews of individual needs, with any agreed actions subsequently implemented.

Despite the important work done by HR specialists and others, and however ambitious or far-reaching the development schemes in your organization, *the ultimate responsibility for development lies with the individual and with their manager*. Given its importance, how then should an individual's development be tackled and what should the manager do?

6.1.1 Analyzing One's Own Development Needs

The process should begin with each individual considering their own development priorities. Where it exists, your organization's own scheme may well prescribe some useful approaches for doing so. Managers will need to exercise their judgement on how well what we suggest below dovetails with their organization's scheme, and act accordingly. Whatever system you use, *your staff need to know that you, their manager, are concerned about their development and prepared to take the steps necessary to help make sure it happens*.

Prior to any discussion about development, we usually recommend that individuals should first consider some basic questions, such as those contained in Fig. 6.1. It is worth making clear to individuals that this is part of a development process: it has been known for some people to complain that they are not receiving development because they have not attended any courses. This is because they take for granted, are unaware of, or undervalue what is done for them day-to-day.

Questions to ask yourself prior to a development discussion

1. What are my main strengths and capabilities relevant to the job? How can these be further developed?
2. When am I most effective at work? How can I become more so?
3. In which areas do I need to develop? Is there anything which prevents me from displaying my strengths at work?
4. When am I happiest at work?
5. Why do I want to come to work, in order to do this particular job?
6. What are my values relative to the work I do? What is really important to me?
7. What constraints does my personal life place on my choices?

Fig. 6.1 Questions to ask yourself prior to a development discussion

Managers can perhaps take the initiative by raising the topic of development with each direct report, saying that the organization is concerned about their development and that this process is designed to help. In advance of an initial meeting to discuss development, it would be helpful if they prepared by thinking about development in their current role in the light of the questions in Fig. 6.1.

Although managers may be able to provide helpful insights into the first three questions, based on their observations of the individuals at work, the later questions are more for the individual to consider.

While the questions are quite simple, the answers require some thought, and they are also subject to change over the course of a career. Indeed it can be useful periodically to revisit questions such as these throughout one's working life. After all, the 20-year-old who chose our original career path will have morphed into a 30-, 40-, 50- or even 60-year-old with a very different set of interests and responsibilities.

At this stage in pinpointing development needs, the focus should be kept for as long as possible on one's current role. Promotion prospects and development in the context of career advancement—the subject of a later section of this chapter—can be considered once development needs in the current role have been discussed. This is important: sometimes people can get too far ahead of themselves thinking about the next career step. Failure to perform effectively in one's current role is likely to hamper promotion to the next level. If you do get promoted, and you have not addressed an important development need in your current job, the problem may become more acute at the next level, leading to stress, poor performance and even the risk of being let go.

6.1.2   What Lies Behind the Various Questions?

The focus on strengths, capabilities and effectiveness in the *first two questions* is important. People are valued and employed for their strengths, what they can do. The start point for any development activity is to develop and facilitate the deployment of these strengths.

Seen in this light, any weaknesses which individuals begin to identify for themselves in their answers to *question three*, are best defined as *those characteristics, traits, behaviours, or deficiencies in knowledge or skill which prevent them from displaying their strengths.* Any development effort should focus on identifying their strengths and addressing any *"disabling weaknesses"*, as we call them. We worked with one individual who was an outstanding professional performer. However his disabling weakness was hypersensitivity to any minor criticisms of his work, which resulted in him often becoming angry and confrontational during meetings. This made him less effective in his role. Because he had developed a reputation for being difficult, people tended to avoid discussions with him. As a consequence, he was frequently starved of the 'soft' information regularly circulating amongst his colleagues, and was even bypassed for certain projects.

People are valued and employed for their strengths, for what they can do. The start point for any development activity is to develop and facilitate the deployment of these strengths

Unfortunately, instead of concentrating on those few weaknesses that prevent people from deploying their strengths, there is sometimes a tendency to get diverted into endless lists of supposed imperfections. This sometimes reaches ludicrous proportions. As organizational consultants, from time to time we have helped clients with selection decisions at senior levels. When there is a choice between internal and external candidates, sometimes far too much emphasis is placed on the known weaknesses of internal candidates, whilst discounting their known strengths. Meanwhile, the assumed strengths of the external candidates are stressed whilst ignoring the possibility of any weaknesses. As we put it rather bluntly to one client: "So the outside candidate you're favouring has no weaknesses then?" This is not an argument for always appointing internal candidates over external ones at senior levels. Rather, we are suggesting the avoidance of a fallacious rationale for their rejection, based on over emphasizing known weaknesses and ignoring strengths.

Question four is designed to help give some insight into the enjoyable parts of any job. Indeed some managers argue that, for the most part in a work setting, what people enjoy doing is generally what they are good at. The answers to this question may give some clues in helping to identify those aspects of their roles for which they would like further development and training, or activities they would perhaps be unprepared to give up, in any future role at work (Schein 1978). This is an important issue when you later start to consider career development. If what you really enjoy is meeting customers as part of day-to-day front line sales, is it sensible to accept a sales manager's role which is likely to take you further away from this activity?

The answers to *question five* sometimes evoke a sardonic response. One manager told us: "I come to work, because the last time I checked, the members of my family were still partial to food and shelter." However, there are other reasons for doing a particular job, in addition to the financial rewards or the need to support a family. For some people the social aspects are important. Others wish to leave their mark professionally, or fulfil their need for achievement whilst carrying out particular types of work. Often individuals will wish to satisfy a variety of such needs. Of course, the reasons for coming to work often evolve over time as one moves through the different phases of one's life.

Question six raises the question of personal values. For some people it is important that the work they do results in some social benefit, improves the lot of other human beings, or results in personal recognition. Our values are often an important signpost to the sort of work we want to do, but only very rarely is it possible for most of us to satisfy all of our value needs fully in our main job. For example, you may have to fulfil your desire to "give something back" by outside activities such as organizing fundraising activities for local charities, or perhaps by serving on the board of the local hospital. Similarly, your increasing concern for the environment can be met through political activity, or perhaps by remaining with your employer and seeking to influence their corporate and social responsibility policy.

For some, the answers to *question seven* will link back to their responses to *question five*.

Question seven highlights the fact that our personal lives frequently constrain our choices. Often we have dependents to consider, geographic constraints, financial and time commitments of various sorts, perhaps even health issues, all of which can impinge on our ability to make free choices. It can sometimes be difficult for certain people to accept that if they themselves are unable to take advantage of particular development opportunities, then those who are able to take advantage may make greater career and salary progress, at least in the short-term.

Once individuals have given some thought to these questions, in most cases they could then usefully discuss them with others—work colleagues, or even friends, partners, or family members. Those working in organizations with a "matrix" or "project" structure can solicit views from both their "functional" and "project" or "line" colleagues, as the case may be. If you are the most senior specialist in your function within your firm, you might consider seeking feedback on yourself or on relevant future trends in your field from trusted and knowledgeable outsiders. A senior director in Finance or Marketing can usefully supplement any internal feedback with the views of specialists from outside—academics, consultants, or other practitioners. Functional specialists, for instance, can consult the relevant institutions for information about trends. In addition to working day by day in your field of interest, the standard way of keeping up to date in any field is to read its literature and talk to functional or other colleagues with relevant specialist knowledge.

Once the questions have been considered, the next step is one or several meetings with one's manager. The aim is to pinpoint the priorities for development, and start to formulate an action plan to address them.

6.1.3   Discussing Development Needs With the Manager

Figure 6.2 sets out a standard five step development cycle. It is a straightforward process, based on identifying the priority development needs and producing and implementing workable action plans to address them. Each of the steps is discussed in turn below.

Step One: Identify Development Need
People have varying degrees of self insight into their development needs in their current roles. On the assumption that the individual and the manager have considered the questions in Fig. 6.1, most managers could usefully start a development discussion with a subordinate by asking them first for their own views. There are two reasons for this. Firstly, we are all perhaps most motivated to address those

Fig. 6.2 The development cycle

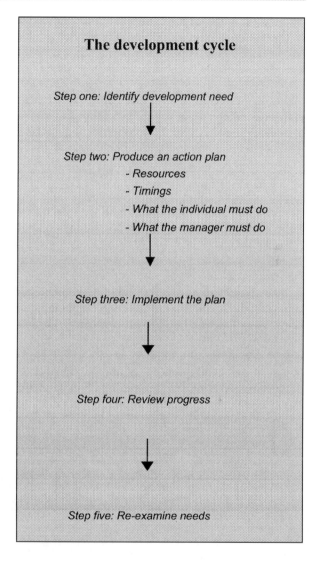

weaknesses we ourselves have identified. Secondly, *Management by Permission* implies that managers should always try to "take their people with them" rather than impose solutions. Development actions need to be 'owned' by the individuals and active cooperation is always easier to achieve when it is their idea. However the discussion will progressively lead managers into sharing their own observations and insights, which will often include telling someone about some of the strengths they have observed, as well as highlighting any gaps between what is required for the role, and the individual's current capabilities.

Sometimes your staff may be unaware of some of their strengths, and they may even see weaknesses where you see strengths. One role managers can usefully play is to remind people of their strengths. However, strengths overplayed can become weaknesses, and strengths in some circumstances become weaknesses in others. For instance, the ability to make decisions quickly, direct others clearly and firmly, and ensure that everyone does exactly as instructed is exactly what is required in a crisis. However, it becomes counterproductive when helping to brainstorm the future of the energy market over the next 10 years. Another example is the individual whose strength lies in taking ownership of problems and working tenaciously to solve them. However sometimes when he runs into obstacles, he is reluctant to ask for others' help before it is too late.

Most of us on occasion probably suffer from some degree of self-delusion about certain of our supposed capabilities. We knew one manager who started every meeting with 5 minutes of light-hearted banter. Far from being a vital ingredient in climate setting, to which he thought his staff always looked forward, in reality they tolerated this time-wasting as the boss's mild eccentricity. If blind spots such as these do not really interfere with performance, then there seems little point in raising them. Remembering that people need to save face is a useful lesson in management as in other areas of human endeavour.

Some people are unjustly proud of "strengths", which their colleagues in fact consider to be the more regrettable aspects of their personalities. Doug thinks he is being direct, tough and assertive, while others see him as aggressive, unreasonable and overbearing. Indeed as pointed out previously, at senior levels in organizations certain individuals are successful *despite* what they consider to be their strengths, not because of them. If Doug's aggressive behaviour becomes counterproductive, it needs to be addressed.

> **Remember**
> - Concentrate on developing strengths
> - Be aware that sometimes we can be proud of "strengths" which our colleagues actually consider to be among the more regrettable aspects of our personalities
> - In different circumstances, our strengths and weaknesses can be the same thing
> - Strengths overplayed often turn into weaknesses

How can a manager best help at this stage in the process? Often managers and staff will have begun to address development planning as part of their discussions about expectations (see Chap. 4). However, it is blindingly obvious that a manager's best opportunity to spot the relevant strengths and disabling weaknesses of staff will be in the course of day-to-day work activities.

The three 'control' approaches discussed in Chap. 3 also provide useful data. For example if the key numbers in a department are unsatisfactory and the explanations given equally so, then this should alert the manager to individual deficiencies. During Work Management Meetings it is often apparent who is struggling and who is coping well with different elements of the work. "Walking the patch"

PART A: "360-DEGREE" FEEDBACK GROUPED INTO CLUSTERS

Cluster One: Communications	Boss	Self	Peers	Subs	Extnl
3. Listens well	8	7	6	8	8
10. Gives feedback effectively	6	7	7	7	8
12. Keeps others informed	8	7	7	7	8
14. Presents ideas effectively and persuasively	6	7	8	8	7
19. Communicates clearly and effectively	6	7	7	8	7
26. Makes clear to others what is expected of them	7	7	8	8	8
32. Adapts their style to fit the situation	6	7	6	7	8
59. Maintains open channels of communication	7	8	8	8	8
66. Explains strategies, objectives and tasks clearly	7	7	8	8	8
Average	6.8	7.1	7.2	7.7	7.8

Cluster Three: Problem solving and decision making	Boss	Self	Peers	Subs	Extnl
7. Anticipates difficulties and develops workable plans to address these	8	7	8	6	6
9. Responds effectively to challenges and problems	8	7	8	7	9
13. Is prepared to take tough decisions	8	7	8	8	7
24. Welcomes suggestions for improvement	8	9	7	8	9
34. Handles emergencies effectively	8	8	9	6	8
36. Is willing to accept help when required	8	8	8	7	6
40. Makes decisions in a timely way	8	8	8	6	8
45. Implements decisions in a timely manner	8	8	7	7	8
53. Is able to understand and take account of issues in a range of technical areas	7	8	8	7	8
Average	7.9	7.8	7.9	6.9	7.7

Cluster Six: Relations with others	Boss	Self	Peers	Subs	Extnl
15. Relates well to others	6	7	6	6	8
20. Recognizes/rewards others' contributions	7	7	7	8	8
28. Is helpful and understanding in others' professional fields	6	8	7	7	7
42. Is sensitive to others' feelings and to own impact on others	5	8	6	7	9
51. Makes sure others get the credit as appropriate	7	8	7	8	8
52. Makes sure others are never left feeling resentful	5	7	5	6	9
60. Works well in teams	5	8	6	7	8
Average	5.9	7.6	6.3	7.0	8.1

	Boss	Self	Peers	Subs	Extnl
Average for all 14 clusters (67 questions)	7.3	7.6	7.2	7.2	7.8

Fig. 6.3 Sample "360-degree" feedback

PART B: VERBATIM COMMENTS UNDER THREE HEADINGS

WRITTEN FEEDBACK FROM BOSS

Strengths
1. Very resilient and tenacious
2. Can always be relied upon in an emergency
3. Very concerned to do a quality job

Improvements
1. Increase knowledge of budgeting and finance
2. Continue to develop conflict handling skills
3. Sometimes you upset people for no reason

If you could give this person only one message
Remember that not everyone is as much of a perfectionist as you

WRITTEN FEEDBACK FROM PEER D

Strengths
1. Very responsive and adaptable as a colleague
2. In-depth knowledge of his field
3. Knows the organization very well

Improvements
1. Perhaps listen a little more before jumping to conclusions
2. Sometimes gives the impression that he is not up to speed on all of the key numbers
3. Gets into conflicts with people which hampers his effectiveness at times

If you could give this person only one message
You would be even more respected in the organization if you fought less with some colleagues

WRITTEN FEEDBACK FROM SUBORDINATE B

Strengths
1. Always available whenever I need advice
2. Maintains enthusiasm no matter what is happening
3. Very supportive

Improvements
1. Sometimes seems unsure of management policy on some topics
2. Maybe trust us a little more
3. Could improve the way he deals with people from some other departments

If you could give this person only one message
Sometimes we are asked to do things at the last minute when we could have been informed earlier

WRITTEN FEEDBACK FROM "EXTERNAL" CUSTOMER C

Strengths
1. Has established good relations at many levels in our company
2. Responds quickly
3. Understands situations and gets to grips with the issues quickly

Improvements
1. Visits to us tend to be too short
2. Very occasionally seems to slip up on some items of detail
3. Introduce us more to the other members of your team

If you could give this person only one message
We are generally very happy with the service we get from you

Fig. 6.3 (continued)

provides the opportunity to probe more deeply and if appropriate, start the process of coaching. Bear in mind that the job of a manager is to try and make sure that people get the development they *need*, not just what they might *want*.

Finally, some organizations make use of "360-degree feedback" and this can provide useful data to help in prioritizing a person's development needs. Figure 6.3 provides a sample extract from one individual's feedback, based on our own web-based "360-degree" process (www.managementbypermission.com). The questionnaire is designed to: highlight the extent to which individuals exhibit the skills and competencies required in their roles; provide respondents with an opportunity to give verbatim feedback on an individual's key strengths and development needs; be easy and quick for respondents to complete.

Part A asks respondents to rate individuals on each item using a 10-point scale, ranging from: 10 = Strongly agree, to 1 = Strongly disagree. There are 67 items in all, which are grouped into 14 "clusters." The average ratings (or individual ratings in the case of the "Self" and the "Boss" columns) are reproduced in Fig. 6.3. The shaded sections in the columns denote particular strengths ▦ or development needs ▨, when comparing the results either against our own database of responses, or against data from colleagues in an individual's own organization. In the example, feedback was obtained from the person's own manager, as well as four peers, four subordinates and four "externals" (in this case, these external contacts were customers).

Part B invites verbatim comments on three strengths and three development needs. A final question asks: "If you could only feed back one message to this person, what would that be?"

Step Two: Produce an Action Plan
Once a need has been identified, the supervisor can have an important role in helping to formulate and implement a development plan. This often involves the manager or the organization in providing the necessary resources or opportunities. In some firms certain types of development assistance have been formalized with employees entitled to a given number of days of off-the-job training per year.

In recent years a "70:20:10" model of development has been applied by some organizations when considering development options (Lombardo and Eichinger 1996). This framework suggests that: 70 % of learning is on-the-job; 20 % results from interventions from others (the boss, mentors, executive coaches, or networking); with the remaining 10 % the result of courses or reading.

Whatever the correct balance between these three methods, it is important to define the priorities for development. Previously, we discussed the need to address *disabling weaknesses*. A typical example of a disabling weakness would be a functional expert from engineering or finance who is sometimes required to make presentations to groups of nonexperts. Instead of tailoring his material to the audience, he uses too much jargon, and the points he wants to make get lost in a welter of detailed charts and tables. His in-depth functional knowledge and expertise is not deployed effectively because he fails to communicate. This is not only a disabling weakness in terms of his current role, it will most likely hold him back from further advancement.

In this case the weakness can probably be addressed through a combination of coaching, learning from a recognized role model, and perhaps a course in presentation skills. The coaching would focus on helping the individual learn to structure an argument, and present information in a way that nonspecialists understand. He could also be introduced to simple techniques such as developing a short summary of the key messages he wants to convey: some people still find it useful to think in terms of an "elevator pitch" whereby one has to distil key messages into a short statement. Watching experts, and then adapting their techniques to one's own requirements, can usefully supplement further formal training.

> Build on people's strengths, but also identify and deal with any "disabling weaknesses" that prevent them from displaying those strengths

Some weaknesses are more difficult to address. For instance, we have observed that a large number of senior people in organizations seem especially adept at reading others' body language, interpreting nonverbal messages, and responding accordingly. Although we have yet to see it defined anywhere as a job requirement, the ability to understand nonverbal signals seems almost a *sine qua non* for many senior roles. Those who do not possess this skill will, for instance, keep talking when others are sending them the message that they should be listening. Making these managers aware of their deficiency will often be enough for them to work out for themselves how they can best remedy the problem. In other cases you may need to go further and try and help them diagnose the reason for their deficiency. For instance, if they are not listening to customers during meetings is it because, for instance, they are concentrating too much on delivering their prepared speeches and other materials, rather than responding to what is actually taking place during the meetings?

There are of course some cases in which individuals may seem genetically incapable of mastering a particular skill. In the last analysis you cannot put in what the creator left out, as writer Stephen King (2000) once remarked. In such instances you will need to help the person find some way of accommodating the disabling weakness. For example, in the above case, an individual could perhaps attend certain key meetings accompanied by a colleague with proven skills in reading nonverbal signals. The colleague could send a prearranged signal—always assuming the person will spot even a prearranged signal—when it is time to listen. In reviewing the meeting afterwards the colleague could share any observations and explain what cues they had observed.

"I've noticed, Cedric, that you have a tendency to drop your right shoulder on the backstroke"

There is a chance that the person could learn from this and be able to look out for similar cues in future when unaccompanied. If they are still incapable of learning the skill then they may need to be supported by others at critical meetings. Such an approach would not necessarily be that unusual. After all, highly successful managers often select members of their teams in part because they help compensate for their own weaknesses. In addressing development needs, there is invariably a key that will open almost any door. With sufficient thought, a solution can generally be found.

6.1.4 Development on a (Practically) Zero Budget

Formal training courses, conferences and seminars may well form part of a development plan. Figure 6.4 sets out twenty further suggestions for development. The

Sample list of twenty development actions

1. Conduct a personal review
   - Set a specific time (daily, weekly, monthly) to review your own performance
   - Write down lessons learned and discuss conclusions with others
2. Keep a logbook/journal
   - Note experiences, ideas; review lessons learned and set targets to pursue
3. Do a time log
   - What patterns are there? Are you allocating your time to your priorities?
4. Obtain feedback
   - From supervisor, colleagues, subordinates, customers, external parties
   - In person or through "360-degree" or other process
5. Interview/meet experts
   - Identify someone who does something very well; ask them how they do it
6. Learn from or shadow an expert
   - Identify a skill or competency you wish to develop (e.g. handling a meeting)
   - Select a role model and try to observe them in action
   - Discuss the issues beforehand, note key points, and review afterwards
7. Undertake special assignments e.g. for difficult or demanding clients
   - Forces you to apply "best practice" standards
   - Their questions and demands help ensure quality outcomes
8. Consider job rotation/temporary placements/secondments
   - Exchange posts with a colleague for a specific period
   - Provide mutual support during the temporary change
9. Increase exposure to other functions/activities
   - Represent the function at meetings one would not normally attend
10. Undertake study/reading/e-learning
    - Read autobiographies– an underrated source of ideas
11. Obtain an internal or external coach/mentor
    - An internal "co-coach" can also bring crossfunctional networking
    - Meet, phone, "plan, do, review"; share experiences and advice
12. Volunteer for leadership/membership of task forces
13. Coach/mentor others
14. Run/host conferences/seminars on relevant topics
    - Deliver presentations internally and externally
    - Invite external speakers and learn from their experiences
15. Carry out benchmarking visits
    - How do we compare against others?
16. Restructure individual roles to add further or unfamiliar responsibilities
    - Lead a meeting one would not normally lead
    - Appoint deputies/understudies
    - Volunteer to take on extra responsibilities
17. Encourage part-time involvement in other organizations
    - Join relevant institutions
    - Work with charities, schools; undertake nonexecutive postings
18. Set up local/international networks for information exchange
19. Get exposure to media and your professional network
    - Publish articles or papers
    - Press, academic journals, radio, TV, Internet, LinkedIn
20. Consider short-term sabbaticals to develop different perspectives/skills

Fig. 6.4 Sample list of twenty development actions

majority of these activities cost little or nothing, and the list may spark other ideas. The ideas are for the most part self-explanatory, however, some comments on some of the items follow.

Item One: Conduct a Personal Review

Professional skills and expertise are generally acquired through practice. We tend to learn most by doing, by reviewing what we have done, and by applying the lessons we have learned. Many development schemes lay great emphasis on attendance at courses whilst ignoring the main source of development which is serious consideration of the work actually done. The purpose of a personal review is to reflect on one's performance and to pinpoint areas for improvement. Staff should take the time to write notes on what they have done, the purpose of the tasks, their rationale for the approaches adopted, what went well and less well, and what they might do differently next time. Over time, patterns will emerge from which they will be able to draw inferences.

It can be valuable to discuss any conclusions with others who can offer constructive criticism and contribute their own experience on the issues. Experienced colleagues are generally very responsive to requests for discussions of this sort, and are often a surprisingly underused source of knowledge and expertise. Even some of the most difficult of people seem more approachable when asked for advice in their specialist fields, especially if the person asking for help has done their homework in advance and asks intelligent and informed questions. By 'doing one's homework' we mean taking the trouble to find out as much as you can before troubling the expert. "I read up on this issue and found that in thirty percent of cases, the standard textbook approach doesn't work. Is there any way of telling when you should carry out the tests? How do you decide? . . .."

Item Two: Keep a Logbook or Journal

"How can I tell what I think until I see what I say?" remarked E. M. Forster. Keeping a logbook has long been a favoured technique for learning from experience and working out ideas. Individuals from a variety of fields use this approach, including software engineers, writers, academics and scientists, and some have specifically recommended it (Wright Mills 1970).

As with the personal review, anyone can learn from their day-to-day activities by recording anything of relevance to their work. Some examples of what to record might include: novel tasks, lessons learned, results of analyses, implications of benchmarking data, summaries of relevant articles or books.

More generally, most of us would benefit from more systematically recording the key points from important discussions, or the highlights from certain meetings. One of Sir Thomas More's standard devices involved sending a summary letter of a conversation he had had with an individual, in order to put things on record (Ackroyd 1999). Few of us are as disciplined with our note taking and record-keeping as we could be, and being able to refer to one's own detailed notes about what occurred months previously and to know "who said what" can be very helpful, especially if others have failed to keep their own notes.

Item Four: Obtain Feedback

Giving positive feedback, where it is merited, is a greatly underused form of development. It is a way of reinforcing desired behaviours, as well as being a source of motivation for the person receiving the feedback. Often little more than a simple "well done" is required. Catching people doing something right, and then praising them appropriately, is a classic technique in motivation. We know as a result of carrying out in-depth interviews in a large number of organizations that one should never underestimate the extent to which people crave recognition for what they perceive as a job well done. However, and as discussed earlier in the book, managers must ensure that any positive feedback *is* deserved. Otherwise your praise becomes a debased currency. Managers should also seek opportunities to pass on any positive feedback they receive from clients or colleagues. This is especially powerful when the source of the feedback is well-respected by the individual concerned. One of us was once told by a boss: "Bill thought you did a great job on that. And Bill isn't an easy guy to impress."

Negative feedback is always more difficult for the manager to handle and some managers avoid giving it at all costs. On occasion, this leads to the ludicrous situation whereby anyone in the organization, plus the birds in the trees, will know a particular individual's disabling weakness, whilst meantime the individual concerned remains in blissful ignorance. They only find out, if they find out at all, when it is too late. As a manager, be very careful you do not make comments about people behind their backs, without making sure they get the relevant feedback direct from you. Your comments are often passed to the people concerned.

Few people like negative messages about themselves or their performance and some people are more sensitive than they appear. Relationships can break down and performance can be affected if feedback is taken badly by the recipient. It is useful to consider how best to feed back development needs while at the same time considering their impact on the 'feelings' of the recipient (Schein 1987). It is worth asking, given your knowledge of a person, how you can give them useful feedback in such a way as to increase the chances they will learn from it and act on it, whilst still maintaining a positive working relationship with you (Fig. 6.5).

Whatever method is chosen, people cannot deal with a weakness of which they are ignorant. If managers do not wish, for whatever reason, to provide the necessary feedback, then one option is to ask an outside consultant to do so, perhaps using "360-degree" feedback and/or other methods. At more senior levels it may be more acceptable for feedback to be given by an external coach, who will often be able to reinforce any messages through their own observations. We have often played this role as part of our coaching work. If an external coach is involved, they too can assist in suggesting ideas for addressing the issue. However, if you do draw upon the services of an external coach, make sure that their values and ethos are consistent with the values and culture of your organization. To state the obvious: a "touchy feely" coach is rarely effective when working in what we call "jungular" organizations (i.e., organizations which exhibit some of the characteristics of the jungle, and in which some people "go for the jugular").

Giving negative feedback effectively

When giving negative feedback, the likelihood of upsetting people is reduced if feedback is seen as a natural part of the management process (for instance, it takes place regularly during Work Management Meetings) and if it is done in the right way.

Subtle hints can be effective and often the well-placed question will be sufficient: ("If you were to do this job again, is there anything you would do differently?" or "When you have finished a piece of work, where do you store your written notes?")

When more direct feedback is required, there are some standard guidelines and many managers will be aware of these. Two of the most important points include:

Facts more than judgements "You no longer seem to contribute much in meetings once the topic is not relevant to your own immediate responsibilities" is better than "You're half asleep." Similarly, "In meetings I have noticed you do not always make eye contact when interacting with colleagues. Are you aware of this?" is better than, "You seem very offhand and uninterested when you talk to people."

Close to the event Rather than store up incidents, managers should seek opportunities for giving feedback in the course of the working day, and as close to the event as possible.

Fig. 6.5 Giving negative feedback effectively

Extremely effective feedback can also be obtained from peers, especially if this is managed in a structured way. In one firm in which we worked, project leaders presented their current new business development projects at quarterly meetings. These meetings were unofficially called "rock throwing sessions" by the participants. Presenters took it in turn to describe and then defend their projects against feedback from the other project leaders and senior functional specialists in attendance. The projects themselves were thus tested and improved, and as well as learning from the comments of their colleagues, each of the project leaders obtained practice in presenting a case to a potentially critical audience.

Item Six: Learn From or Shadow an Expert

Often we can learn more from our failures or difficulties than from what has gone according to plan. Or as Bertrand Russell stated rather more elegantly, "there is a thousand times more experience in pain than in pleasure" (Russell 1978). Whenever we have interviewed successful executives and discussed their memorable learning experiences, it is notable how many of them report that some of their most valuable lessons arose in working with people they liked the least. So, for example, whilst they may have disliked the disciplines or rigour which others (sometimes their bosses) brought to situations, in retrospect they acknowledged that these very disciplines helped to fill gaps in their own make-up.

In working with large numbers of managers, we have observed that after a certain age, a desire to pass on one's experience and expertise to more junior colleagues can be a strong motivator, and research supporting this has been known for many years (Dalton et al. 1977; Schein 1978). These individuals may also be 'role models' given the manner in which they carry out some of their tasks. It may be appropriate to ask for their help as coaches or mentors to less experienced staff, which will in turn help develop them as well as the staff.

Item Ten: Undertake Study/Reading/E-Learning

In addition to bespoke development and other packages designed to address specific knowledge and skill gaps, useful insights and ideas can be found in autobiographies, memoirs, and biographies of public and other figures in the world of politics, business, sport, and the media.

The biographies about, and autobiographies by, those who have performed at top levels in various sports often contain "nuggets" or philosophies which can be adapted for use in organizational or business settings. Self-evidently, it is a matter for the individual to find a sport or field in which they are interested (even if it is a minority activity) and uncover suitable materials from which lessons can be learned. For example, one Chief Executive of our acquaintance considers the biography of Irish hurling coach Ger Loughnane (Scally 2001) as the best management book he has ever read. In addition to the Harvard Business Review article aiming to distil Sir Alex Ferguson's management wisdom (Elberse 2013), the latter-day Harvard lecturer's own autobiography also provides a detailed insight into some of his methods and ideas (Ferguson 2013). Similarly, former world champion Gary Kasparov (2007) draws upon his experience of the game of chess to set out his strategy for success away from the chessboard.

Political biographies and autobiographies are a useful source of material for understanding how others, 'get things done through other people', as well as cope with the vagaries of organizational life. The ideas of Jack Welch continue to prove popular amongst many executives (Welch 2001). The experiences of any former country leader, president or prime minister can be worth studying, as can the inside accounts of well-placed political "spin doctors" or journalists (Blumenthal 2003; Mandelson 2010; Powell 2010). Theodore White's series of studies into the 'making of various US Presidents' is well-regarded and informative (see for example, White 2010). Kearns Goodwin's account of Abraham Lincoln (2009), "the one book Obama could not live without in the White House", provides a detailed description of how Lincoln successfully assembled a team of former rivals to work together towards a common purpose.

In addition to the plethora of business and leadership books on the market, many of which repay further study, and are cited at the end of the chapter, it is also worth reading accounts focusing on events within particular institutions, as well as high-profile case histories. Leeson (1996) describes his role in the downfall of Barings; Fox (2003) discusses the rise and fall of Enron; Isaacson (2011) provides an in-depth account of Steve Jobs and Apple; and Brooks (2014) sets out 12 readable US business case studies and discusses the lessons to be learned.

Churchill once explained that he attributed his ability to anticipate the actions of others as, in part, owing to his study of history (Lord 2003). History books often contain interesting perspectives on strategy and tactics, whether these relate to centuries past—for instance, the account of Henry VIII's minister Thomas Cromwell (Hutchinson 2007)—or more recent publications in the field of war studies (Kennedy 2013). To cite the sorts of insights to be obtained, amongst the most pertinent advice on public speaking is to be found in the memoir of Jones (1978) describing his time working for British Scientific Intelligence during World War Two. He recommended: (1) believing you have something worth telling your audience; and (2) imagining yourself one of that audience. He adds that nearly all of the advice given to would-be presenters deals with the trimmings without mentioning these fundamentals.

Item Twelve: Lead/Participate in Task Forces
Giving people a chance to develop their leadership skills as early as possible can bring advantages to those in early career, especially if the individuals concerned are called upon to supervise those from a different technical background to their own. Unable to rely on their own technical expertise, the experience seems to force them to develop the interpersonal and other skills they need in order to manage others (Evans et al. 1989).

Many managers encourage using a type of "trial promotion" in order to test an individual's suitability for supervisory responsibility. Rather than formally announcing that someone is being considered for a management role, they ask a given individual to take responsibility for a small project, and typically one which involves some degree of supervision. This can help the individual as well as their manager to assess whether they are cut out for some of the demands of leadership. While some will demonstrably enjoy the experience and look as if they have grown around 3 inches taller, others will become "obstacle-dominant", constantly complaining about the difficulties: they could not get the information; their emails and phone calls went unanswered; or another department refused to cooperate. These sorts of reactions can be an indicator of an individual's unsuitability for management in certain types of organizations.

6.1.5 Developing a Plan

We noted above that your current organization may well issue development planning guidelines and forms to be completed. While the approaches vary in complexity and emphasis—for instance some company schemes focus heavily on development plans set against a framework of organizational competencies—in most cases it makes sense to make use of what already exists in your organization. Notwithstanding this, there is little need for a complicated form in order to record a handful of priority development needs together with some activities which will help address them.

Figure 6.6 presents a worked example of a very simple approach which will suit most circumstances. The form is designed to record up to four development needs, together with a set of actions aimed at helping meet these needs. The actions are

Sample development plan

DEVELOPMENT NEEDS (Use the space below to identify up to four development needs to be addressed in the coming 6-12 months)

1. *Further develop strengths, especially in advanced design.*
2. *Improve monitoring and control of activities of direct reports.*
3. *Learn company's new management accounting system.*
4. *Improve working relationships and contacts with sales function.*

DEVELOPMENT ACTION PLAN (Use the space below to record the action plan to address the above needs)

1. *Contact Prof. Jones and discuss our current position.*
2. *Attend Annual Conference of Institution.*
3. *Implement Work Management System; review progress and report back (discuss with JK her approach to this).*
4. *Attend two-day internal management accounting seminar.*
5. *Spend two days accompanying sales reps. on customer visits (Manager to arrange).*
6. *Make state of the art presentation to the Exec. Group.*

Fig. 6.6 Sample development plan

designed to take place over a six to twelve month period, with progress reviewed at various predetermined points. As the priority development needs or disabling weaknesses are addressed, so further development actions can be agreed and implemented, and the cycle recommences.

Development resembles Schubert's Eighth Symphony: it is destined to remain forever unfinished. There is always the opportunity to: deepen one's professional skills and knowledge; build up one's confidence in some aspects of work; learn more about the impact of one's work on other parts of the organization; improve one's performance; or simply keep up to date with developments in our fields. Even the best trained amongst us sometimes find that many of our qualifications, no matter how impressive, are of a mature vintage, and some of our certificates might as well have been written in disappearing ink.

In the example in Fig. 6.6, the development action plan draws on on-the-job activities as well as an internal course. Retaining the involvement of the manager in helping to realize a development plan can be helpful for a whole host of reasons. One of the actions here—the sales visits—requires the facilitation of the manager in order to set up the programme.

> **Remember**
> * OUR BEST DEVELOPMENT COMES FROM THE WORK WE DO
> * Help your staff to learn as much as possible from their current work activities
> * Where practicable enable people to expand the range of their experience
> * Help people to analyze their own development needs
> * Use your Work Management System to help identify needs and progress plans
> * Concentrate on the deployment of strengths – develop the strengths and minimize disabling weaknesses

6.2   Development Towards Other Roles

In this section we will show you how to:

* *help employees develop practical, realistic career plans*
* *help people understand the cost as well as the benefits of progression in an organization*
* *help them appreciate the constraints which can have a bearing on career development*
* *deal with people when they leave*

As part of an in company career development workshop, we once asked an experienced Technical Director to address a group of high potential staff about his own career, the lessons he had learned, and the messages he wished to pass on. Following the event, we realized that the issues he raised in his speech, although personal to him, had resonance for a much wider population than just one firm's high potentials. Ever since, we have often used a transcript of his address in career development discussions with managers at all levels (see Fig. 6.7).

Not everyone wishes to advance to the level of Technical Director, although some will aim even higher. The level to which one wants to rise is a matter of ability, opportunity and personal choice. But whatever the extent of someone's ambition, or even their career stage, his views are useful background reading for those considering their options. He raises a number of points to take into account in considering one's future.

"Take what you want and pay", runs the old proverb. If it emphasizes anything, the Technical Director's case is a reminder that if you want any job, you must be prepared to pay the price that goes with it. The upper echelons of organizations are not *necessarily* populated by the most intelligent, the most highly skilled, or even by those with the greatest common sense. However you do usually find at the most senior levels those who have a sufficiency of these characteristics, and critically, people who want to be there, and are willing to pay the price.

Paying the price: getting to the top and staying there

"When I left University and joined this firm, I decided that I wanted to be Technical Director by the time I was thirty. I soon learned that there is no point in making a rigid career plan. If you do that, you'll fall at the first hurdle. You need to know the sorts of jobs you must do en route to the top, and then keep a look out for them. If someone wants you to go somewhere, you go. This may not please your partner or your family, but if it is a job en route, then you have to go. This is particularly the case if you are asked to move by senior management.

If you want to progress rapidly, you have to be noticed by your boss. You can do this by your attitude, your enthusiasm, and your energy. I like to see people who move rapidly, and who are obviously keen to get on and get things done. People who rush off on the dot of finishing time are unlikely to impress.

It doesn't apply everywhere, but many people at the top of organizations can be quite conservative. They don't always like strange hairstyles, tattoos and outlandish or scruffy dress. If you want to become a senior manager, then look at the senior managers in your organization as one guide to what might be expected. The old "Peter Principle" –that in hierarchies we tend to rise to the level of our incompetence –does apply in some cases. But by doing parts of the job above you, you can demonstrate to yourself as well as the organization that a promotion would not be beyond your level of competence. You can do this by volunteering to take on some elements of the more senior job, by just doing them, or simply by asking for more scope in your work.

Don't try to undermine your boss or stab them in the back. It will rebound on you. Your boss only has to tell his own manager that you are "trouble" and you are sunk in the organization. Support your boss, and don't contradict them in public in a way that makes them look foolish. They won't forgive you if you do. You need to show respect. By all means put your point of view, but do it constructively and helpfully. At all costs, don't get a reputation as a "whinger." Nobody likes people who are constantly complaining, and they don't get promoted.

You must take responsibility for your work, and show appropriate guilt or concern when you get it wrong. I don't like people who just shrug it off. So if you make an error, show some remorse, and a determination to put things right.

What do I get out of my job? A great sense of satisfaction, when I see new products going into the factory, and our people with a more secure future. I enjoy the responsibility and the continued interest. I have never been bored; there is always too much to do. I like the power, and at senior levels you do have this, both for good, and for ill. The money can be good, but you are unlikely to be very rich, at least at my level. If you want to be really well off, you have to be Chief Executive, or possibly set up your own business. The rewards can be very high, but so can the risks of failure.

Fig. 6.7 Paying the price: getting to the top and staying there

Some foreign travel is interesting, but mostly it is very tiring and involves travelling in an aluminium tube, to an office just like your own, probably in a not very interesting town. You then sleep poorly in a functional hotel, possibly after an indifferent meal, after which it is late to bed, early to rise, some stressful meetings, after which you return in the aluminium tube to your own office. In fifteen years of intensive travel, I reckon I could count my "pleasurable trips" on the fingers of one hand.

The downside is time, time, time. I really could use a thirty-six hour day. In a good week I will put in fifty hours, and in a long one, seventy or eighty. I try to keep Saturdays to myself, but Sunday is always dedicated to the job. In today's organizations, there simply aren't the people around to delegate things to. Your family suffers, and it puts a great strain on relationships. Another effect is that as you progress your character changes, and you also change the way you look at the world. Not all relationships survive this intact. You need to spend a lot of time on your network of business contacts. This means that you no longer have time for old colleagues and often you lose touch with them.

To stay at the top you need a number of characteristics. You must be resilient, and be able to keep dozens of balls in the air. Sometimes I deal with thirty or forty issues in a day, and you have to remember where each one is. What annoys me is when people come into my office with an urgent matter which could have been dealt with routinely three days ago, if only they had been on top of the job.

You need to have courage, or at least have some strategies for controlling the outward signs of fear. Courage will also help you to face difficult issues, such as choosing who is to be laid off and how you make the decision. It is the senior manager who has to break the news. Some people find it hard to stay sober the evening after having to tell people that they no longer have a job. On the other hand, you have to be able to relax. You must be able to sleep without having to resort to pills, or the bottle.

Perhaps most of all you need a sense of humour. If you sometimes hear gales of laughter coming from the management team meeting, it's probably because some particularly stressful item is under consideration. The laughter relieves the stress. You should never stop laughing altogether."

Fig. 6.7 (continued)

In most organizations, really wanting a senior job means being prepared to do what is necessary to get there—for instance taking an assignment when it is offered, regardless of how it might fit with your private life or personal circumstances at the time—and being prepared to do what is necessary to stay there. This usually requires putting in the hours required, making daily sacrifices, and to some extent losing control over aspects of one's life. It also means dealing with organizational politics. The branches at the top of the organizational tree are thinner, as is the air. The stresses and strains associated with organizational politics are not for everyone.

When people think about their future careers, they do not always appreciate the personal cost required for effective performance at senior levels. While this Technical Director speaks positively about the benefits he gains from his job, he is also very clear about the price he personally has paid, and it is one which often lies hidden beneath the surface glamour of successful executive careers. Those who are ambitious to reach the top may not like it when they get there, and they may not like doing what is required to stay there.

This is far from an argument against taking on senior roles: as the Technical Director points out, these roles can provide a great deal of personal satisfaction as well as bringing benefits and security to others. Many people are understandably driven to strive for the top. However, it is as well to be aware of what might be involved in the decision to pursue certain avenues.

One way of helping to identify what is required for career success in a given organization is to ask a question we first heard posed by INSEAD's Professor André Laurent. He asked a client: "who gets ahead around here and why?" While in some organizations getting ahead means inventing new products, in other places it means having succeeded in a key organizational role, or perhaps simply being ready and available to deal with organizational issues at all hours. In some firms, a certain division or business will gain a reputation for being a development "hothouse" for high flyers. Elsewhere it can be that running a particular country organization, or heading up a given function seems to be a route to seniority. Having identified what is necessary to get ahead, people can decide for themselves if that is what they want to do. Sometimes they will find the medicine they might have to take to get there simply too unpalatable.

6.2.1   "You Can't Always Get What You Want" (Helping People Develop a Realistic Career Plan)

Helping someone in preparing for a future role follows essentially the same development cycle as set out in Fig. 6.2. The process involves: deciding upon the future role (which may be a stepping stone to a bigger role later on); identifying any gaps between an individual's current capabilities and what the future role requires; and then developing workable plans to address these gaps.

Some development activities require thinking about years in advance. For example, if an individual aspires to be Chief Executive, it may be important for them to run a particular Division or undergo certain external training several years ahead of the likely vacancy. In many other cases an individual may already possess some of the background or training necessary to a given role. It now needs enhancing with further development. An example would be the accountant who wishes to become an accounting manager. She already has the basic technical knowledge of finance. The priority now is for her to undertake supervisory responsibility and get her ticket punched, for instance by leading an internal project team which will be of assistance in developing her management skills.

A career ladder containing behavioural objectives in an engineering test department

Junior Test Engineer

- Apply standard tests within a defined programme, interpret results, produce reports and liaise with engineer
- Obtain materials, samples and equipment for standard test programmes
- Present results at project conferences
- Visit customers with an engineer and discuss results

Test Engineer

(In addition to the above)

- Design and prescribe test programmes to suit customer/commercial requirements
- Supervise work of junior engineers and develop their capabilities
- Liaise with and visit customers along with "Sales and Marketing" for routine progress reviews

Senior Test Engineer

(In addition to the above)

- Design, develop and implement novel test processes and procedures as required
- Develop test programmes with customers and agree with them any changes required as the programmes are progressed; keep manager and others fully informed of problems and progress
- Supervise work of engineers and develop their capabilities.

Fig. 6.8 A career ladder containing behavioural objectives in an engineering test department

Many organizations provide career paths for those who remain in similar roles but at increasing levels of professional and operational capability. This is recognized in such job titles such as "Senior Accountant, "Accountant" and "Junior Accountant." Often a set of behaviours or behavioural objectives will have been defined so that individuals will know what they need to be able to do in order to achieve a higher grade (see Fig. 6.8).

It can be very useful to define the requirements at various levels of a professional ladder in this way. If the information is not available, then as part of a development discussion the manager is often asked: "What must I do to be promoted to a higher grade?" Bluntly, in many organizations the real answer boils down to a combination of: being there a long time; ingratiating oneself with the boss; or threatening to leave at a critical point.

A more constructive and professional way of dealing with the situation is for managers to consider, preferably before they are asked, what they want from an employee at each grade, both in terms of professional capability and of behaviour. The simple question is: "What do I want people to DO at each level?" Once the answers are clear, then the development goals become apparent, the criteria for promotion may be set, and a programme initiated.

Helping someone arrive at a realistic career plan can be difficult, especially in cases in which the manager believes that a direct report's aspirations are overambitious or inadequately thought through. At times like these it can be helpful to encourage people to try and obtain information about what any proposed future role actually involves, as well as the capabilities and background required. Once someone has an accurate understanding of what a job entails, they are in a better position to arrive at a realistic judgement about their likely prospects, and whether they would want it.

Having considered the matter, they may well decide to remain where they are, often despite encouragement from their manager and others to be more ambitious. After all, being the right person in the right job, and continuing to perform well, can often yield the greatest career satisfaction of all. Some people are happy once they find a post which suits them, and they will remain there for the rest of their careers, valuing the security, and getting their satisfaction through being solid, experienced, successful professionals or practitioners in their fields.

It is often the opportunity to ply their trade which motivates such people. "What I love, is the sheer pleasure of doing law" said one of our clients. Meanwhile, individuals such as these still have the time to enjoy their outside interests and private lives. This may well have been the situation regarding the two senior IT engineers in the case study in Chap. 2. They showed no interest whatsoever in the management vacancy in IT. And when Paolo eventually gets around to discussing their development with them, the focus may well be on deepening and updating their skills in their chosen technical field.

For those seeking information about a potential future job, it is not often possible to experience, or to examine in detail, the content of many organizational roles in order to discover what may be of interest, or make best use of our strengths. The reality of what many jobs entail has often been edited out (de Botton 2004). Sometimes people can have quite erroneous impressions of what a particular job involves, and it is worth recommending that they discuss with some current jobholders the content of any posts to which they might aspire. Most people both within and outside an organization are prepared to talk about their jobs to anyone who is genuinely interested.

Managers can sometimes help in this by using their own contacts to set up meetings between their direct report and an appropriate jobholder. Before meeting a jobholder, staff should first do their homework on the role and then prepare a set of informed questions in advance (e.g., "I have read in several articles recently that Finance Directors are having to meet a whole new set of legislative reporting requirements. How is that likely to affect existing work practices?") During the discussion, they must focus on getting an accurate picture about what the person actually does in their job *day by day*. Broad statements such as: "As management accountants, we are responsible for preparing management reports", are quite uninformative to a prospective incumbent. The following is much more helpful: "I spend a third of the day on the telephone chasing up the information I need for management reports, and the rest of my time in front of the computer inputting the data and running the reports."

Having listened and learned, and gained an understanding of a role as it actually is, individuals can decide for themselves whether or not an activity really appeals. They should consider in particular whether the more routine parts of a job are worth tolerating in order to carry out its more interesting elements. It should be said, however, that almost all jobs have their "grunt" aspects, those unpleasant little chores that no-one really likes doing. Not all of the activities comprising a job are always entirely pleasant.

One important role managers should play in career development is to 'hold up the mirror' to their staff. By this we mean giving your honest reaction to their plans and ideas based on your insights and observations. For instance, when we have interviewed executives about their experiences in moving to more senior jobs, a number of them have mentioned that they had completely underestimated the extent of the loneliness and isolation involved in making important decisions.

One of them expressed this as follows: "All the issues have been discussed and mulled over. And now a decision has to be made. This is the point at which you have to sit in the office with the door closed, and call it. You have no safety blanket. You're on your own." If you manage an individual who has difficulties in making decisions, or seems to lack confidence in backing their judgements, then it is appropriate to highlight the decision-making aspect involved in most senior roles, and ask your staff member how they would feel about the buck stopping with them. Some people are initially excited by the prospect of having power and authority and being at the centre of decision-making. On reflection, some others are decidedly not.

In a similar vein, sometimes when discussing career development with some staff, they will tell you they want a job which involves working with people. Yet their current work behaviour suggests that they do not seem to want to work with people at all: they typically work alone, may take lunch alone at their desks, and their social contacts with others seem minimal. In fact they appear to avoid people. In such cases the manager would hold up the mirror by sharing their observations. The aim is not to make judgements, merely to provide people with some food for thought. It is worth remembering that very often we infer our attitudes from our behaviour: if we seem to avoid people in our day-to-day activities, then this might suggest that we do not necessarily want to take a new job which would involve interacting with others all day long.

> Often people tell you that they want a job involving working with people. Yet their day-to-day behaviour suggests they don't like working with people at all. If you find working with people difficult, it may be a grave error to take a job with a large interpersonal content in an attempt to make yourself good at it.

"You can't always get what you want", goes the song, and sometimes people's ambitions and their ability are out of kilter. It is as well to bear in mind that most of us will face career disappointments at some stage in our lives. As the management writer Peter Drucker argues, it is sensible to develop a hinterland of other interests to help prepare for these disappointments when they do come. Mailer (2004) quotes the saying amongst boxers that, 'the punch you see coming hurts less than the one you never saw at all.'

6.2.2   Some Patterns of Career Development

Career progression can of course involve sideways as well as upward movement. Those moving across an organization to another field or department often do so because they want a change, which is usually the opportunity to do new and interesting work. By developing fresh interests and knowledge, very often at the end of their working lives such people can look back on a fascinating time, if not always a highly rewarding one financially.

When considering changing fields most of us will appreciate that some activities demand highly specialized knowledge, training and experience, and acquiring this can be a barrier to entry. Examples would be in technology related areas such as engineering, IT, and medicine, as well as the law and finance. Specialists can move out of these professions into general management or even into some of the less "technical" organizational fields. However, it is usually very difficult to move into them after the age of 30, or without obtaining a degree or other formal qualification.

Sometimes people who have remained for a number of years in their own technical or functional "silo" can often discover an interest in management comparatively late on in their careers. There can be a variety of reasons: their self-confidence has increased; they want to see things done to the right professional standards and they consider that helping to establish these will be their legacy; they have started to enjoy coaching and developing younger staff (often those whom they perceive as more junior versions of themselves); they have discovered late on that they enjoy the responsibility of taking decisions; following the resignation of their boss, they are afraid that if they do not manage the group they will find themselves being managed by someone they do not like or respect, and it would be more trouble staying where they are.

> Partners and spouses have a much greater influence than is generally realized on: employees' behaviour at work; their feelings about how they are treated at work; the decisions they make about their careers

Financial or other pressures can also spark a sudden career interest in the hitherto unambitious employee. The arrival of children, an expensive divorce, a poorly performing pension fund, a new spouse or relationship, can all awaken ambition.

We referred above to the role spouses or partners sometimes play in scanning job vacancies. We would also add that in our experience the influence that spouses and partners can sometimes have on career or other workplace decisions is greatly underestimated. People go home and discuss situations and events in their place of work, and their subsequent reactions and responses often depend on the reactions and advice they receive at home. Some managers would do well to be more mindful of this fact when meeting the partners of their direct reports at social gatherings and on other occasions.

There are many methods that organizations use to identify their "key people." An interesting approach is to imagine you are to leave your firm tomorrow. Now ask yourself: "Which people would I take with me and why?"

Some people's career ambitions will inevitably lead them towards other organizations. Moving can involve a loss of networks, status, in-depth knowledge of how an organization works, sources of information, and sometimes friends. These factors concern some more than others.

We have noticed that sometimes individuals leave one department for another section or another employer in the search for "greener grass", only to find that the problems within the new role are worse than those they perceived within the old. In addition, in the new role, one may no longer have the consolation of the networks and the understanding of "how things are done." When a decision to leave an organization is being considered, it can be very difficult to obtain reliable, relevant information about the new firm prior to making the move.

"That's the last time I apply for a job in a flat structure with no prospects of promotion"

As stated above, development in one's current role should be the first priority. Once these development plans are in place, attention can turn towards pinpointing

---

Self-analysis questions about career development

1. At the end of my career, what would I ideally want to look back on and say, "I am glad I did that"?
2. What choices are realistically open to me?
3. What job do I want to do and why do I want to do it?
4. What skills, behaviours, qualities, knowledge and experiences are required for the post to which I aspire?
5. What skills, behaviours, qualities, knowledge and experiences are required for any posts I need to take en route?
6. What price would I have to pay and am I willing to pay it?

Fig. 6.9 Self-analysis questions about career development

development actions for the future. These can be added to the actions already set out on the form (Fig. 6.6). In Fig. 6.9 we again provide some brief questions which can help an individual in considering their options.

6.2.3 Trying to Prevent the Resignations of Key People: The "Organizational Stake"

If a manager makes sure they develop their staff, then these staff will be more productive and easier to manage. And as we said at the beginning of this chapter, even the most ambitious of them will tend to stay longer with their employer. As a manager, you will reduce the chances of resignations, or at the very least extend the length of time that staff will stay with you, if you also apply the other ideas and principles as set out in this book.

6.2.3.1 If You Develop Them, They Will Stay
When they are kept busy on interesting projects which also develop them, staff are less likely to think that they would benefit from a change of scenery. It also helps if they are told periodically that their contributions are valued, and that they are wanted. Such words should also be backed up by deeds: you demonstrate your concern for people and their development by taking action—seconding them to projects which extend their knowledge into new areas, for instance.

If you are developing an individual as a potential replacement candidate for your own role, then you should start giving them practice in those activities they will need to carry out once they have replaced you. This could mean progressively giving them more exposure, by, for example, taking them along with you to meetings with senior managers, involving them in discussions with important external contacts, or even allowing them to present specific items at meetings.

You can begin to take them through your thought processes on certain issues, ask them how they themselves would approach such matters, and consider with them their proposed courses of action. Some organizations allocate executive coaches to their high potentials as a way of providing support, accelerating learning, and supplementing the advice and guidance from their own manager.

> An individual's "organizational stake" is made up of those factors, beyond pay and the formal contract, which seem to bind them to their organizations. By helping your staff to build up their organizational stake, you encourage them to stay longer

One practical way in which managers can assist in retaining valued people is by helping them to build up what we call their "organizational stake." We define the organizational stake as those factors, beyond pay and the formal contract, which seem to bind employees to their employers.

We gradually became aware of the organizational stake concept as a result of carrying out large numbers of interviews in the course of our organizational consulting work. On many occasions we found ourselves interviewing people who had become highly disaffected. They were unhappy for a variety of reasons, but what they had in common was that they felt they had been in some way badly treated by their employers. As they told us their stories, we could see some of them reliving the anger all over again.

We learned of people who had been passed over for promotions which, according to them, they had either been promised, or been given to understand were theirs. In other cases individuals were bitter because, despite their strongly expressed views to the contrary, decisions had been taken which would have an adverse impact on them or how they were able to do their work. Occasionally, employees were angry because important decisions had been made without consulting them, when they felt that they were the organizational experts on the subject in question. For some interviewees structural changes were a bone of contention: these made their jobs more difficult, and in some cases new reporting relationships were either a demotion or perceived as such.

Often it was the way in which the decisions were communicated which proved especially galling: sometimes there was little or no advance warning of a change, although they might have heard some whispers or information would begin to leak. Discussing his non appointment to a new job, following an internal competition, one employee told us: "I didn't get the job. But no-one told me officially for weeks. I kept hearing rumours. Everyone else seemed to know but me." In some cases interviewees perceived these sorts of communication failures as a public humiliation, a loss of face or personal embarrassment. One manager told us that he had first learned of the decision to reduce his position to a part-time role at the same time as his team, and in the course of a monthly management briefing.

Yet despite their strong feelings, and the fact that many of these disaffected individuals were marketable and could indeed have moved on, they had decided to remain with their employers. At first we were puzzled by this. Why would so many of them want to stay given their strength of feelings about their treatment? Perhaps we were simply dealing with a self selected sample—by definition we were interviewing those who had decided to remain. Perhaps the interviewees did not feel that strongly after all, although their body language, and the vehemence with which they expressed themselves, made us feel that this was not the case. But as we explored the issue in more depth, in some cases later returning to these selfsame interviewees for further discussions on the issue, we gradually came to realize that these staff had become tied to their organizations in ways that sometimes even they did not fully understand. We began to identify some of the reasons why they were reluctant to leave.

In most instances these were people with a number of years of service. During that time they had built up a strong network of colleagues to whom they felt a considerable loyalty. They were well-known to these colleagues and in many instances were appreciated and valued by them for their contributions. Often they had built up strong internal reputations as acknowledged organizational experts on certain topics, and were highly respected in these areas.

Over time, many of these colleagues had become friends, as well as business associates. Progressively, this network sometimes even included their firms' customers as well as some outside advisers. In some organizations many of their colleagues lived in the same locality and were often part of the same social and other networks external to the organization. Their positions had given them a degree of status in the local community: their firms had strong local reputations and these individuals benefited from this by association. The benefits were even more marked in cases in which the organizations tended to set high barriers to entry. People value more what it has cost them to obtain. If it is harder to get a job with a given organization, once one has succeeded, their job holds a greater value in the incumbent's eyes as well as in the eyes of outsiders, and one is even more reluctant to give it up.

A shared history in the organizations and the communities in which people live and work gives them an important professional and emotional stake which becomes inextricably entwined with their organizations. To leave is to throw all of this away. As a consequence, the greater their number of years of service, the less likely they were to want to leave. They knew their organizations, the people, and the rules of the game. They had spent years building up their network of contacts, and they knew instinctively that they would not wish to walk away lightly from all of this.

Leaving an organization, you lose your network and you have to start afresh, friendless in a more uncertain environment. The longer one stays in an organization, the greater one's stake in that organization, and the harder it is to decide to leave.

> For most people in large firms, "organizational loyalty" is loyalty to colleagues rather than to Boards of Directors or business owners

Although as we have described it, this organizational stake seems to grow independently of the management, nonetheless managers can help to encourage, enhance and deepen it in a number of ways. Consulting people about matters in their perceived areas of expertise is an obvious one. They can be given the opportunity to pass on their knowledge and wisdom by being appointed as designated coaches or mentors to more junior staff. They can be encouraged, for instance, to work on longer term projects which will help cement their commitment. Indeed any activities which involve longer term commitment can help to foster an individual's organizational stake. It has struck us more than once that the advantage for a company of the longitudinal, in company MBA or other in-house development programme, may lie in its long term nature as much as in its content.

6.2.4   How do I Cope With Resignations When They Happen?

Despite your best endeavours, however, some of your better staff may resign from your organization. Opportunities will inevitably arise for them elsewhere, and where possible managers should always have one eye on succession planning in their own areas just in case people leave, especially the key employees.

While resignations can be inconvenient, in fact they are not always a problem. Indeed a complete lack of staff turnover in an organization limits succession opportunities amongst existing staff, and also constrains the introduction of new blood from outside. However, high levels of staff turnover in a short period can be a challenge, especially if it is the key employees who are resigning.

When key people do resign, what should you do? If you have been following our advice on the importance of control, as set out in Chap. 3, then your Work Management System will ensure you have a handle on the person's current work-load. Your control system will also enable you quickly to take the decisions necessary to ensure continuity and the smooth handover of any leaver's work. All of the information sharing which has taken place during Work Management Meetings guarantees that the Department as a whole will have a reasonable awareness of each person's work and what is involved. Furthermore, if people feel that you have treated them fairly, they will usually cooperate in ensuring a smooth changeover.

> When discussing their resignation with someone don't ask, "Why are you leaving?" Instead, ask them, "Why did you start looking?"

With respect to the person resigning, should you try to retain them? There is no hard and fast rule. We have seen situations in which great efforts have been made to retain someone who has tendered their resignation. In one case the person resigning had been on the point of being promoted as a replacement for his own manager, who was due to be appointed Director within a few months. In the event both appointments were brought forward and the individual was retained. By all means try your best to keep those people you want to keep, using whatever suitable means you have at your disposal. But do be mindful of the dangers of setting precedents. Offering them more money can be a solution, but it can cause a ripple effect which unsettles other members of staff. It also brings a potential risk of being held to ransom at some future point. It may encourage the view that, 'the only way to get on around here is to find another job.'

Some organizations are fairly successful with their structured approaches for preventing resignations in the first place, and when they do happen, getting employees to reconsider. Success in 'turning around' resignations seems to be based on: (1) responding rapidly; (2) involving senior managers in intensive discussions with the individual during which the focus is on listening to the employee's concerns; and (3) seeking to understand and then resolve the employee's "problem." If you are engaged in attempting to turn around a resignation, it can be worthwhile making sure people have fully thought through the advantages of their current position, and the upside of staying. All too often, people focus on the downside of their current situations, discount what they will be giving up when they leave, and they may later regret their haste.

However, when people are determined to leave, and some of them inevitably will, in your discussions with them, you should avoid the mistake made in many exit interviews when people ask the question: "Why are you leaving?" Rather, you should ask, *"Why did you start looking?"* If you ask why people are leaving, rather than the real reason, you tend to get a rationalization of their decision, such as a description of their new benefit package, or their terms and conditions (which you probably cannot match, and even if you could, things have probably gone too far now). Asking why they started looking potentially gives you important information about what was either present or lacking in the working environment, and what made them want to leave in the first place. This information can help to pinpoint potential problems which could affect others, enabling any necessary remedial action to be taken.

When valued people have left, you can contact them periodically to see how things are progressing with their new employer. In some instances you may wish to ask some of your other staff members to get in contact with them. By keeping in touch you show your interest, extend your organization's network, and more specifically, you learn whether they have actually found greener grass on the other side. A call placed six to nine months after a key employee has left can find them just on the point of frustration with their new organization. Promises made may not have been kept, and some disillusionment may have started to set in.

Sometimes such people are even prepared to come back. If they do, there is no loss of face; after all they have now been headhunted. In such circumstances they will return as more experienced, and as a consequence, more valuable employees. They may also subsequently provide more stability in your organization: they have returned and will justify their decision vis-à-vis their colleagues.

> **Remember**
> - There is often a personal price to pay for promotion.
> - There are many satisfactory patterns of career, and people vary in what they find satisfying.
> - People have a personal stake in the organization beyond the work and the mission statement.
> - If people do resign, ask them why they started to look, not why they are leaving.
> - When competent people move on, keep in touch, you may have an opportunity to get them back.

References

Ackroyd, P. (1999). *The life of Thomas More*. London: Vintage.

Blumenthal, S. (2003). *The Clinton wars: An insider's account of the white house years*. London: Penguin.

Brooks, J. (2014). *Business adventures: Twelve classic tales from the world of wall street*. London: John Murray Learning.

Dalton, G. W., Thompson, P. H., & Price, R. L. (1977). The four stages of professional careers - a new look at performance by professionals. *Organization Dynamics, 6*, 19–42.

de Botton, A. (2004). *Status anxiety*. London: Hamish Hamilton.

Elberse, A. (2013). Ferguson's formula. *Harvard Business Review, 10*, 116–125.

Evans, P. A. L., Doz, Y. L., & Laurent, A. (Eds.). (1989). *Human resource management in international firms: Change, globalization, innovation*. London: The Macmillan Press.

Ferguson, A. (2013). *My autobiography*. London: Hodder & Stoughton.

Fox, L. (2003). *Enron: The rise and fall*. Hoboken, NJ: Wiley.

Handy, C. (2006). *Myself and other more important matters*. London: Arrow Books.

Hutchinson, R. (2007). *Thomas Cromwell: The rise and fall of Henry VIII's most notorious minister*. London: Phoenix.

Isaacson, W. (2011). *Steve Jobs*. London: Little, Brown and Company.

Jones, R. V. (1978). *Most secret war*. London: Coronet.

Kasparov, G. (2007). *How life imitates chess*. London: William Heinmann.

Kearns Goodwin, D. (2009). *Team of rivals: The political genius of Abraham Lincoln*. London: Penguin.

Kennedy, P. (2013). *Engineers of victory: The problem solvers who turned the tide in the second world war*. New York: Random House.

King, S. (2000). *On writing: A memoire of the craft*. London: Hodder & Stoughton.

Leeson, N. (1996). *Rogue trader*. London: Little, Brown and Company.

Lombardo, M. M., & Eichinger, R. W. (1996). *The career architect development planner*. Minneapolis: Lominger.

Lord, G. (2003). *Niv: The authorised biography of David Niven*. London: Orion.

Mailer, N. (2004). *The spooky art: Thoughts on writing*. New York: Random House.

Mandelson, P. (2010). *The third man: Life at the heart of New Labour*. London: Harper.

Powell, J. (2010). *The New Machiavelli: How to wield power in the modern world*. London: Vintage Books.

Russell, B. (1978). *The autobiography of Bertrand Russell*. London: Unwin.

Scally, J. (2001). *Raising the banner: Official biography of Ger Loughnane*. Dublin: Blackwater Press.

Schein, E. H. (1978). *Career dynamics: Matching individual and organization needs*. Reading, MA: Addison Wesley.

Schein, E. H. (1987). *Process consultation volume II: Lessons for managers and consultants*. Reading, MA: Addison Wesley.

Welch, J. (2001). *Jack: What I've learned leading a great company and great people*. London: Headline Book Publishing.

White, T. (2010). *The making of the president 1964*. New York: Harper Perennial.

Wright Mills, C. (1970). *The sociological imagination*. Harmondsworth, Middlesex: Penguin.

Conclusion: Coping When You're Poorly Managed; and Why Management Jobs Are Still Worth the Bother

> *Work is of two kinds: first, altering the position of matter at or near the earth's surface relative to other such matter; second, telling other people to do so. The first kind is unpleasant and ill paid; the second is pleasant and highly paid*
>
> Bertrand Russell
>
> *We cannot be taught wisdom, we have to discover it for ourselves by a journey which no-one can undertake for us, an effort which no-one can spare us*
>
> Marcel Proust
>
> *Be yourself. Everyone else is already taken*
>
> Oscar Wilde
>
> *My boss is like the tattoo of St. George on the horse. He sits there day after day, but he never goes anywhere*
>
> Anon

The modern world desperately needs competent managers. As we have argued from Chap. 1, the job of management has become more difficult, and for a number of reasons. This book is our solution. To summarize: *Management by Permission* (MBP) comprises four ingredients: (1) get control; (2) clarify expectations; (3) run interference; and (4) develop the people. Get these four ingredients right and you will manage effectively.

In drawing together the various strands of the book, this final chapter addresses two issues: (1) how, if you are being badly managed by your own boss, you can use these four ingredients as a guide to improving your situation; and (2) why, despite the levels of opprobrium directed at managers from so many quarters, we believe that management jobs are still attractive and worth taking.

© Springer International Publishing Switzerland 2016
T. McNulty, R. Marks, *Management by Permission*, Management for Professionals,
DOI 10.1007/978-3-319-25247-6_7

7.1   What to Do if You Are Being Poorly Managed

Whilst most readers of this book will be responsible for managing others, almost all readers will work in hierarchies in which they themselves are subject to management control. Even at the most senior levels, almost everyone has someone to whom they are directly accountable. And the blunt truth is that not all of these bosses will be equally competent. This raises the question about what to do if you are being poorly managed.

"And so I said to him, 'Skipper, you're paid to know your way through the rocks. I'm not going to tell you how to do your job'"

There are a number of reasons why managers perform poorly. The most common ones include: they are overworked; they lack the right experience or training; they have never seen effective management role models in action; or they simply lack interest in the role (perhaps they took it for the money, or the status, or, in the case of some entrepreneurs, they suddenly found themselves running something much bigger than they ever envisaged). Some of these managers may have a business qualification; others may even have read up on management *theory*. However they do not always know what to do in *practice*. As a result, the performance of some managers can be inept.

The management cadre also contains its fair share of bullies, power maniacs and manipulators. Such individuals can be quite unpleasant, causing untold stress, belittling others, and generally abusing their position. Many of them see everything through a prism of their own power, status and self-aggrandisement. For example, when there are issues to be discussed, rather than focusing on the topics in hand, they take things personally, playing individuals rather than the ball. Sometimes they even try to get subordinates to behave in inappropriate ways by camouflaging the truth or misleading others.

At the end of this section we will return to the subject of what to do when faced with the latter sorts of bosses. For the most part here, we will be focusing on managers who are well-meaning, but inept. Inept managers typically fail to provide the support and framework you need to do your job and they can inadvertently create interference rather than run it.

Whether you are an individual contributor, or the manager of a team, you have a duty to yourself and your team to make sure you are being properly managed. If this is not happening, you need to take steps to make sure it does happen. Otherwise you will become frustrated and ineffective.

It is important to recognize that everyone reporting to an underperforming boss is invariably tainted by association. It is not in any subordinate's interests for their boss to fail. A failing boss means failing subordinates. As a consequence, you have a vested interest in being managed properly and in helping your manager to perform. If your manager is poor then they need your urgent support.

Successful management is a cooperative venture in which subordinates have to play their part. Both managers and the people they are managing have a joint responsibility for making their working relationship effective and for getting the work done. So sometimes you will be your manager's eyes and ears, helping to run interference on their behalf. You will also need to provide them with your best advice, showing them where problems might lie, even if they think they already know. If you fail to do this, you too can end up cast on the resulting wreckage.

As we discussed in Chap. 2, poorly managed staff run the risk of losing all of the advantages that having an effective boss can bring. In the case of an inept boss it can sometimes even appear an attractive option to be managed incompetently: comparative freedom; little discipline; few constraints; working on your pet projects; surfing and socializing. But at best these are short-lived pleasures. In the long run careers are derailed, projects get cancelled, and you become disconnected and lose touch with organizational reality. The work becomes less interesting, your professional reputation is destroyed, your professional capability is eroded, and you are undermined. Your contribution will not be properly recognized, and decisions may well be taken which will affect you adversely.

7.1.1 Some Practical Steps You Can Take

If you and your boss do not work well together, the constant stress can be costly to you and personally wearing. If you feel you are being badly managed, start by thinking through what your manager needs from you in order to do their own job, and provide it as best you can. For example, when they are concerned about an issue, volunteer the information they *need*, not simply what they say they *want*.

If you want to ask your boss for a meeting in order to keep them briefed, or discuss any topics, prepare a short agenda in advance setting out the issues you would like to cover. Sending this to your boss beforehand gives them a chance to prepare. Few people like issues, especially contentious ones, to be sprung on them without warning, and your manager may well appreciate the opportunity for some prior thinking about your topics, and as necessary, to do some prior fact gathering. An outline agenda helps to keep any meeting on track and also acts as a spur in making sure you yourself prepare properly. Remember that it is more helpful to a boss to be able to focus on a handful of well-defined discussion points, supported by facts and evidence, as opposed to a catalogue of moans and groans.

You do not have to like your boss (liking them is a bonus), nor do you have to respect them necessarily (although work life is probably more comfortable if you do). Remember they are human beings, with all of their strengths, flaws and idiosyncrasies, and like the rest of us, they face a daily struggle to cope with life's challenges.

Do not get into a battle with your manager, try to score points off them, dig holes for them, whinge, or fail to watch their back. Helping and supporting your manager is enlightened self-interest—if you help your boss, it also works in your own interest. The fact that if you perform well, your manager will get some of the credit, is an immutable law of nature in a hierarchy. The converse may not apply: if you perform poorly, your manager will not necessarily get the blame.

The four ingredients to *Management by Permission* help not only your organization and your manager, but you too, in your capacity as someone who is being managed. Below is a summary of the advantages of each of the ingredients seen from the perspective of the subordinate, together with our recommendations as to what you should do if your manager is not providing what is required in any one of the four areas.

7.1.1.1 Control

Control, especially by means of an effective Work Management System, gives a subordinate: access to the organization and to the resources of their boss; an up to date view of the organization's priorities; better acceptance and understanding of the problems; and performance assessments based on a dossier of factual information, rather than innuendo, the last few weeks' work and any major errors you may have made during the year.

Top management can get access to a list of the work you are doing and take comfort from the fact that it is progressing. If they wish to know what you are doing, the information is readily available. They have the comfort blanket, while you have some degree of protection from emotional or ill-informed opinions circulated about you or even decisions made about you. Being part of an effective process of Work Management helps ensure that you keep on learning, that you get credit and recognition for work well done, as well as the support and information you need in order to be effective.

If control is inadequate you should use one of the formats for setting out lists of jobs as suggested in Chap. 3. Write out a list of the work which you and, as appropriate, your team are working on. Put time estimates on these activities, and then take the list to your manager and go through each of the items. Make sure that you are covering all of the activities and tasks your boss would wish you to cover. Afterwards, you can add notes on priorities, progress, and external developments and add any extra projects to your list. Then send a revised list to your manager. Additionally, think of any numbers you could use to track performance in your area, get hold of them, discuss them with your boss, and decide how they should be used to monitor progress.

As the work progresses, provide your manager with updated copies of your list of jobs and the latest numbers. Request a periodic discussion—perhaps monthly but certainly at least quarterly—to review progress and obtain your manager's input. This will enable you to provide an updated progress report, get their feedback on how things are going, and keep your list of priorities up to date. By providing your manager with a list of work, you have also given them something which they in turn can take to their own manager.

Organizational strategies often evolve by trial and error, accident as well as design, such that some issues and activities become more important as time goes on, and you may well need to change focus in your own work. The above meetings give you an opportunity to keep abreast of any changes known to your boss. If you disagree with any of the changes in emphasis or strategy, remember that senior management may well be party to information of which you are unaware. Often there is a bigger organizational picture which can explain decisions and actions, and one which is not necessarily available to you.

Nevertheless you owe your boss your best advice based on your knowledge and perspective. If you think an approach or the strategy is flawed then explain to them why you think as you do, presenting your best professional opinion based on the facts as you see them. Give your best advice and do not sulk if it is not taken. If your manager says that they are doing something else then you have to assume that there is a good reason. Give your boss the information they need in order to do their job. They have pressures on them as well.

7.1.1.2 Clarifying Expectations

Clarifying expectations means you know where you stand: it gives you a clear understanding of your activities, the extent of your responsibilities and hence the chance to succeed in an area of importance to the organization. You get to know the ground rules and targets, and even the parts of the job you may dislike—the little chores which need to be done and the non-negotiable issues. You also get a chance to clarify the more pleasurable aspects of your role. The process reduces the elements of surprise. You get an opportunity to articulate what you want from the job, the organization, and to have these needs satisfied, or at the very least, considered. Most people are usually able to obtain some of what they want.

If your manager has not clarified what is expected of you, then make some notes on what you think might be expected in your current role, as well as what you yourself expect, and ask for a meeting with your manager. Present your list and say to him or her: "This is what I think the organization expects of me, am I right?" Make clear that you fully support any effort your manager may make to improve the management of the group, and that you will continue to be supportive. As appropriate, also make clear that you will give your best professional advice and that if another course of action is decided upon, you will continue to provide support.

Managers are not mind readers and if you have some expectations of your own, or there are elements to your psychological contract you want to share, then do so:

I would like keep up to date with the developments in my field. I get the principal journals and I follow developments on the Internet but I would also like to attend the Annual Conference of the national society and perhaps submit a paper.

I think there are some more opportunities for our business overseas and I would like to develop a plan for tackling some of these territories which I will share with you.

My partner has a senior nursing job and needs to be late at work on Fridays. Could I leave an hour early on Fridays to pick up my daughter? As you know I often work late and I will make up the time that way. I will also make sure that everyone else on the team knows that this is the arrangement.

"If every part of a manager's job were fun, Arnie, we wouldn't pay you, we'd sell tickets"

7.1.1.3 Running Interference

Running interference gives you: a source of coaching and advice; protection from disruption when you need time to focus on important work; hands-on help in getting any boulders on the race track removed; assistance in your day-to-day work; as well as access to the organization's resources. It also gives you access to your manager's own network, and remember that once accessed, you can often use it subsequently. When your manager helps to run interference for you, your interests are represented and you are given the freedom to focus on your job. You are protected from some of the barriers, irritators and impediments to performance, and as a consequence your chances of job satisfaction and your effectiveness are greatly enhanced.

If your manager is not running interference on your behalf then try to consider how best the problems or barriers could be overcome. As always, work on the actual problems, not on someone else's definition of what the solution might be. If you are able to do so, sort the problems out yourself. If that does not work, then make sure your manager knows what the problems are. Explain to him or her what you have done and suggest a workable solution if you have one. To get your boss to move a boulder that you could move yourself is a waste of his or her time and they may well think you incompetent.

On occasion you may need to make use of the resources or contacts of your boss. When you do, do not lead your boss into a minefield or expose them. As one of our clients rather bluntly put it, alluding to his (male) CEO: "I always ask myself: will the Chief Executive's bum look big in this?" Make sure you have spoken to those who could help remove the barriers, such as the owners of the systems or information. Listen to them and understand their points of view. When you have all the information and an understanding of the issues, write a note and go and see the boss.

Remember that your manager is a resource and is there to help, although they will rightly expect you to have done some thinking about the issues first. Do not, however, think that you have to act as a hero and solve every problem yourself against all the odds. What for you may be intractable at your level, can be something your own manager can easily address. There is no shame in going to your boss. Remember that they too have a vested interest in making sure you are not prevented from performing. Bumps in the road are normal and few of us carry out all of our assignments exactly to plan.

Do not get your boss to use up their own "blue chips" on political or other issues which you could resolve yourself. It wastes their time and potentially renders them less able to help you in the future. If the problems are interpersonal in nature consider whether you could use some of the techniques described in Chaps. 4 and 5. In the last analysis, goodwill on your part and a willingness to listen and understand seem to help in resolving most relationship problems.

7.1.1.4 Development

Development gives you the satisfaction of increased skill and competence in your current role, greater potential earning capacity, further career options, better job performance and very often enhanced status and reputation. It can also ensure that your changing career aspirations and life goals can be taken into account, and you may get help in achieving them.

If you are not getting development, remember that whilst your manager, as a representative of the organization, *should* be interested in this, if nothing happens then your development is your problem and you need to attend to it. Sort out what you need to do to help improve your current job performance and ask for it.

Reread Chap. 6, which should spark ideas for how you can develop. Ask for what you want—a coach or a mentor, for instance. Ask for "360-degree" feedback. You need to be aware of any disabling weaknesses you might have; they are probably holding you back or making you less effective. If you work in a larger organization, talk to your HR Department about available courses and development opportunities. Find people who could help you and ask them for their advice. Keep a logbook or journal. Analyze your professional work and consider what lessons you could draw. For example, what information or learning would you want to pass on to a junior whom you were coaching?

Ask yourself, if I had to brief someone as to my job, what would I tell them? Try writing a two page note: "Janet and John (or Dick and Jane) take charge of my job for a year." In writing out the activities, tasks and challenges involved, what conclusions would someone draw about the skills or capabilities required by the jobholder? (This can also be a helpful technique to use if you are taking over from a previous manager—ask them to write the "Janet and John run the department" note, and then arrange a follow-up discussion at which you ask questions. We have advised clients to do this when taking over from someone else, and it has proved very useful).

Find out best practice standards in your field; carry out benchmarking; talk to colleagues in similar roles to your own in other organizations, and take steps to meet or exceed these standards. Above all, just because you are being poorly managed, do not allow your own professional standards to drop. To do so is unprofessional, corrosive, hard to recover from, and would be difficult to justify to a new manager should your existing one be replaced, or to a new employer should you move on.

Look for opportunities to train and develop others. Keep up to date—read the journals, review relevant research, attend conferences, talk to the experts. Look at how things work in other areas—what lessons transfer? Sort out what you want to do in the future. Use this book, follow the advice, ask for the help you need. Develop a hinterland—careers can often end in some degree of disappointment, so you should consider developing your interests in other areas. For some people, this may include rekindling old friendships as well as personal relationships. Towards the end of their careers many managers say they wished they had much earlier started to invest more time in their families, and in particular, in their partners.

> Irrespective of whether you are managing others, or you yourself are being managed, following the four ingredients to *Management by Permission* is enlightened self-interest—you further the interests of others, whilst furthering your own.

7.1.2   If, Despite All Your Efforts...

"Guarantees? You want guarantees? Buy a toaster," suggested Clint Eastwood. There are few absolute guarantees. If it looks as if you will not be managed properly, and you have exhausted all of the above suggestions without success, then you may need to transfer to another department, get a new job or leave. There is little point in making a fuss or threatening. Faced with threats to resign unless you get your way, as a general principle any manager would be well advised to accept your resignation. For them to respond to your threats would be to encourage a further threat later on, as well as being a poor example for others.

"These are my principles. If you don't like them, I have others", noted Groucho Marx. If you work in organizations it is inevitable that at some point you will deal with some people whose values you do not share. Some of their behaviour, personal lifestyles and outside activities may be anathema to you or clash with your own beliefs and values. Your ethical system may differ from that of your manager or other business associates. Provided people's values, beliefs and lifestyles do not impinge adversely on the work or on your organization, these may be of little relevance. You and they are there to do a job.

You may, however, have evidence of corrupt behaviour. Some examples would be: blatant abuse of power which destroys, threatens, takes advantage of or damages others (e.g. destroying someone's career through malicious comments or references); bullying or "mobbing"; behaviour which damages the organization or its reputation; or actions which could jeopardize the safety of the public or exploit individuals.

If any of these are the case then a "rotting rhino" is on the table in front of you, and you have to deal with it. Under these extreme, and very unpleasant circumstances, there is little point in doing battle with your manager. They hold most of the trump cards. Your best defence probably lies in keeping good records of your work, so that you have available documented evidence of your achievements, expectations and actions, including the content of any significant discussions held with your manager and others. A subordinate who has at hand the documented evidence that they are performing is more difficult to bully and manipulate. However, you may need to consult HR, take professional advice, or blow the whistle, with all the consequences that such actions may entail. And in the last analysis, you may need to get out.

7.2   Management as a Maligned Profession: Are the Rewards Worth the Effort?

At the start of this book we raised the question of whether management jobs were still worth taking, given all the pressures faced by managers in the modern world.

Certainly the profession of management itself is maligned in many quarters. Some people have an inherent antipathy towards the 'management class' and, as a consequence, an instinctive dislike for anyone in a management role. And more generally, whenever there is a problem in any organization, invariably its managers get the blame. Yet people also take good management for granted. They never think twice so long as: there is food in the stores; water in the taps; ATMs get refilled; planes get refuelled; and the lights go on at home when they press a switch. What people are really railing against is *poor* management, such as when you are kept waiting for 2 hrs. for a hospital appointment because there is some failure in the system, resulting in your file being in the wrong place.

Society really does need competent, committed managers who will improve efficiency and effectiveness, provide employment, make the best use of resources, and, in the case of those working in the private sector, deliver profits which will ultimately help fund public and other services. So, what are some of the personal rewards of management, and is the price worth paying?

Certainly not everyone wants managerial responsibility, and it often does have a personal price attached. This is especially so at the more senior levels, as the Technical Director in the last chapter reminded us. However, he also stressed that management jobs could be very satisfying, as does Bertrand Russell, albeit he is being slightly jocular in the quotation at the start of this chapter.

Having worked with large numbers of managers at all levels, our strong view remains that despite the potential disadvantages (longer hours, more worries, "the 4 am Think Tank"), for many people the rewards of management will continue to be worth the effort. We believe that there are at least four reasons for this. These four may not be the only reasons, but for many managers they seem to be a more than adequate reward and they make the job worthwhile.

7.2.1 First Reason: Job Interest and Professional and Personal Development

Many knowledge workers and individual contributors tell us that if they do not take a management post, they face the prospect of repeating the same "technical" work for most of their careers. After a number of years, their day-to-day job becomes a cycle in which the same tasks repeat, and similar projects recur.

Whilst this prospect does appeal to some individuals, many others want to do something new, which will give them a different sort of "buzz." For some of this group, the tipping point into management is sometimes the feeling that they can do their manager's job better than their manager can. And once they get onto the managerial ladder, a similar feeling will often be the trigger that they are ready for promotion to the next rung.

In the majority of cases management roles actually increase professional job interest and development. As one moves up the management tree, some of the sheer "grunt" work associated with many jobs can be left to others. Taking a broader role enables you to control bigger and more complex jobs than would be possible as an individual contributor. You gain access to more information, as well as a greater knowledge and understanding about how and why certain decisions are made. Seen from a management perspective, the challenges become more complex and multi-faceted, and they tend to be set in a wider business or organizational context, thus producing richer problems and in turn greater satisfactions.

When you are a manager, your work often expands to include the activities and the know-how of related disciplines, as well as some less familiar areas. Non routine contact with clients, customers and stakeholders increases, as does the opportunity to operate on a wider stage. The financial and intellectual resources available to you also grow. Many managers further expand their knowledge by attending conferences and seminars, and some are given the opportunity to follow courses and gain qualifications in management.

Overall, work becomes more interesting in a purely professional sense, and depending on their role, many managers even find they do not necessarily have to leave behind their former area of expertise just because they have entered management. It is often the case that those in quite senior management roles remain their organizations' top specialists in certain fields.

7.2.2 Second Reason: Power, Influence and Status

A classic assumption is that managers want power, influence and status. This is certainly true for some individuals, and there are people who have always had the desire to take control and direct others. They like being in positions of authority and enjoy the limelight and the responsibility that goes with it. They also like taking decisions and seeing their decisions implemented. For most people, being able to exert greater control over one's environment can be a route to more happiness and less stress, and some management roles do provide this.

For other people, the desire for management responsibility grows on them more gradually. This sometimes happens when, over time, individuals develop strong convictions and ideas about what should be done in their organizations, as well as how it should be done. They realize that the only way they can exert greater influence on the decisions made is by becoming a manager. They know that their views will be taken more seriously if they speak with management authority, and their position in the hierarchy will increase the chances that things will be done their way. For others the drive can be more complicated: perhaps after a number of years' experience, they are no longer prepared to be forever subject to those they feel may make poor decisions. Or they may have reached a point where they no longer wish to take instructions from those whom they feel do not know as much as they themselves do.

A strong need for personal achievement can still be met in a management position, albeit by getting the work done through others, rather than always doing it yourself. And taking a mediocre organization and turning it into an effective and professional unit is a satisfaction not available to the purely technical employee.

The pursuit of status is often jeered at, but given the choice, most people would generally prefer others to have a positive opinion of them, and status is a route to being respected for some. Within most organizational hierarchies, there is a clear link between status and influence, and hence to desire influence, requires status: those with higher status have a greater chance of getting things done their way. A desire for status is probably very fundamental to human beings, although we should not slip into thinking that higher status within an organization represents a higher value as a human being (de Botton 2004). Often people who have a comparatively low position in an organizational hierarchy are of very high standing in the wider community: they might arrange sponsored walks for a local charity, for instance. We worked with one medium-sized firm which at one point provided the local Mayor, several councillors, as well as chairpersons and officers for a number of local societies. None of these individuals held down top-level organizational roles within their firm.

As a manager you also have the ability to influence the continued employment of the workforce. Quality management leads to a successful organization and that in turn leads to reliable employment. Whether your business is large, or only employs a handful of people, others still have a living in part as a result of the efforts you put in. As one small business owner put it to us when describing his own motivations: "When I see the people leave the office on a Friday afternoon, I know that I have had some considerable part in providing them with worthwhile employment. And that is a tremendously rewarding feeling."

Even when organizations need to be radically downsized, managers often have the satisfaction of knowing that they are helping to secure the futures of the 70 % who are staying, whilst probably also helping to provide funding for the exit packages and future pensions of the 30 % who are to leave.

7.2.3　Third Reason: Financial Rewards

"Money is better than poverty, if only for financial reasons", noted Woody Allen. Whilst a few people might consider their earnings mostly as a scorecard representing their personal success, the actual material rewards of a management position can be significant in and of themselves, and this should not be underestimated. Money tends to confer greater choices, with financial rewards boiling down to a better standard of living, and the freedom to indulge in a more comfortable lifestyle. Some people crave the security money brings; others want a second home and to be able to indulge in more expensive pastimes, hobbies and interests, which can include more travel.

For those in relationships or with families, greater material rewards bring more freedom to improve your own, your partner's, or your family's lifestyle. Some people want to be in a position to provide private health care for their families, private education for their children, or even long term care for parents. Others wish to support various charities or religious institutions. For your partner there are the opportunities to develop personally by pursuing academic interests or hobbies. They can start a business, or as the case may be, stay at home and focus on child rearing or other activities.

Some people provide continuing financial and educational support for their children, and this can extend to helping with an initial property purchase. On the other side of the equation, others may need to fund an expensive divorce or perhaps support a new relationship, both of which are likely to increase the need for money as one heads towards retirement.

7.2.4 Fourth Reason: Developing and Growing Others

When they look back on their careers, many managers report that one of their greatest satisfactions at work has been the opportunity to help develop and grow the next generation of talent. Some managers speak with pride about the part they played in training and retaining people who subsequently reached the very top of their organizations. Others look back with pleasure at their involvement in helping to develop their replacements or even those who go on to have successful careers elsewhere. Helping these people on their way is a strong motivation for some managers and they greatly enjoy providing the interesting work opportunities and coaching which help people hone their skills.

Talented young professionals want to work with people they can learn from, and their managers are often strong role models in their eyes. Those reporting to you often look to you to see how to act. When managers have been successful role models, it can give enormous pleasure to see and hear your former staff repeating actions or words they first learned when working with you.

As a manager, you are uniquely placed to pass on best practice and professional standards in your field. You also have an opportunity to coach the members of your team, helping them to identify and build on their strengths, and eradicate or reduce the impact of any disabling weaknesses they might have. Much of what is involved in providing development opportunities, such as giving access to training and education, is usually in the direct gift of the immediate manager. Further, it is the manager who is best placed to produce an environment in which people are encouraged to learn from their work, and then share this learning with each other.

7.3 Hello to Management by Permission, Goodbye to Shawshank

As suggested at the beginning of this book, the highly directive approach to management is unlikely ever to disappear entirely. When a business is doing badly or there is a downturn in the overall economic cycle, the focus of organizations tends to be on maximizing efficiency and cost-cutting. When this turns into a crisis, hard decisions have to be made and made quickly, with little time for endless debate and consultation. This can lead in some places to a return to a more autocratic, command and control management style, with people feeling they are treated as little more than commodities.

People are usually prepared to accept a less consultative approach for a short period. They understand that if management is under pressure, and the very survival of an organization is at stake, there is a need for strong leadership and that sometimes less than palatable decisions have to be taken and implemented quickly.

Leaving aside these particular situations, however, we believe that the hard-nosed consensual management approach which is *Management by Permission* will increasingly become the norm. It will no longer be possible to manage people by issuing edicts, by waving rulebooks or imposing contractual agreements—the latter will always be open to interpretation and dispute.

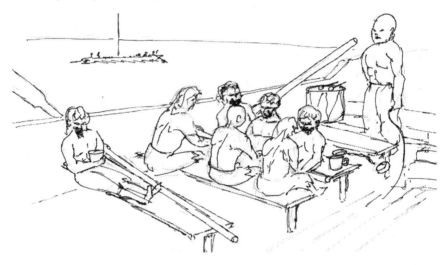

"I don't care who's texting you. Row NOW!!"

Recessions may come and go, but as respect for traditional institutions, organizations and hierarchies continues to wane, so individuals at all levels in a modern, less deferential society will expect more consultation about matters which affect them. No-one will want to be taken for granted, and people will not accept being background noise. The greater levels of participation required will be time-consuming and energy sapping and will place yet more demands on managers. Increasingly, management will only be possible with the active cooperation and consent of the people being managed.

Yet it really *is* possible to manage effectively in the twenty-first century. We have seen it done in many places. Take the four ingredients and get started. Good luck.

Reference

de Botton, A. (2004). *Status anxiety*. London: Hamish Hamilton.

Appendix

More Advanced Work Management System

This is a more ambitious approach than that described in Chap. 3. In our experience, and especially in the more 'technical' or 'project-based' departments, once managers have used this more advanced system, they seem reluctant to return to other methods. Given the amount of detail required, however, it may not be suited to all contexts.

The main difference between the attached "Job List" and what was described in Chap. 3 lies in the additional three columns devoted to estimating and monitoring the number of hours (or days, as the case may be) devoted to particular projects or activities.

"Initial estimate of hours" records the length of time it is assumed at the outset that the work or activity will require. The number of hours recorded here represents the total number of hours for all of the staff working on the project. This figure is based on a discussion between the manager and the individual responsible for the work. Managers will be given a detailed explanation of what is involved if the nature of the work, or parts of it, are unfamiliar to them.

Getting the job explained in some detail is helpful for a number of reasons: (1) it ensures clarity (often when an expert explains something to someone unfamiliar with all of its technical aspects, it helps the expert to think it through in more detail, thus increasing the likelihood of exposing any flaws); (2) managers learn about what is involved and are then in a better position to assess whether the time estimates and resources required are realistic, suggesting a revision, as necessary (over time, project definitions within the team become tighter, since staff know they have to account for their hours, if only to themselves); (3) everyone's estimation skills will improve; (4) the need for contingency plans can be assessed and developed as required.

© Springer International Publishing Switzerland 2016
T. McNulty, R. Marks, *Management by Permission*, Management for Professionals,
DOI 10.1007/978-3-319-25247-6

The *"Current estimate of hours"* is updated monthly, or if appropriate, weekly. It will change as the job progresses and is used to record the on going revised estimate of the time required for the activity. Individuals will each find a way of recording the time they spend on projects—in most circumstances, it is convenient to note this at the end of the working day. The number of hours for the month can then be shared at the next meeting. This column is *not* intended to be a method of accounting for all of the hours of the staff. Rather, it records their hours spent on the projects on the Job List. However, it does give some clues as to how much more work a department could handle at any one time, and even more important, enables managers to gauge immediately the consequences of any new projects which their bosses may allocate: "Yes, of course we can deliver this new job. The consequences for deadlines relating to these other tasks you have asked us to do will be . . ."

The *"Actual hours to date"* column is also updated monthly. In providing an up to date record of the time expended thus far on a task, it can act as a warning sign of potential problems or the need to allocate extra resource. For some staff, it also acts as a competitive spur to bring in a job under time.

One final point: if, as the work progresses, the scope of the job changes substantially, then inform the client, close the job, and open a new job with a new job number and a re-estimated time.

Job List

Job No.	Responsible	Client	Date of request	Description of job	Progress	Initial estimate of hours	Current estimate of hours	Actual hours to date	Completion date/ comments
261	JEB	PTR	6/6/2015	Develop paper on automation strategy for presentation at December Board meeting	All Directors interviewed and briefings conducted with three potential suppliers. Project has now been extended to take into account French subsidiary. Next steps: (1) supplier needs to be reviewed in next 14 days. (2) benchmarking visits to three user sites to take place in next 3 weeks. (3) Initial paper to be presented to Work Group Meeting during next month.	80	95	70	28/11/2015 est.
264	DT	AC	12/6/2015	Develop and implement revised working arrangements at company call centre	–	100	–	120	Completed 6/9/15 Completed policy documents/project files are all located in Central File under "Call centre" Staff involved were AC, JWP and RET. The project took slightly longer than envisaged owing to the need for additional staff briefings

Index

© Springer International Publishing Switzerland 2016
T. McNulty, R. Marks, *Management by Permission*, Management for Professionals,
DOI 10.1007/978-3-319-25247-6

Printed in the United States
By Bookmasters